Modernism
and the Law

NEW MODERNISMS SERIES

Bloomsbury's *New Modernisms* series introduces, explores, and extends the major topics and debates at the forefront of contemporary Modernist Studies.

Surveying new engagements with such topics as race, sexuality, technology, and material culture, and supported with authoritative further reading guides to the key works in contemporary scholarship, these books are essential guides for serious students and scholars of Modernism.

Published Titles
Modernism: Evolution of an Idea
Sean Latham and Gayle Rogers

Modernism in a Global Context
Peter J. Kalliney

Modernism's Print Cultures
Faye Hammill and Mark Hussey

Modernism, Science, and Technology
Mark S. Morrisson

Modernism, War, and Violence
Marina MacKay

Forthcoming Titles
The Global Avant-Garde
Christopher Bush

Modernism and Its Media
Chris Forster

Modernism, Sex, and Gender
Celia Marshik and Allison Pease

Race and Modernisms
K. Merinda Simmons and James A. Crank

Modernism and the Law

Robert Spoo

BLOOMSBURY ACADEMIC
LONDON · NEW YORK · OXFORD · NEW DELHI · SYDNEY

BLOOMSBURY ACADEMIC
Bloomsbury Publishing Plc
50 Bedford Square, London, WC1B 3DP, UK

BLOOMSBURY, BLOOMSBURY ACADEMIC and the Diana logo are trademarks
of Bloomsbury Publishing Plc

First published in Great Britain 2018

Cover design: Daniel Benneworth-Gray
Cover image © The Old Bailey, circa 1899, from *The Queen's Empire*. Volume 3.
Cassell & Co. London

A catalogue record for this book is available from the British Library.

Library of Congress Cataloging-in-Publication Data
Names: Spoo, Robert E., author.
Title: Modernism and the law / Robert Spoo.
Description: London; New York : Bloomsbury Academic, 2018. | Series: New
modernisms series | Includes bibliographical references and index.
Identifiers: LCCN 2017056562 (print) | LCCN 2017056911 (ebook) |
ISBN 9781474275828 (ePub) | ISBN 9781474275835 (ePDF) | ISBN
9781474275811 (Hpod) | ISBN 9781474275804 (pbk. : alk. paper)
Subjects: LCSH: Culture and law. | Obscenity (Law) | Censorship.
| Pornography in literature. | Copyright. | Publicity (Law) | Libel and
slander. | Extortion. | Modernism (Christian theology)
Classification: LCC K487.C8 (ebook) | LCC K487.C8 S67 2018 (print) |
DDC 340/.115–dc23
LC record available at https://lccn.loc.gov/2017056562

ISBN: HB: 978-1-4742-7581-1
          PB: 978-1-4742-7580-4
          ePDF: 978-1-4742-7583-5
          eBook: 978-1-4742-7582-8

Series: New Modernisms

Typeset by Integra Software Services Pvt. Ltd.
Printed and bound in Great Britain

To find out more about our authors and books visit www.bloomsbury.com and sign up
for our newsletters.

*For my brother Richard Spoo and my friend
Joseph Kestner—a lumi spenti.*

CONTENTS

Figures viii

Acknowledgments x

Introduction 1

1 Oscar Wilde, Man of Law 15

2 Obscenity and Censorship 45

3 Copyright, Patronage, and Courtesy 79

4 Privacy, Publicity, Defamation, and Blackmail 103

5 Ezra Pound, Man of War 127

Annotated List of Statutes, Treaties, and Cases Cited 152

Works Cited 170

Index 185

FIGURES

1.1 Marquess of Queensberry's calling card left for
   Oscar Wilde, February 1895. Courtesy Merlin
   Holland 21

1.2 Napoleon Sarony, *Oscar Wilde No. 18*, 1882.
   Courtesy Merlin Holland 36

2.1 John Sumner (hatted), New York Society for
   the Suppression of Vice, helping to incinerate
   objectionable materials. From *New York Journal
   American*, November 27, 1935. Courtesy Harry
   Ransom Center, University of Texas at Austin 53

2.2 John Munro Woolsey, US District Court for the
   Southern District of New York, 1931. Courtesy
   John Woolsey III 73

3.1 Workers, Riverside Press, New York City, February
   1917. Photograph L.W. Hine. Courtesy Library of
   Congress Prints and Photographs Division 91

4.1 Telegraph operators, 1908. Photograph John
   Robert Schmidt. Courtesy Library of Congress
   Prints and Photographs Division 112

4.2 Illustration by Sidney Paget for "The Adventure of Charles Augustus Milverton," *Strand Magazine*, April 1904. Image reproduction courtesy Gina Bradley 116

5.1 Ezra Pound, mug shot, US Army Disciplinary Training Center, May 26, 1945. Photograph US Army. Image reproduction courtesy Gina Bradley 146

ACKNOWLEDGMENTS

I wish to thank the series editors, Sean Latham and Gayle Rogers, for their support and ideas at all stages of this project. The anonymous readers of my book proposal offered excellent early advice that remained with me throughout the process. Thanks go to David Avital, Mark Richardson, Clara Herberg, and the Bloomsbury staff for their creativity and flexibility. I am grateful for early support shown by Barton Beebe, Mike Groden, Peter Jaszi, and Paul Saint-Amour, and to those who provided ideas, suggestions, and corrections during the drafting of chapters: Russell Christopher, Stephen Galoob, Mike Groden, Richard Hix, Thomas Keymer, Tamara Piety, and Simon Stern. For assistance with or permissions regarding photographs, I wish to thank Gina Bradley, University of Tulsa; Jay Gertzman; Joseph Hassett; Merlin Holland; the Library of Congress Prints and Photographs Division; Rick Watson, Harry Ransom Humanities Research Center; and John Woolsey III. I am also grateful to the John Simon Guggenheim Foundation for a 2016 Fellowship, which, along with the support of the Chapman Trust and a sabbatical semester provided by the University of Tulsa, greatly assisted the writing of this book.

A few paragraphs of Chapter 4 appeared in a different form in my essay, "'Ah, You Publishing Scoundrel!': A Hauntological Reading of Privacy, Moral Rights, and the Fair Use of Unpublished Works," *Law & Literature* 25.1 (Spring 2013): 85–102. Portions of Chapter 5 appeared in a different form in my essays, "Pound and the Law," *Ezra Pound in Context*, ed. Ira B. Nadel (Cambridge, UK: Cambridge UP, 2010), 125–35; and "Ezra Pound, Legislator: Perpetual Copyright and Unfair Competition with the Dead," *Modernism and Copyright*, ed. Paul K. Saint-Amour (New York: Oxford UP, 2011), 39–64.

Introduction

Modernism's laws often came in clusters, one legal problem implicating another until authors, publishers, or readers felt stifled by the cumulative force of regulation. In an introduction to his novel *The Power and the Glory* (1940), Graham Greene counted the ways in which secular and religious interdictions had pursued him and his book, almost as if he had inherited some of the persecuted fate of his character, the whisky priest, in flight from anticlerical Mexican officials (Greene 1–5). Greene's introduction served as a kind of confession box into which he whispered his encounters with law, beginning with a libel action brought by the child actress Shirley Temple and her movie studio for a review he had published of her film *Wee Willie Winkie* in 1937. Greene had written of the "dimpled depravity" of the girl's performance, and of the "middle-aged men and clergymen" who secretly "respond[ed] to her dubious coquetry" (qtd. in Sherry 619). The distributor W.H. Smith refused to carry the magazine containing the review; and, after a hearing in the King's Bench, the defendants agreed to a settlement of £3,500, £500 of which was to be paid by Greene. When the settlement was announced, he was in Mexico, researching the persecution of the Catholic Church there, and he was worried that he would be arrested on his return to England (621–2; Greene 1). It was not his first brush with libel law. The author J.B. Priestley had threatened to sue over a satirical portrait he had spotted in proofs of Greene's earlier novel *Stamboul Train* (1932), forcing him to make costly changes to the text (Shelden 164–5).

Greene began his paratextual confession with his sin against Hollywood's sacred Temple, but he did not stop there. From libel he passed to religious transgression. On two occasions, French bishops had denounced *The Power and the Glory* to Rome, he noted, and the Holy Office had condemned the novel for recounting "extraordinary circumstances," such as the alcoholic priest's having fathered a child in a random, lonely rut (Greene 4–5). The Church had urged Greene to revise the book in future editions, but he had declined "on the casuistical ground that the copyright was in the hands of [his] publishers" (5). His word "casuistical" hovers between its two senses of religious reasoning and specious equivocation, and he leaves little doubt that Church officials were unpersuaded by his claimed inability to redeem his fallen novel because of a transferred copyright. Copyright sometimes mixed promiscuously with modernists' machinations. James Joyce in 1930 contrived to avoid paying his New York lawyers' bill—some three thousand dollars owed for their efforts to obtain damages for the use of his name in connection with an unauthorized serialization of *Ulysses* (1922)—by transferring all rights in the book to his Paris publisher, Sylvia Beach, and by telling the lawyers that he would not pay for legal work that concerned someone else's property. Beach was outraged over Joyce's copyright casuistry and was further appalled when he later demanded the rights back from her so that he could have a free hand to negotiate for an authorized edition of *Ulysses* in America (Spoo, *Without* 230–2). Joyce and Greene pleaded copyright as a way of dodging monetary and spiritual creditors, respectively.

Libel, blasphemy, copyright. Such a combination might seem surprising, but it was not unusual in modernism's congested legal culture. In later years, firmly established as a major figure, Greene took to discouraging scholarly excavations of his career by claiming he had "a 'copyright' to his life ... and was willing to use legal means to frighten away potential biographers" (Shelden 15). On one occasion, he turned his lawyers loose on an unauthorized biographer and claimed in the press that the man had used "false pretenses" to gain access to a university archive, even though the archive welcomed all researchers, whatever their motives were (16). The collateral use of copyright to enforce privacy has been a preoccupation of modern authors and their estates. Privacy is the prized residuum left behind when celebrity has exhausted its self-display. As we will see in Chapters 3 and 4, the dream of propertizing privacy has haunted writers and heirs from the time of Henry James to that of Sylvia Plath and J.D. Salinger.

This book offers a concise account of law as it shaped transatlantic literary modernism. There are a number of ways in which law and literature can be brought together for critical purposes. My approach leans heavily on two. First and foremost, I examine the ways in which law regulated modern literature, or, more precisely, how legal and extralegal mechanisms—statutes, courts, prosecutors, purity groups—intervened in what Robert Darnton calls the communications circuit. Obscenity laws, for example, targeted publishers and printers—intermediaries that carried the signal from author to reader—along with the conductive tracks of modernism's circuit board: bookstores, mailing privileges, and customs imports. These laws shaped, inhibited, and sometimes deformed literary production and dissemination. Just as libel law was "an organizing component" of modernist works, "constrain[ing them] by its potent ability to adjudicate fact and thereby define the limits of fiction" (Latham 19), so obscenity laws led authors to employ euphemism, indirection, irony, or silence, and caused publishers to sanitize books or issue private editions, all in order to avoid legal consequences. This focus on regulatory forces in legal and literary history is sometimes called the "law of literature" (Barendt 481).

The law of literature includes copyright law. At first glance, copyrights might seem to encourage rather than restrict discourse. According to Anglo-American theory, copyrights stimulate creativity by giving authors the confidence to enter the communications circuit. By artificially raising the cost of imitation, copyrights replace freeriding with licensed uses and theoretically permit authors and publishers to capture all or most of the economic value of creative works (Lemley, "IP" 462, 482). But making imitation costly is also a tax on creativity. Copyright's legal monopoly controls the ability of others to imitate, alter, and adapt protected works. "Immature poets imitate; mature poets steal," wrote T.S. Eliot, referring to poetic daring or directness rather than to lawbreaking, since he did most of his costless thieving from works that had long since entered the public domain ("Philip Massinger" 153).

Today, intellectual property is thought of as a vaporous cargo (Barlow), but information wanted to be free long before the digital era. From its inception, US copyright law freed much information by legislative fiat, withholding protection from non-US authors for most of the nineteenth century, and granting it as of 1891 only upon satisfaction of statutory conditions that authors and publishers often found burdensome. Works thought to be immoral, unsuitable, or too experimental were vulnerable to these protectionist laws, and many modernist works lacked copyright in America. US copyright laws thus warped the conditions of modern authorship, generating vast transatlantic asymmetries in the protection and circulation of works. The resulting copyright vacuum allowed publishers like Samuel Roth to become lawful though reviled purveyors of an unauthorized literature. Sometimes, only obscenity laws stood in the way of lawful piracy. The functional antagonisms and surprising affinities between copyright and obscenity laws are recurrent themes in the chapters that follow.

The law of modernist literature thus reveals a struggle to control the costs and benefits of authorship. State and private actors, employing obscenity, libel, and privacy laws, tried to force authors to internalize (or absorb) the social costs of their creativity (indecent words and incidents, injurious falsehoods, intrusions upon seclusion), while copyright, privacy, and publicity laws aided authors in internalizing (or capturing) the economic benefits of their creativity and celebrity (Frischmann; Posner, *Law* 320). The internalizing of social costs took the form of censorship and self-censorship; the internalizing of economic benefits entailed the scarcity-producing effects of monopoly. As I suggest throughout this book, both forms of internalization arguably disserved readers. Moreover, the personal and dignitary impact on artists' expressive rights—what Oscar Wilde called "the rights of intellect" (*Complete Letters* 434)—gave poignancy to the often harsh operations of these regulatory forces.

In addition to the law of literature, there is a second analytical approach that examines the ways in which literary texts register and represent the forces of law. This approach focuses on the mutually constitutive relationship between law and literature, the ability of creative texts to respond to their jailers, as it were, by reimagining the effects and affects of regulation. As I employ it, this critical method reveals texts as both "occupied" and "preoccupied" by law (Saint-Amour, *Copywrights* 12). Thus, although regulatory contexts are my chief interest here, I also examine modernist texts for their imagination of law and legal problems. Chapters 1 and 5—about Wilde and Ezra Pound, respectively—blend this approach with the law of literature, as does Chapter 4, in which I discuss what I call the reputational cluster: blackmail, defamation, privacy, and publicity. Because legal protections for private life and public image were scant and undeveloped during much of the modernist period, authors often resorted, as a form of self-help, to textual representations of the modern self grappling with invasive technologies or the temptations of image crafting. Henry James's "The Aspern Papers" (1888) and "The Real Right Thing" (1899) are tales of threatened authorial privacy and also, in their way, amicus briefs for better privacy laws. Similarly, Arthur Conan Doyle's "The Adventure of Charles Augustus Milverton" (1904) explores the predatory crime of blackmail and, less overtly, the dilemma of the self torn between the need for privacy and the pleasure of selective self-display.

We usually think of the law as acting on persons, but law's power often targeted modernist works themselves. For example, the Obscene Publications Act of 1857 (known as Lord Campbell's Act) was not employed to prosecute individuals for selling or distributing immoral writings and images. Rather, it was a quasi-criminal statute that empowered British magistrates to authorize the search and seizure of indecent materials and, after adjudication, to order their forfeiture and destruction. Such forfeitures might lead to the prosecution of persons, but prosecution would be carried out separately under the common law of obscene libel. Henry Vizetelly, the English publisher of translations of Émile Zola's novels, was personally prosecuted in 1888 for publishing obscene libels, whereas D.H. Lawrence's *The Rainbow* (1915) and Radclyffe Hall's *The Well of Loneliness* (1928) were attacked in forfeiture proceedings under Lord Campbell's Act. Vizetelly went to prison; Hall's and Lawrence's books were fed to the furnace or the guillotine. The law distinguishes between proceedings *in personam* (against the person) and proceedings *in rem* (against the thing). In the early twentieth century, for example, libel actions, typically begun *in personam*, often concluded with a judgment or settlement *in rem*, requiring the destruction of the offending *res*, the stock of books containing the injurious falsehood. *In rem* solutions disabled the communications circuit by simply removing the signal.

Chapter 1, "Oscar Wilde, Man of Law," serves as the full introduction to the subject of this book: modernism and the law. Wilde's private prosecution of the Marquess of Queensberry for criminal libel and the Crown's subsequent prosecution of Wilde for acts of gross indecency with males are among the most famous *in personam* proceedings in modern history, and I use them to highlight the roles of honor, defamation, and blackmail in Wilde's career and the later decades of modernism. I also explore the multivalent concept of "posing" in Wilde's trials and its later use by judges, prosecutors, and purity groups to taunt transgressive modernism for its purportedly indecent and elitist tendencies.

But Wilde's encounters with law began long before he sought an indictment against Queensberry. His struggles with copyright law and American piracies, as well as his clashes with censorship, obscenity, and blasphemy, made him a precursor of modernism's legally embattled posture. Like Henry James, he was outraged by popular culture's invasion of privacy and the law's impotence to provide a remedy. His warnings that the memory of deceased authors was being desecrated by eager biographers—"the mere body-snatchers of literature" ("Critic" 1010)—matched James's cautionary fictions about the vulnerability of dead authors to commemorative spadework. Wilde's anti-moralistic demand that individuals be "let alone" ("Soul" 1100) joined other contemporaneous uses of that phrase, not only by James but also by lawyers and legal scholars. During his American tour in 1882, Wilde coyly complained of losing his private life to newspaper reporters even as he hungrily courted publicity, marketing his own privacy in ways that would become a fixed feature of modernity (Hofer and Scharnhorst, eds. 87). His own need for privacy was twofold: he wanted domestic privacy for himself and his family, and he paid blackmailing boys not to reveal the increasingly open secret of his homosexuality. Wilde thought of himself as an exception within or outside the law. His exceptionality was in part a self-willed emergency, a suspension of normativity comparable, on the level of the individual self, to forms of political exception identified by Carl Schmitt and Giorgio Agamben.

Chapter 1 introduces many of the discrete though overlapping areas of law to be examined in later chapters: obscenity, copyright, blackmail, defamation, privacy, and publicity. Together, Wilde and modernism constitute a sort of legal call and response. Just as the printer of *The Ballad of Reading Gaol* (1898) feared a libel action by prison officials (Wilde, *Complete Letters* 983 n2), printers' concerns over James Joyce's naming of real persons and places delayed the publication of *Dubliners* (1914) for nearly a decade. The deletion of homoerotic passages by the publisher of the magazine version of

The Picture of Dorian Gray (1890) (Gillespie 50–1) prefigured what Katherine Mullin calls the "auto-censorship" resorted to by Pound, Margaret Anderson, and other editors and publishers of modernist writing (Mullin, *James* 8). Wilde's complaints about unauthorized American reprints of his poems—a "hellish infringement on the right of an English author" ("The Poet" 1)—were echoed forty-five years later by Joyce, Pound, and Eliot, who also refused to believe that mere statutes could destroy authors' natural rights in their creative work. Modernist authors shared the incarcerated Wilde's exasperation with "the whole of this law-business" (*Complete Letters* 819).

Obscenity and censorship are the subjects of Chapter 2. My approach here is to trace important sociolegal issues—the concept of immoral tendencies and the special vulnerability of children; indiscriminate circulation of indecency and the institution of private editions; and the troublesome regulatory anomaly of literary classics—back to their articulation in the 1868 case of *Regina v. Hicklin* and forward to their development in modernist culture. Once Victorian moralism had extended its censure to serious literary and educational works, obscenity law lost its coherence as a tool for regulating explicit commercial pornography and became an arm of capricious meddling. Long before *Hicklin*, English jurisprudence had been troubled by the seemingly victimless nature of literary obscenity; and with the advance of prudery, there seemed no logical way of keeping the classics from being swept into the suppression campaign. Prosecutors and purity groups attacked the writings of Boccaccio, Rabelais, and other venerable authors, but courts were often uncomfortable with such retroactive purging and found reasons to allow the classics to escape through what Morris Ernst, defense counsel for modernism, likened to a "statute of limitations on obscenity" (Ernst and Seagle 55).

Jurists and scholars have struggled with Judge Augustus Hand's conclusion that there were only two persuasive methods for testing the value and propriety of literature: time and expertise (*United States v. One Book Entitled Ulysses* 708; Glass, "Redeeming" 344). If a classic had stood the test of time, courts often presumed that its apparent salaciousness would do little harm, especially if the work was old and likely to be read by a comparative few. But when the work was modern, and time could not be called as a witness, courts were urged to allow experts to substitute their judgment.

Loren Glass has argued that expert testimony turned obscenity trials into "rituals of consecration whereby modernist texts could be affirmed as 'classics'" and the test of time was replaced by "the patina of professionalism" ("Redeeming" 344). Prosecutors and purity groups, in their turn, were seeking to dispense with the test of time by substituting a patina of moralism. Obscenity litigations, by their nature, collapsed the slow operations of the moral and literary marketplace into a justiciable question. The notion of the "modern classic" owes much to the institutionalized impatience of the judicial process.

Judges were often reluctant to permit writers, critics, and other experts to invade the province of the fact-finder (whether a court or a jury). Moreover, in the 1930s, American judges might have felt an unarticulated discomfort with New Deal progressivism and its willingness to submit the choices of government to a select brain trust, a "patrician or technocratic vision [that] eschewed popular opinion in favour of scientific knowledge and expert opinion" (Nowlin 36). Ernst's marshalling of educated opinion in the *Ulysses* customs case and other obscenity litigations reflected this politics of top-down, administered progressivism. Judge Martin T. Manton, in his dissenting attack on Judge John M. Woolsey's decree lifting the customs ban on *Ulysses*, complained that the views of "those who pose as the more highly developed and intelligent" had been deferred to at the expense of vulnerable readers (*United States v. One Book Entitled Ulysses* 711). Manton felt that Ernst and Woolsey had hijacked the legal process by allowing cultural experts to supplant the intuitions of the larger community. His contemptuous glance at the "pose" of cultural elites was a direct legacy of the Wilde trials.

Chapter 2 concludes with two issues critical for understanding the complexity of modernism and obscenity. First, I offer the case of *Ulysses* to illustrate the uncoordinated, patchwork regulation of obscenity in America during the 1920s and 1930s. Concurrent state and federal legislation, together with multiple federal laws and jurisdictions (postal and customs prohibitions), could render the defense of accused books a game of legal whack-a-mole. *Ulysses* was subjected to piecemeal prohibition—multiple postal suppressions; prosecution under a New York criminal statute; at least two adjudicated customs seizures—yet never received full legal absolution from the US Supreme Court. (The government decided not to seek *certiorari* after Random House's victory in the US Court of Appeals.) The role of the Supreme Court is the subject of the chapter's final topic, "modernism constitutionalized." I reframe this familiar narrative as a realization, on the legal plane, of a desire expressed decades earlier by Wilde, Pound, Jane Heap, and others that art be treated as immune from the ordinary demands of law and morality. The story of obscene modernism's transformation into free speech is more than "the received liberal view of the battle against literary censorship" (Parkes, "Censorship" 67); it was a momentous *lex ex machina* that resolved the factual dispute over modernism's indecency, perhaps unsatisfyingly, by placing almost all cultural expression under First Amendment protection. Modernism was part of a vast manumission. I conclude by suggesting that the slow process of granting legal immunity to erotic modernism, in Britain and the United States, delayed modernism's full development as a historical moment into the 1960s.

The delay of modernism's growth continues into the present under laws that permit copyrights to endure for a century or more, hampering both creative adaptation and scholarly study of modern works. Chapter 3 takes up this theme of modernism propertized, along with the cultural and market effects that copyright shared with scarcity-producing obscenity laws. I also examine copyright and patronage as coexisting institutions of modernism. Patrons' gifts might be thought to have rendered the economic incentives and rewards of copyright unnecessary, but many modernists were keen to protect their copyrights, if only as dignitary badges of authorship. Writers wrote for many reasons besides money: aesthetic pleasure, competitiveness, prestige—the imponderable inducements that make creativity "messy" and copyright's incentive theory incomplete (Tushnet 546). Perhaps Wilde was thinking of the elusiveness of artistic incentives when he described the modern artist as a mocking dandy who found protection "not in Prince, or Pope, or patron, but in high indifference of temper, in the pleasure of the creation of beautiful things" (*Complete Letters* 520). Pound, too, contrasted the extrinsic attractions of money with "inherent activity, artist's desire to MAKE something, the fun of constructing and the play of outwitting and overcoming obstruction" ("ABC" 239). The true artist doubled as self-patron, internalizing the seductions and rewards of creativity.

Chapter 4 is devoted to law's reputational cluster: blackmail, defamation, privacy, and publicity. Blackmail might seem a misfit here inasmuch as it was a crime rather than a form of legal protection. Yet it did offer illegal or extralegal protection, purchased from the very person who posed the reputational threat. If prepublication censorship constituted prior restraint in the realm of obscenity, blackmailers trafficked in prior self-restraint, like a home insurer offering a policy against its own pyromania. Angus McLaren defines sexual blackmail as "a tax on reputation" (16). In one of modern culture's stranger extortionate schemes, Algernon Swinburne was coerced into exchanging the copyright of his poem "A Word for the Navy" for the return of letters in which he had recorded his flagellation fantasies (57; Wise 69). Even more bizarrely, the blackmailer had acquired the letters from Charles Augustus Howell, Swinburne's business adviser and the original of Conan Doyle's professional blackmailer, Charles Augustus Milverton (Chew 67). If Thomas Macaulay was right in calling copyright "a tax on readers" (Macaulay 201), Swinburne paid a reputational tax in the currency of a reading tax.

Blackmail exploited the power of knowledge. In fact and fiction, servants and other menials—the disempowered—often used blackmail to acquire lucrative control over their indiscreet masters. Conan Doyle's story traces a furtive economy in which a capitalist blackmailer, Milverton, purchases incriminating documents from proletarian thieves, the servants of the rich and famous. That Milverton is murdered by one of his aristocratic victims posing as a treacherous servant underscores the class struggle inherent in many blackmail narratives of the period. The tale of Dorian Gray, who fears blackmail at the hands of his servant, Victor (a name suggesting both the power of the invisible domestic and the source of that power in Victorian sexual prudery), ends with Dorian lying dead—withered and wrinkled—attended by his servant, coachman, and footman (1890:63, 100). This final tableau of retainers keeping stunned vigil over the libertine's corpse hints at a reversal in which the lower orders at last possess the terrible secret their master has withheld from them.

Privacy invasion is similar to blackmail in that disclosure of intimate facts diminishes a person's autonomy by making her a prisoner of her past (Solove 531). Henry James so feared what he called the "pestilent modern fashion of publicity" (qtd. in Salmon 79) that late in life he made a "gigantic bonfire" of his private papers and notebooks (qtd. in Edel 664). In Chapter 4, I read James's fictions of posthumously harassed authors alongside Samuel D. Warren and Louis D. Brandeis's call for common-law safeguards for privacy. I also suggest that James satirizes the very nexus between privacy and intellectual property that Warren and Brandeis made central to their lawyerly brief for a right to be let alone. My discussions of James and Conan Doyle, balancing the law of literature with textualizations of the law, attempt to do for privacy, publicity, and blackmail what Sean Latham's monograph does for libel, Celia Marshik's for obscenity (*British*), and Paul Saint-Amour's for copyright (*Copywrights*).

Chapter 5, "Ezra Pound, Man of War," offers a concluding counterpart to the opening chapter on Wilde. Like Wilde, Pound is a capacious figure whose life and writings testify to a tempestuous engagement with what he considered sociolegal pathologies: protectionist book tariffs, discriminatory copyright laws, obscenity statutes that reduced literature to an article of commerce, passport regulations that restricted the mobility of bodies and minds. Pound's vision of patronage, of which he was a recipient and a provider, mirrored his idea of copyright. Rewards for authors, he argued, should have spillover effects that benefit readers and other authors; both patronage and copyright should produce social dividends that go beyond the private economic needs of authors and their heirs. Yet his generous theories of copyright, patronage, and money did not keep him from drifting foolishly into anti-Semitic prejudice and fascist ideology, and his indictment for treason in 1945 brought him face to face with the law he had always treated as a personal foe. Deemed mentally unfit to stand trial, he never had a chance to confront his accusers in a public forum—as Wilde did in his three trials—much as he had hoped to put on a defense blending the Constitution with Confucius. The incarcerations of Pound and Wilde bookend modernism and its legal turbulence. Treason and gross indecency were at odd angles to most of the laws that superintended modernism; they originated in deeply personal forms of rebellion and fulfilled an intimate logic of temperament. Yet these two authors, contending with law throughout their careers, embodied, even in their final trials, something of modernism's legal transgressiveness.

I have tried throughout to write a prose that neither simplifies nor obfuscates modernism's passages with the law. My careers as literature professor, journal editor, law professor, and lawyer have taught me that interdisciplinarity is never easy and that writing for multiple learned audiences requires clarity, flexibility, and humility. I have employed words and phrases that lawyers and legal scholars use in discussing their subjects, in the belief that the stereoscopic interdisciplinarity that I am attempting would not benefit from blurred paraphrase and bloodless substitution. Legal language has its place in law and literature, just as the learned shoptalk of literary critics does, but I have tried to include brief definitions or explanatory context whenever I employ vocabulary or concepts that might seem puzzling. I occasionally make use of terms and ideas found in law-and-economics scholarship (such as costs and benefits, incentives, monopoly effects, freeriding, above-competition pricing, and artificial scarcity). Economics continues to be such a large presence in legal scholarship that it should find its way into law and literature as well. I have appended, along with a list of works cited, an annotated list of statutes, treaties, and cases cited in the chapters.

Every book is written from strengths and weaknesses, shaped by personal and professional experiences, and limited by its conceptual structure and physical length. I have included legal categories that I see cutting across much of Anglo-American modernism—obscenity, copyright, moral rights, blackmail, defamation, privacy, name appropriation, publicity, free speech—along with a few exotics like treason and gross indecency. But there are inevitable and regretted omissions. Any truly comprehensive study of modernism and law would have to include, for example, suffragism and the development of women's property rights (see, for example, Hynes, *Edwardian* ch. 6; Irr ch. 1; Scott pt. 1); race and its relation to obscenity; racial identity and literary form; and Jim Crow segregation and African-American disenfranchisement (see Dore ch. 4; Seshagiri; Smethurst).

Although I touch on the use of wartime laws (Defence of the Realm Act; Espionage Act of 1917) to censor disobedient authors and texts, there is more to say on that subject (see Hynes, *A War*), as well as on the laws, ideologies, and texts of war, interwar, and total war (Saint-Amour, *Tense*). The power of the Lord Chamberlain and the Examiner of Plays to ban perceived blasphemy and obscenity from the British stage deserves more attention than I have been able to give it (see Hynes, *Edwardian* ch. 7). Paris—magnet for controversial publishing—makes frequent appearances in Chapters 2 and 3, but more discussion could be devoted to that city's accommodation of obscene modernism (see Ford; Potter).

My jurisdiction in this book is limited to literature, but other arts and media would round out the picture of law and modernism. For example, as Peter Decherney shows, copyright law grew in important ways through disputes over film in the early twentieth century.

Finally, I feel that a book on modernism and law must take account of the role of non-law: informal norms, social codes, private ordering. In Chapter 2, I examine informal and quasi-official networks—purity groups and circulating libraries—that assisted and sometimes exceeded law enforcement in the war on suspect books. And the story of the transatlantic effects of copyright and obscenity laws would be incomplete without a discussion of the practice known in American publishing as the courtesy of the trade, or trade courtesy. Courtesy was an informal, norms-based system in which publishers agreed among themselves to treat copyright-deprived works as if they actually enjoyed legal protection, and sometimes paid royalties or honoraria to the authors of prematurely public-domain writings. I have written extensively on courtesy elsewhere (*Without*; "Courtesy"). For this book, I have compressed the history of courtesy, tied it more closely to issues of obscenity and intellectual property, and integrated it into the broader legal terrain that I survey.

1

Oscar Wilde, Man of Law

More than a decade after Oscar Wilde's death, his friend and literary executor Robert Ross wrote an introductory note for Stuart Mason's *Bibliography of Oscar Wilde* (1914). By turns satirical and admiring, amused by the obsessive archeology that underlay the hundreds of entries, Ross began his cameo appearance by playfully suggesting that he might sue Mason:

> Pius the Ninth, when invited to assist the sale of a certain writer's book, promised to put it on the Index Librorum Prohibitorum. The kindest act which I could do for Mr. Stuart Mason would be to injunct the result of his toil on the ground that he or his publishers had committed some breach of the Copyright Laws. This would have tempted the dealer in unauthorised literature, who would, I am sure, have invested at once in what might promise to become "curious" and "scarce." But Mr. Mason has pedantically observed all the principles of the Berne and Berlin Conventions and those other conventions which have no other authority than courtesy. (Mason, *Bibliography* v)

The sardonic faux-legalism of this endorsement suggests that Ross, mired at the time in litigation arising from his friendship with Wilde (Murray 182–8), could scarcely think of the disgraced wit as a subject distinct from the law. Ross figures himself here as the plaintiff in a lawsuit against the bibliographer, seeking an injunction for infringements of Wilde's copyrights—even though forced sales and bankruptcy had stripped Wilde of many of his copyrights in the aftermath of his trials and burdened Ross with the ongoing task of recovering the alienated rights for Wilde's children (Ellmann, *Oscar*

588). Bitter and court-weary, Ross cannot resist pointing to other features of the legal landscape of the early twentieth century. He notes that books tainted by legal scandal—whether from charges of obscenity, blasphemy, or piracy—often acquired value in the underground markets that exploited law-induced scarcity. And he casts a skeptical eye on international copyright conventions that had been adopted in previous decades for combatting cross-border piracies but that, lacking the signature of the United States, often did little to inhibit transatlantic exploitation of European writers. Only "courtesy"—informal norms of respect for authorship, discussed below and in Chapter 3—might persuade American publishers to treat foreign authors and their executors as if they were entitled to control the printing of books and the collecting of royalties.

The primary target of Ross's imaginary legal action is the book itself, "the result of [Mason's] toil," which he playfully threatens to "injunct" and so consign to a booklegger's heaven of forbidden wares. He does not suggest, as some executors might, that he will seek damages to compensate beneficiaries. His litigation scenario is mostly *in rem*, directed against the offending thing, rather than *in personam*, against the actors—Mason and his publisher—who are responsible for the imaginary infringement. Ross thus models his friendly suit on one of the period's chief legal strategies: to assail books themselves as the source of harm to morality, property, or reputation.

Ross evokes in his brief fantasia the law-saturated culture in which Wilde lived and wrote—a culture of authorial regulation, moral didacticism, banned books and performances, infringed copyrights and lawful piracies, and informal and sporadic courtesies extended to vulnerable authors. Wilde himself had come to recognize that he was a product or precipitate of the law. Writing in his prison cell at Reading in 1897, he observed that "[t]o be entirely free, and at the same time entirely dominated by law, is the eternal paradox of human life that we realise at every moment" (*De Profundis* 704). This melancholy philosophy—confided in a letter to his friend and lover, Lord Alfred Douglas—figured the law almost as an erotic force, imposing its will on consciously free subjects just as Dorian Gray's personality "dominates" the artist Basil Hallward in *The Picture of Dorian Gray* (1891:25), and as Wilde "dominated" various young men, according to the barrister who cross-examined him at trial (Holland 268, 270, 273). As a convict, Wilde at times thought of himself as a victim and plaything of the law; at other times, he imagined the law as a retributive fury exacting a righteous toll for his private conduct. But mostly he lamented "the unintelligent violence of the Law" as a thing that crowded and consumed his postlapsarian life (*Complete Letters* 819, 1142; *De Profundis* 758).

Yet law's pervasive force had been there all the time, even if Wilde only became fully aware of it as he looked back on his road to Reading. In *De Profundis* he observed, "I am a born antinomian. I am one of those who are made for exceptions, not for laws" (732). He returned to the figure of the exception later in the same letter while discussing Christ as the supreme example of individualism: "Christ had no patience with the dull lifeless mechanical systems that treat people as if they were things.... For him there were no laws: there were exceptions merely" (750-1). Wilde imagined himself to be, like Christ, an exception shining in the darkness of homogenizing laws, a figure whom norms and normative systems could never assimilate or fully comprehend.

When he characterized himself as an exception among laws, did he mean that he was an exception in the conventional legal sense? If this was his meaning, then he thought of himself as occupying law's ambit of grace, a person whose individualism merited a special juridical accommodation. If, on the other hand, he meant that his exceptionalism was outside law's framework altogether, something unaccounted for by the law, then he was imagining himself and his predicament as constituting a state of exception analogous in some ways to the condition described by the political theorist Carl Schmitt: an emergency or extreme peril that troubles the shared legal order and cannot be reconciled with known facts or made to conform to preexisting legal codes (Schmitt 6). The exception in this sense—and it seems to be Wilde's sense—is charged with dangerous novelty, with "the power of real life [that] breaks through the crust of a mechanism that has become torpid by repetition" (15). In this respect, Wilde was a solvent of norms, a human emergency that dared the Victorian legal order to regulate and remedy him. His personal state of exception implied "a suspension of the judicial order itself" (Agamben 4).

But Wilde was not the only sociolegal emergency. The very laws that he challenged were in a state of perilous flux. The legal regimes that regulated literary piracy, obscenity, privacy, sexuality, and other aspects of British life at the *fin de siècle* contained gaps, negative spaces, undeveloped rationales, and ambiguous standards—legal black holes and grey holes that either defied the law to fill them or invited the law to act arbitrarily and capriciously in regulating deviant subjects (Vermeule). Even before an English court sentenced him to two years at hard labor for the statutory offense of gross indecency, Wilde's life had become defined by the laws of late nineteenth-century Britain and its combative, legalistic culture. His immersion in law, forced and voluntary, makes him both a representative and an exceptional figure within his legal culture and a precursor of literary modernism's complex interactions with law in the decades that followed. Just as Wilde's state of exception collided with the regulatory forces of Victorian law, so modernist writing would be a challenging emergency within the transitional normative systems that sought to regulate it.

Honor and libel

In Britain in the late nineteenth and early twentieth centuries, there was a fierce culture of honor among writers and artists, often manifested in real or threatened litigation or in public accusations and recriminations. Men who felt that their professional or personal reputations had been impugned instituted civil or criminal libel proceedings, seeking damages for themselves or prison terms for their opponents. In 1878, James McNeill Whistler sued the art critic John Ruskin for publishing a critique that assailed one of Whistler's paintings as the work of a "coxcomb ask[ing] two hundred guineas for flinging a pot of paint in the public's face" (qtd. in Whistler 1). Whistler prevailed in the libel action, but the jury awarded him only contemptuous damages of a farthing, and the judge denied him the costs of his suit (Pennell 242). In *The Gentle Art of Making Enemies* (1890), Whistler revisited the Ruskin litigation and other artistic and literary quarrels, including his public feud with Wilde for allegedly plagiarizing his ideas (236–43). In the decades following Wilde's death, Lord Alfred Douglas was the plaintiff or the defendant in several libel proceedings involving books about his relationship with Wilde, accusations of homosexuality, and his work as an author and editor. Even Douglas's father-in-law prosecuted him for criminal libel in the course of a family dispute (Murray 168–9).

In this culture of honor, the combatants spoke the language of law as if it were a sturdy vernacular. When Douglas's father, the Marquess of Queensberry, confronted Wilde at his London home to warn him to stay away from his son, Wilde went on the offensive: "I suppose you have come to apologise for the statements you made about my wife and myself in letters you wrote to your son. I should have the right any day I chose to prosecute you for writing such a letter." To this threat of a libel prosecution, Queensberry retorted, "The letter was privileged, as it was written to my son" (qtd. in Ellmann, *Oscar* 447). Queensberry's reply alluded to the law's qualified privilege for communications made to protect the interests of family members (Odgers, *Outline* 124–5). Less menacingly, George Bernard Shaw wrote to the author and journalist Frank Harris in 1921 to discourage the making of a film about Wilde's life. He lectured Harris colorfully if pedantically on the application of libel law to living and deceased persons and on the distinction between copyrighted expression and unprotected ideas. If the "film people" attempted to use Shaw's name, he warned, he would "be down on them instantly with all the legal thunderbolts [he could] throw" (qtd. in Harris 209–11).

These honor feuds were sometimes not far from physical violence. In the quarrel leading up to Wilde's attempt to prosecute Queensberry for criminal libel, the principals threatened each other with beatings and shootings. In response to an insulting telegram, Queensberry wrote his son that he would give him the "thrashing" he deserved. In return, Douglas informed his father that, in addition to a possible libel action, he had armed himself with a "loaded revolver" with which he or Wilde would be "completely justified" in defending themselves against "a violent and dangerous rough" (qtd. in Murray 58, 64). Queensberry himself claimed that he would be justified in shooting the "monster" Wilde in the street, and he showed up at restaurants armed with a horsewhip, vowing to administer a public lashing if he found Wilde and his son together. A concerned friend made Wilde a present of a sword stick with which to protect himself (73–4), and Wilde warned the Scarlet Marquess during a heated interview that, whatever the Queensberry boxing rules might say, "the Oscar Wilde rule [was] to shoot at sight" (qtd. in Ellmann, *Oscar* 447). These mutual menacings blended legalism and mayhem in a potent antisocial brew. (Fascinated by the romance of wounded honor, Wilde included duel motifs in at least two unproduced dramas [411–12].)

Turbulent quarrels over reputation were the chief reason for the historical growth of criminal libel law (Latham 75–6). A remedy in the criminal courts was meant to take the place of duels, public brawling, and other breaches of the peace (Odgers, *Outline* 177–8). Lord Alfred Douglas referred to his own libel actions as attempts to obtain "satisfaction," a transfer of the duel from the field of honor to the courtroom, with attorneys playing the role of seconds and the jury's verdict replacing the épée and the pistol (Murray 187). Aesthetes and decadents who resorted to honorable violence were imitating the habits of the hereditary leisure class, for whom dueling, according to Thorstein Veblen, was the survival of an archaic predatory instinct (Veblen 249). Queensberry and Wilde—the one a blood aristocrat, the other a dandy mimicking the dress and airs of the upper class—might have traded threats of violence, but in the end they submitted their honor-based aggressions to the criminal courts, which had long before assumed jurisdiction over public violence committed in the name of wounded honor.

Wilde's formal indictment against Queensberry recited the dual rationale underlying the law of criminal libel as it existed in 1895. Wilde alleged that the calling card left by Queensberry at Wilde's club, bearing the message "For Oscar Wilde posing as somdomite [*sic*]," was maliciously intended "to deprive [Wilde] of his good name fame credit and reputation" and "to excite him to commit a breach of the peace" (Holland 285–6). Wilde in effect charged that Queensberry should be held accountable for both a private wrong and a public harm because he had sought to injure Wilde's reputation and to incite him to violent retaliation. Although harm to reputation had long been recognized as the basis for civil libel actions, and breach of the peace as the basis for prosecuting criminal libels, jurists in the nineteenth century were coming to view criminal libel as protecting against private and public harms equally (*Report from the Select Committee* 35; Veeder 41–7). Criminal libel's threat to the public peace had given rise to several traditional rules. First, unlike a libel in a civil action, a criminal libel need not have been published to a third party to be punishable; a libel communicated solely to the injured party was sufficient to provoke violence (Odgers, *Outline* 187–8). Second, although only statements about living persons could be the subject of civil actions for libel, a libel aimed at the dead was a punishable

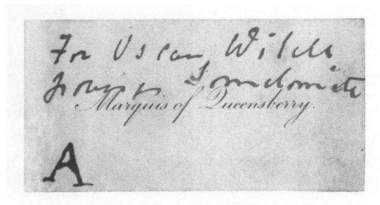

FIGURE 1.1 *Marquess of Queensberry's calling card left for Oscar Wilde, February 1895. Courtesy Merlin Holland.*

crime because it could lead to family feuding or other public mischief (184). Third, while the truth of an injurious statement was a complete defense in a civil action, truth alone could not justify a libel in the common-law criminal courts, because telling an inflammatory truth might provoke retaliation just as easily as stating a falsehood. Hence, the old maxim, "The greater the truth, the greater the libel" (188).

Because Wilde was prosecuting him for criminal libel, Queensberry could not defend himself simply by proving the truth of his statement that Wilde had been posing as a sodomite. Instead, Queensberry had the twofold statutory burden of showing that his words were true and that he had published them for the public benefit (Libel Act 1843 § 6; Latham 76). Publishing a truth for the public benefit was deemed to justify a libel because it offered a "countervailing advantage to compensate the public for the risk of a breach of the peace" (Odgers, *Outline* 188). In other words, publishing an unsettling truth for a broadly beneficial purpose was thought to balance out any threat to the public safety. The law of criminal libel, while it shared elements with its civil counterpart, in this respect remained rooted in the public interest. Throughout the trial, Queensberry—although his public-spiritedness had previously shown itself in threats to beat and disinherit his son—maintained, through his counsel, that he had sought to "save" Douglas and to expose Wilde's corrupting influence on other young men, for the public benefit (Holland 249).

Posing

The "hideous words" written on Queensberry's calling card read, "For Oscar Wilde posing as somdomite" (Ellmann, *Oscar* 438). Or did they? At least three different readings of the crabbed scrawl have seemed possible. Some scholars contend that what Queensberry wrote was "For [or To] Oscar Wilde posing Somdomite" (438; Holland 300 n41). At Queensberry's committal hearing in March 1895, the hall porter of Wilde's club, to whom the Marquess had handed the card, testified that the message was "For Oscar Wilde ponce and somdomite," but Queensberry interrupted and insisted that the words were "posing as sodomite" (Holland 4). Queensberry's self-serving version—"posing as" was easier to defend than other possibilities—was the one that came to dominate the proceedings, but what did it mean to pose as a sodomite? Wilde's indictment itself seemed undecided. His first count alleged that the words accused him of "commit[ting] and [being] in the habit of committing the abominable crime of buggery with mankind" (285). The second count offered no interpretation at all, suggesting, probably, that the words meant just what they said: "*posing* as a sodomite." Queensberry's plea of justification mirrored this dual reading by claiming, first, that "the natural meaning of the words" was that Wilde "did solicit and incite" more than a dozen young men "to commit sodomy and other acts of gross indecency and immorality with him"; and, second, that certain writings by Wilde described or were related to "sodomitical and unnatural habits tastes and practices" (286–91). These allegations all converged in the notion that Wilde had "created a public persona for himself as a 'sodomite'" (Latham 65), yet the litigation never quite settled on a single meaning for Queensberry's cryptic slur. Was Wilde accused of *posing* or of *being*, and did it really matter which?

In fact, the meaning of "posing" multiplied throughout the libel trial, overtaking Queensberry's simple dichotomous equivalency: "to pose as a thing is as bad as to be it" (Holland 214). Wilde himself introduced the first variation when defense counsel Edward Carson caught him in a flattering miscalculation of his age. Wilde flared, "I have no intention of posing for a younger man at all" (64). This flippant parody of the Marquess's calling card glanced, unconsciously perhaps, at *The Picture of Dorian*

Gray, which Carson would shortly adduce as evidence of Wilde's immoral posing. In the novel's second chapter, Dorian literally poses for the painter Basil Hallward and grows jealous of the portrait that will "remain always young" while Dorian himself will become "old, and horrible, and dreadful" (1890:19). After his prayer for perpetual youth is answered, Dorian lives a life that enables him, as the years pass, to pose as a young man about London, while his portrait, shut away in the attic, registers the reality of his moral corruption and physical aging. Worship of youth is at the center of the story's bizarre moral alchemy. Dorian is his own living portrait, perpetually posed and posing. His unchanging body circulates in society, as Jonathan Goldman has shown (19–54), while the changing canvas keeps a secret tally of his sins. Basil Hallward also fears that the picture reveals a secret, but it is "the secret of [his] own soul," the "extraordinary romance" and "idolatry" that he has felt for Dorian (1890:6, 10, 57). Dorian and Basil both worry that the canvas will betray a shameful truth that has its roots in worship of male youth and beauty. Wilde once remarked that Basil was the character he felt he most resembled but that "Dorian [was] what [he] would like to be—in other ages, perhaps" (*Complete Letters* 585). The faint quibble on "ages" foreshadowed Wilde's chronological posing in the witness box.

In *Dorian Gray*, posing is mostly characterized as a false or feigned attitude. When Basil chides him for his cynical "pose," the dandy Lord Henry Wotton retorts that "[b]eing natural is simply a pose" (1890:5). Confronted by Basil about scandalous rumors, Dorian attacks the hypocrisy of the middle classes "who pose as being moral" (1891:118). Later, when Dorian hints that he has murdered Basil, Lord Henry chaffs him for "posing for a character that doesn't suit [him]" (160). These are poses that seek to conceal the truth. Queensberry, in contrast, seemed to charge Wilde with a pose that revealed the truth. At trial, Carson sought to collapse the distinction between posing and being, appearance and reality, by showing that Wilde's poses were simply a performance of his sexual being (Danson 107; Novak 82). When Wilde refused to condemn a homoerotic story, "The Priest and the Acolyte," which had appeared in the same magazine that printed some of his epigrams, Carson pressed him: "I want to see what position you pose in." Wilde objected to this taunt, but Carson had scored his point, implying that Wilde's poses were actually antisocial positions that could be unveiled by aggressive questioning. Wilde's writings, Carson argued, showed him "pos[ing] as not being concerned about morality or immorality" (Holland 70, 74). Under the stress of cross-examination, the meaning of posing was changing from public persona to private belief, from exteriority to interiority, just as the trial as a whole, according to Alan Sinfield and Ed Cohen, helped to establish homosexuality as an intrinsic type of sexual identity. Seeking leave from the court to read from Joris-Karl Huysmans' *À Rebours*, which had suggested some incidents in *Dorian Gray*, Carson contended that establishing what was "in [Wilde's] mind" when he wrote the novel would help the jury to determine whether he was "posing as a sodomite" (Holland 100). Wilde's "writings and [his] course of life," Carson argued, permitted the jury to infer that he "was either in sympathy with, or addicted to, immoral and sodomitic habits" (255). Posing was no longer simply a form of public display. It was the essence of Wilde.

In the course of the trial, Carson developed a further specialized meaning of "posing" with which he mocked Wilde's artistic pretensions. When Wilde stated that only "brutes and the illiterate" would think that *Dorian Gray* was "a sodomitical book," Carson sprang to the defense of unsophisticated readers and asked Wilde if he thought "the majority of people live up to the pose that you are giving us ... or are educated up to that" (Holland 81). Wilde took the bait. When Carson belittled the artistic merits of one of his letters to Douglas, Wilde retorted, "I think everything I write extraordinary.... I don't pose as being ordinary—good heavens!—I don't pose as being ordinary" (110). Carson had cleverly driven a wedge between Wilde and the jury, making the playwright out to be an elitist snob whose very art was a pose. This made it all the easier for the barrister to argue that in consorting with unemployed male prostitutes (or "renters"), Wilde was not nobly disregarding class distinctions as he pretended, but simply using the young men for his indecent needs. As we will see in Chapter 2, the pitting of aesthetic cliques against the moral masses, the posing artist against the ordinary reader, was a common ploy of judges, prosecutors, and social purity groups in the early decades of the twentieth century.

Blackmail

The three trials of Oscar Wilde indelibly linked blackmail and defamation law as mechanisms for preserving reputation in the modern world—and as platforms for the ritual sacrifice of reputation. Wilde's initial libel prosecution featured his letters to Lord Alfred Douglas, which had fallen into the hands of blackmailers and were read out in court to establish Queensberry's plea of justification. After the libel action ended abruptly in a conceded jury verdict for Queensberry, the government prosecuted Wilde over the course of two trials for committing the crime of gross indecency. Section 11 of the Criminal Law Amendment Act of 1885, known as the Labouchere Amendment, made it a misdemeanor, punishable by up to two years' imprisonment at hard labor, for any male, in public or in private, to commit, procure, or attempt to procure "any act of gross indecency with another male person." The conduct proscribed by the statute was notoriously indeterminate, and it could occur anywhere, in public or in private, whereas older British law had imposed liability only if a grossly indecent act occurred in "an open and public place" (Mead and Bodkin 68–9). Acts of sodomy would certainly fall within the scope of the Labouchere Amendment, but so would less overt kinds of intimate contact. Replying to a journalist's charges that *Dorian Gray* was an indecent work, Wilde in 1890 declared that he had tried to surround Dorian "with an atmosphere of moral corruption [that was] vague and indeterminate and wonderful." "What Dorian Gray's sins are no one knows," Wilde contended. "He who finds them has brought them" (*Complete Letters* 439). The nebulous language of the Labouchere Amendment similarly invited subjective reader response on the part of fact-finders. It posed scandalous riddles that prosecutors and juries might solve as they pleased, vindictively or sanctimoniously.

During Wilde's second and last criminal trial, his attorney Edward Clarke argued that the proceedings seemed to be "operating as an act of indemnity for all the blackmailers in London" (qtd. in Ellmann, *Oscar* 476). He meant that some of the young men who had appeared as witnesses were notorious for blackmailing and other rogueries. In 1893, a group of blackmailers had subjected Wilde to what was known as the badger game, tag-teaming him as they attempted to extract serial payments for an amorous letter he had written to Douglas. Blackmail in this pre-digital era often took the form of payment demanded for the return of an embarrassing physical document. In Wilde's play *An Ideal Husband* (1895), the action turns on two incriminating documents—a letter written by Sir Robert Chiltern early in his career and a recent note penned by his wife—that threaten professional and marital ruin, respectively. Only Sir Robert's letter is actual evidence of wrongdoing, but both writings serve the purpose of the blackmailer, Mrs. Cheveley, for whom extortion is "the game of life as we all have to play it" (*Ideal* 495). In a twist on the Wildean motif of intangible honor being menaced by a tangible object, Lord Goring at one point turns the tables on Mrs. Cheveley by confronting her with a diamond brooch she once stole and threatening to have her prosecuted if she doesn't hand over Sir Robert's letter (488, 535–7).

Wilde's plays are filled with ingenious variations on blackmail's coercions, as when Mrs. Cheveley agrees to surrender Sir Robert's letter if Lord Goring will marry her (*Ideal* 532–3), or when Mrs. Erlynne, who has been extorting money from Lord Windermere by threats that she will reveal that she is Lady Windermere's mother, repents and vows that she will ruin her daughter's life if he now tells Lady Windermere the truth (*Lady Windermere's* 425–7). Mrs. Erlynne's maternal change of heart takes the form of counter-blackmail. Whereas she formerly promised silence in exchange for Lord Windermere's cash payments, she now obtains his silence by threatening to behave in ways that will cause her daughter pain. The theme of blackmail floats playfully over *The Importance of Being Earnest* (1895) without ever settling into real menace. The first act opens with Algernon refusing to hand over Jack's "private" cigarette case until Jack agrees to explain its mysterious inscription from "little Cecily" (324–6). From innocuous coercions like this to Dorian Gray's cruel threat to disgrace a former friend unless he agrees to dispose of Basil Hallward's body (1890:89–92), motifs of extortion pervade Wilde's mature writings. Sometimes blackmail is figured as a slow-gathering retribution. "Sooner or later we all have to pay for what we do," declares Mrs. Cheveley (*Ideal* 496). In most cases, however, it is rooted in the pose of excessive morality—the "monstrous pedestals" erected by Victorian ideals (521)—which Angus McLaren associates with the rise of sexual respectability and of privacy as a proprietary good (McLaren 3–4, 11, 278).

In the nineteenth century, blackmail often appeared as a revolt of the lower orders. Servants, gamekeepers, coachmen, and other employees became dangerous when they decided to use the intimate knowledge they had acquired during their service to coerce their employers, thus turning the household *heimlich* into the criminal *unheimlich* (McLaren 43). The crime of blackmail, seen in this light, was a vehicle for protecting the moneyed and privileged classes from a knowledge-empowered proletariat (Alldridge 373). Wilde complained from prison about Douglas's careless treatment of his letters, left "lying about for blackmailing companions to steal, for hotel servants to pilfer, for housemaids to sell" (*De Profundis* 716). *The Importance of Being Earnest* opens with a comic glance at the danger of the all-hearing domestic when Lane, the manservant, remarks that he "didn't think it polite to listen" while his master, Algernon Moncrieff, was playing the piano (321). Dorian Gray, who cultivates the power of knowing other men's secrets, worries that his servant, under a "placid mask of servility," might become a "spy" in the house, using his access to Dorian's altered portrait to blackmail him for the rest of his life (1890:59, 63). Dorian takes pains to cover the picture with a heavy fabric before asking a frame-maker and his "somewhat rough-looking young assistant" to carry it up to the attic (60–2). His great fear is that servants and workmen, paid to do the living for their masters, will thereby acquire forbidden knowledge and become as gods, turning old transgressions into a source of endless tribute.

One of Wilde's letters to Douglas, in which he compared the young man to Apollo's lover Hyacinthus, fell into the hands of opportunists who attempted to "rent," or blackmail, Wilde. Somehow—probably through the renters—a copy of the letter found its way to the theater manager Herbert Beerbohm Tree; and when the badgers set upon Wilde, the latter shook them off by saying that he would have paid a large sum for the letter as a "work of art," but that Tree's copy made buying it back unnecessary. He also informed them that the letter would shortly be published "in sonnet form in a delightful magazine"—a reference to *The Spirit Lamp*, an Oxford undergraduate magazine that in 1893 printed Pierre Louÿs' free French translation of the letter (a ruse, argued Queensberry's attorney, for laundering the letter's indecency) (Holland 50–5, 111–33). The existence of copies of the Hyacinthus letter foiled the blackmail plot, which depended on a unique tangible document passing from renter back to rented after payment. The multiplication of copies in effect introduced the logic of copyright into the mechanics of blackmail, substituting the benign prospect of authorized dissemination of a public good for the danger of a unique incriminating artifact. With the aura of blackmail dissipated by the reality of mechanical reproduction, the asking price for the original document fell sharply (50–5).

Affirmative defenses

Wilde's encounter with blackmailers revealed a characteristic feature of his art and legal imagination. When one of the renters claimed, to start the bargaining, that a man had offered him £60 for the Hyacinthus letter, Wilde facetiously urged him to accept that offer, as he himself had never "received so large a sum for any prose work of that very small length" (Holland 53). Wilde's retort was typical: an epigrammatic parry that converted a black market for secrets into a white market for literature, and a dangerous love letter into a work of art. When Lord Henry, whom Dorian Gray calls the "Prince of Paradox," attacks realism in literature by announcing that "[t]he man who could call a spade a spade should be compelled to use one" (1891:147), he is engaging in a similar gesture of transvaluing values, equating intellectual effort with manual labor and treating literary taste as a mark of social class. Throughout his trials, Wilde deflected adversarial questioning—whether about the purported immorality of his writings or of his friendships—by shifting the context to artistic meanings and values. He insisted in the witness box, "I cannot answer any question apart from art," in effect positing a transvalued aesthetic morality at odds with the discourse of law and legal proceedings (Holland 105).

Wilde's instinct, both in his heterodox maxims and in his answers on cross-examination, was to assert a form of what the law calls an affirmative defense, a pleading strategy whereby a defendant does not deny the truth of the complainant's factual claims but instead attacks her legal right to assert them (*Black's* 60). For example, a person charged with murder might raise the affirmative defense of insanity, without actually denying that he had killed the victim; or the defendant in a copyright action might concede that she had copied from the plaintiff's work but argue that her copying was privileged as a fair use. The rhetorical posture of the affirmative defense is "yes but," just as Wilde's paradoxes and epigrams quip, "yes but." His aphoristic art—described by critics as "a perverted mimicry of public speech" and a practice of "inverting Victorian truisms" (Gagnier 7; Goldman 25)—was a form of affirmative defense, prefiguring his law-for-art's-sake posture during the legal proceedings: "What is abnormal in Life stands in normal relations to Art" ("A Few Maxims" 1203). Wilde consistently exploited the logic of the affirmative defense, wearily acknowledging a state of facts but wittily pointing to a larger moral or aesthetic dimension ignored by his adversaries. One of the least witty things he ever did was to cave to external and internal pressures in prosecuting the Marquess of Queensberry for libel. But once he found himself in the dock, he regained his levity and elevated the affirmative defense to an art form. The great speech during his first criminal trial in which he discoursed movingly on "the love that dare not speak its name" translated the fact of male–male desire to the moral plane of noble love, and allowed Wilde, for a Platonic moment, to dominate the Old Bailey as he had formerly ruled dinner tables in society (Ellmann, *Oscar* 463).

Privacy, publicity, and name appropriation

In attempting to prosecute Queensberry for libel, Wilde pursued a remedy that was plainly ill-adapted to the real outrage. The insult scribbled on Queensberry's card served Wilde as a pretext for invoking the law to free himself from the Marquess's escalating menace. Wilde brought the libel action, in part, to reclaim his threatened privacy, to draw a line between his public poses and his private actions. The trial did the opposite, of course, turning his private conduct into public notoriety and collapsing his cherished distinction between surface and secret. By the late nineteenth century, privacy had come to seem a proprietary entitlement of the middle and upper classes, as McLaren notes (4, 11, 61–2). Blackmailers recognized this property as a monetizable good, just as commercial journalism created a mass market for artistic celebrity and saleable image. Wilde lived in a time when privacy and publicity as yet enjoyed few recognized legal protections (North). Privacy was a juridical exception, a lacuna that the clumsy mechanisms of defamation law, copyright law, and even extralegal dueling sometimes sought to fill. Wilde typified the contradictory subject of modernity—the self that seeks to enjoy the benefits of selective public display while fiercely asserting the right to be let alone.

For Wilde, individualism meant freedom from external compulsions. Individual goodness flourishes "when [people] are let alone," he wrote in "The Soul of Man under Socialism" (1891) (1100). His feeling for privacy was intense and genuine. In 1885, he was outraged over a public sale of John Keats's love letters and responded with a sonnet that lamented the dead poet's loss of privacy to "the brawlers of the auction mart." The poem, of which Wilde was especially proud, decried the "small and sickly eyes" that pored over Keats's letters, and compared the auction to the dividing of Christ's garments by dicing Roman soldiers who had failed to perceive "the God's wonder, or His woe" ("On the Sale" 815). The public sale struck Wilde as a further invasion of Keats's privacy— the letters had already been published several years before—and as a sullying of art by bourgeois market values. In particular, Wilde deplored the hawking of Keats's "poor blotted note[s]," the tangible remains of his private passion; and he managed to purchase several of the letters himself, almost as if he were paying a blackmailer's price to retrieve his own intimate confessions (Wilde, *Complete Letters* 254 n2).

Wilde himself would know the shame of merchandised privacy ten years later when, following his failed libel action, his creditors forced a sale of his books, manuscripts, and other effects, including the original manuscript of a Keats sonnet, which the poet's niece had given him (Wilde, *Complete Letters* 157–8). James Joyce, writing in 1909, proposed a line from Psalms as a fitting motto for Wilde's tombstone: "They part my garments among them, and cast lots upon my vesture" ("Oscar" 205). Although Joyce was primarily referring to Wilde's tragically divided legacy as a man and writer, the words also echo the sonnet on the sale of Keats's letters and mark Wilde as a celebrity dandy whose defiant posing could not in the end prevent the public sacrifice of his personal privacy.

Wilde was as protective of his family's privacy as of his own. In 1889, the journalist and author Herbert Vivian published some humorous details concerning Wilde's children, claiming that the wit had offered to stand as "fairy-godfather" of the book (154–8). Wilde objected to this "extremely vulgar and offensive" publication and denied that Vivian had "the right to make one godfather to a dirty baby against one's will," especially when Vivian added the insult of reproducing the text of one of Wilde's letters without his permission. Wilde was even more disturbed that the story had upset his wife Constance, who, he said, did not "wish to see her children paraded for the amusement of the uncouth." He accused Vivian of combining "the inaccuracy of the eavesdropper with the method of the blackmailer"—an invasion of domestic space coupled with an exploitative use of private correspondence (*Complete Letters* 426–7). Vivian's journalistic predation had put Wilde in mind of the close proximity between invaded privacy and blackmailed reputation as comparably intractable legal problems.

Wilde complained that Vivian had published a book "with which no gentleman would wish to have his name associated" (426). Vivian had appropriated his name for the purpose of spreading gossip "in the public press," in effect violating two rights that Wilde held dear: the right to privacy and the right to control the publicity of his name (427). Yet Vivian's perceived wrongs were largely immune from legal retaliation in 1890. Wilde might have sued him for infringing a copyright in his letter, but such an action would not have gone to the essence of Wilde's grievance: the assault on his domestic seclusion and the exploitation of his marketable name.

In 1890, privacy and publicity occupied a negative space in the law, a gap for which English courts offered little satisfactory redress apart from the unwieldy law of defamation and the limited tort of confidentiality. That same year in the *Harvard Law Review*, Samuel D. Warren and Louis D. Brandeis famously called on the common law to protect "the right to be let alone," but the law's full response was decades away, as we will see in Chapter 4. Without clear causes of action for privacy invasion and name appropriation, authors often resorted to homemade remedies. Wilde's self-help took the form of shaming Vivian for his "wilful surrender of that position you hold as a gentleman" and a "Cambridge man" (*Complete Letters* 426). Vivian had not acted properly from "a gentleman's point of view, or from the point of view of literary honour" (427).

Wilde was appealing to an extralegal concept of class-based honor, decrying a breach of propriety that in a more dangerous setting might have led to violence on the field of honor. In the absence of a legal remedy, he invoked informal norms of courtesy to fill the juridical void that Warren and Brandeis were urging American common-law courts to address.

Wilde's writings foreground privacy as a primary desideratum, whether in Dorian Gray's "terrible pleasure of a double life" (1891:134) or in the comedy of Algernon Moncrieff's theory of Bunburying (*Importance* 325–6). *The Picture of Dorian Gray* is, in one respect, the story of a compulsively public man who wishes to keep his personal life private, and who secretes the record of that life—his portrait—in the attic room where as a boy he often hid himself in a *cassone*, an ornate marriage chest where brides traditionally stored their personal effects (1890:61–2). Fearing the kind of public gossip that led Warren and Brandeis to call for a right to privacy, Basil Hallward admits that he loves "secrecy ... the only thing that can make modern life wonderful or mysterious to us" (1890:5). Even after his public disgrace, Wilde insisted on a modicum of privacy, refusing Douglas permission to quote in print from the intimate letters he had written him from Holloway Prison after his arrest. Although the forced sale had stripped him of many of his literary and performance rights, he could still invoke the undivested "legal copyright" in his private correspondence (*De Profundis* 722). He was shocked that his lover would consider disseminating letters that he should have guarded as "sacred and secret beyond anything in the whole world," and he reminded Douglas of the sonnet he had written to express his "sorrow and scorn" over the sale of Keats's letters (717).

In *De Profundis*, Wilde also rebuked Douglas for planning to use his name without permission on the dedication page of a volume of poems (684, 721–2). Wilde knew that his name had lost its power and respectability; after his arrest, his name had been pulled down from theater hoardings where his comedies were playing, and he acknowledged in prison that his children would no longer bear his name (654; Ellmann, *Oscar* 458). Yet he clung to the remnants of dignity and refused to allow Douglas to appropriate his name for a dedicatory paratext, just as he had upbraided Herbert Vivian for using his family to boost a journalistic effort. Wilde could no longer feel, as Basil Hallward and Lord Henry Wotton do in *Dorian Gray*, that names were powerful and talismanic (1890:5; 1891:147), but he could deny Douglas the use of his name to play keeper of the Wildean flame. Douglas was the love that dare not publish Wilde's name without permission. Honor, courtesy, and friendship demanded at least that.

Piracy, copyright, and courtesy

In "The Soul of Man under Socialism," Wilde wrote that private property had "crushed true Individualism" and that only with the abolition of property could healthy individualism flourish. The "perfect personality" would not "admit any laws but its own laws; nor any authority but its own authority" (1083, 1084–5). As attractive as this hedonic anarchism may have seemed to Wilde the essayist, Wilde the man of property was far from relinquishing his copyrights. He took pains to secure rights for his plays in copyright-unfriendly America and made special arrangements to reserve the book rights to "The Portrait of Mr. W.H." (1889) and *The Picture of Dorian Gray* after their magazine appearances (*Complete Letters* 150, 400, 425). He was deeply distressed when forced sales and bankruptcy took away "my copyright in my published works, my copyright in my plays, everything in fact ... down to the staircarpets and door-scraper of my house," as if the law had compounded tragedy by erasing any distinction between his intellectual creations and his gross chattels (*De Profundis* 774). Even after his release from prison, Wilde hoped to buy back some of his copyrights, and he schemed to secure rights for *The Ballad of Reading Gaol* (1898) in the United States, where copyright protection for foreign authors depended, after 1891, on simultaneous transatlantic publication and other stringent conditions (*Complete Letters* 970; Chace International Copyright Act § 4956; see also Chapter 3).

When Wilde made his celebrated lecture tour of the United States in 1882, American copyright law offered virtually no protection for foreign authors. He was indignant when he learned that his *Poems*, published the year before in London, was being hawked on American trains for ten cents in the unauthorized Seaside Library edition published in New York. In addition to his poems, the flimsy volume contained his lecture on the English Renaissance, the centerpiece of his cross-country tour. He complained about this "hellish infringement on the right of an English author" and told the train newsboys that such piracies "must have a disastrous effect on poetical aspirants," espousing the theory, as Wordsworth had done a half-century before, that creative incentives would dry up unless authors could legally control their writings ("The Poet" 1; Wilde, "Impressions" 178). Wilde claimed that the pirated version of his lecture was thinning attendance at his appearances—"people think they know it, and stay away"—so he hurried together two new readings for the remainder of his tour (*Complete Letters* 147; Ellmann, *Oscar* 193). Piracy no less than copyright could sometimes spur creativity.

Wilde also made efforts to secure US copyright for his play *Vera; or, the Nihilists* (1880), which he wanted to see produced in New York, but when asked by a reporter if copyright had been his reason for coming to America, he loftily ignored the impertinence (Hofer and Scharnhorst, eds. 14). Fantasizing with a friend years later about producing a deluxe volume containing his unwritten thoughts, Wilde quipped that there should be "five hundred signed copies for particular friends, six for the general public, and one for America" (qtd. in Ellmann, *Oscar* 392). The remark was only partly a sneer at American culture; given the rapidity with which unauthorized publishers reprinted British writings, a single imported copy would have sufficed to supply bookstores in all major American cities within a week or two. As with Dickens before him, Wilde's celebrity in America soared, and his lectures filled up, in part because his writings were reprinted so freely and cheaply.

Lawful piracy was an aggressive, often volatile business in America in the 1880s, but not all publishers exploited the letter of the discriminatory copyright law. For decades, certain established publishers had agreed among themselves to divide up the commons of foreign works and to respect each other's claims to certain authors and books. This informal cartel was known as the courtesy of the trade, or trade courtesy; its participants, which included the Harpers, Scribner's, Henry Holt, and other major houses, even paid honoraria or royalties to foreign authors when they could. As a response to the law's creation of a teeming public domain and legalized piracy, trade courtesy brought a fragile order to American publishing by improvising a facsimile of copyright law and enabling publishers and authors to benefit from informal norms of neighborly self-restraint (Spoo, *Without* 13–64). Foreign authors were so grateful to be treated courteously that they sometimes wrote statements or letters of authorization, which their American publishers reproduced in the front matter of their editions. These courtesy paratexts extolled the virtues of honest publishing and served to legitimize the authorized text (Spoo, "Courtesy"). The US copyright vacuum for foreign authors was a kind of juridical void, yet this void was not filled by a sovereign or executive power but rather by informal, voluntary trade norms. Trade courtesy was to the copyright gap what Wilde's appeal to honor and gentlemanliness was to the privacy-law gap.

Although distressed by the piratical Seaside Library, Wilde took consolation in Roberts Brothers of Boston, which had published an authorized courtesy reprint of *Poems* in 1881. It is not known whether Roberts Brothers made payments to Wilde, but he was pleased to have a "genuine" American edition and remarked scornfully of the pirate houses that "a country gets small good from the literature it steals" (Hofer and Scharnhorst, eds. 121, 123 n7). On one occasion when he was traveling by train, Wilde scolded a newsboy for selling the pirated *Poems* for the "beastly figure" of twenty-five cents for three copies. The plucky boy laughed at him and refused to believe that he was the author of the volume. Later, after being assured that Wilde was indeed who he said he was, the boy returned and offered him half a dozen oranges "to call it square" ("The Poet" 1). Here was a rude, spontaneous pantomime of what courtesy publishers were doing on a larger scale: offering legally uncompelled honoraria for the exploitation of foreign authors' unprotected writings.

Wilde came to America under contract. The producer Richard D'Oyly Carte had agreed to pay his expenses and half-profits from his lectures if he would go about the country as a living advertisement for the authorized American production of Gilbert and Sullivan's *Patience, or Bunthorne's Bride* (1881), a comic opera satirizing the aesthetic movement and based in part on Wilde himself. The contract required Wilde to lecture in aesthetic garb, complete with knee-breeches, black hose, and satin coat (Goldman 25; Rose, *Authors in Court* 71), and it was in such a costume that he posed for a series of photographs taken by the celebrity photographer, Napoleon Sarony, shortly after he arrived in New York. Sarony insisted on

FIGURE 1.2 *Napoleon Sarony*, Oscar Wilde No. 18, 1882. *Courtesy Merlin Holland.*

an exclusive agreement that made him the sole photographer of Wilde during his American tour, an arrangement that Wilde later regretted when he saw the high quality of professional photography in other cities (Hofer and Scharnhorst, eds. 127). Sarony's exclusive contract was responsible for the dearth of other photographs of Wilde in America and for the compensatory profusion of cartoons and caricatures that followed the aesthete from city to city. When a company marketed unauthorized lithographs based on his photograph "Oscar Wilde No. 18," Sarony sued for copyright infringement and took the case all the way to the US Supreme Court (*Burrow-Giles Lithographic Co. v. Sarony*). In this era before celebrities enjoyed rights of publicity, Wilde, the posing subject of the infringed image, had no standing to claim his own damages in litigation (North 187).

Wilde's role as "advance poster" or "sandwich man" for *Patience* has been much discussed (Lewis and Smith 22–5; Gaines 80–1). Less well understood is the copyright dimension of his arrangement with Carte. *Patience*, like other Gilbert and Sullivan productions, enjoyed doubtful copyright protection in the United States, and pirate productions sprang up in various American cities to exploit the English team's popularity. Wilde's appearances were intended to impress on the public that only Carte's was the authorized version (Lewis and Smith 7; North 189; Rose, *Authors in Court* 71, 73). In this respect, Wilde played a role analogous to the courtesy paratexts printed in the opening pages of authorized American editions of British authors' works, guaranteeing the quality and authenticity of the approved Carte production. Wilde's relationship to *Patience* was also trademark-like, a sort of official Bunthorne brand, prefiguring the efforts of today's content industries to use trademark and branding to reinforce questionable or expiring copyrights in movies, cartoons, and other media (Foley; Rosenblatt).

Wilde publicly posed as the original of the fleshly poet Reginald Bunthorne of the opera, yet he was also a copy of Bunthorne, contractually required to model a parody of aestheticism that had already been popularized by Gilbert and Sullivan and, before them, the cartoonist George du Maurier in *Punch*. The fundamental distinction in copyright law between original works and copies became perversely transposed in Wilde's life and art. In "The Decay of Lying" (1891), he grounded the theory that "Life imitates Art," or that the original copies the copy, in references to mechanical reproduction and copyrighted dissemination: "Life tries to copy [Art], to reproduce it in a popular form, like an enterprising publisher" (982). Wilde was the original of Sarony's photographs, but his popularity grew through mass reproduction of those posed images, both in authorized copies bearing Sarony's signature and in thousands of infringing copies for which Sarony collected damages, as well as in countless cartoons and illustrations that copied Wilde as he toured America. The humorist Eugene Field turned himself into a human copy of Wilde by driving about Denver in a carriage, got up in a wig and fur-trimmed overcoat, imitating the languid gestures of the Bunthorne lookalike (Ellmann, *Oscar* 191).

Whether Dorian Gray is the original or the copy of the hidden portrait that does the changing and suffering for him is a question that haunts the novel. As he circulates in London society, unaltered for decades, he is more like a photograph than a person. Scholars have probed motifs of the commodified self, mass reproduction, and photography in the novel (Gaines 43–52; Novak 84–8; Rose, *Authors in Court* 88–9). One measure of Lord Henry's worship of Dorian is the twenty-seven photographs of the young man that he keeps in his house (1890:22–3). Sarony is known to have photographed Wilde in twenty-seven different poses (Rose, *Authors in Court* 72). When Wilde revised the novel for its book appearance, he altered the number to eighteen (1891:47), perhaps an allusion to Sarony's copyright lawsuit over his photograph, "Oscar Wilde No. 18." (In Wilde's story "The Canterville Ghost" [1887], the brash Americans who purchase a haunted English estate replace its ancient portraits with "large Saroni [*sic*] photographs" of themselves [204].) Dorian may be an infringing photograph, a copy that has illicitly traded places with the original and is passing itself off as authentic to a public enamored of mass-reproduced experience. The ambiguity of "picture" in the novel's title opens the text to visual possibilities beyond a painted portrait (Novak 82–3). Challenged to defend the novel in the libel proceedings, Wilde described it as "a picture of changes" (Holland 103).

After his release from prison, Wilde lived abroad, spending freely when he could, often hard up, supported largely by an allowance from his wife and gifts from friends. He had learned the humiliation of bankruptcy while incarcerated—an experience, Paul

Saint-Amour suggests, that prepared him for a new understanding of intellectual property as a basis for intersubjective community. Wilde had challenged the "privatizing of imaginative expression" in earlier counterdiscourses, notably his plagiarized lecture on the literary forger Thomas Chatterton and in "The Portrait of Mr. W.H.," where belief in a theory about Shakespeare's sonnets circulates "exactly like alienable material property"—a chattelizing of intangible thought (Saint-Amour, *Copywrights* 96, 109). In prison, Wilde transformed bankruptcy and dispossession into "the renunciatory grace of a public domain" by writing *De Profundis*, an intertextual *cri de coeur* that was "post-property, post-copyright, post-genius" (97, 118).

Wilde had one more subversion in store for the idea of property. In his last years, he sold the scenario of an unwritten drama for £100 to several persons, each apparently believing that he or she was the sole purchaser. Frank Harris also paid £100 for the scenario. After expanding the sketch, Harris staged the play in London as *Mr. and Mrs. Daventry* (1900), but not before the other purchasers—at least five—threatened legal action unless they were paid. Wilde was unmoved by Harris's predicament and only complained that "Frank has deprived me of my only source of income by taking a play on which I could always have raised £100" (*Complete Letters* 1211–2). Wilde had turned his investors into something like blackmail victims, uncertain that their payments would ever really buy peace.

By selling the same scenario to multiple buyers, Wilde created what Michael Heller calls a tragedy of the anticommons—a resource endangered by underuse and stagnation because of the difficulty of coordinating conflicting ownership claims. Whereas a commons is sometimes threatened with overuse—too many exploiters of a single unowned resource, such as overgrazed land—an anticommons is threatened with underuse: too many owners of a single proprietary resource. This was Wilde's final drama—not the scenario itself, but the anticommons tragedy he blithely created as he seduced investors. The gesture summed up all his witty contempt, and passion, for property. The renunciatory commons he had imagined in prison now became a lucrative anticommons, serially sold and forever saleable, Keatsian in its passionate permanence, a golden alms bowl for collecting tributes to his genius. There was a certain flamboyance in Wilde's repeated sale, a wish to live in the memory of his investors. Perhaps tragedy is not the right word, since Harris managed in the end to pay off all the indignant purchasers. Rather, this was Wilde's tragicomedy of the anticommons.

Obscenity and blasphemy

Wilde viewed censorship as a bullying blend of psychic repression and poor reader response. He held that all efforts of governments to suppress "imaginative literature" were "monstrous," and that "Public Opinion" was "monstrous and ignorant" when it tried to "control Thought or Art" (*Complete Letters* 431; "Soul" 1094). Lord Henry Wotton sketches a parallel theory when he tells Dorian Gray that denial of desire sickens the soul by enacting "monstrous laws" that render desire "monstrous and unlawful" (1890:14). Desire becomes monstrous because social taboo and self-denial make it so, not because the mind itself, apart from action, can do any evil. Wilde argued that the true moral of *Dorian Gray* was that "all excess, as well as all renunciation, brings its punishment," and that Dorian suffers from "an exaggerated sense of conscience" that leads in the end to self-mutilation and suicide (*Complete Letters* 435–6). When challenged to explain why he opposed censorship, Wilde asserted that "[t]he rights of literature ... are the rights of intellect" (434). He was not referring to intellectual property rights but rather to the notion that the mind possesses inalienable rights of self-expression that the world has a correlative duty to respect. This was the basis of the aphorism he added to *Dorian Gray*: "[t]here is no such thing as a moral or an immoral book" (1891:17). In court, he similarly insisted that "[t]here are no views in a work of art" (Holland 80). Ethical demands confused literature with life. Governments had no competency, and courts no jurisdiction, to dictate morality to authors.

Wilde's libel trial doubled as an inquisition into the morality of his writings. Queensberry's plea of justification accused *Dorian Gray* of being "an immoral and obscene work ... calculated to subvert morality and to encourage unnatural vice" (Holland 290–1). Carson's cross-examination articulated a didacticism that would haunt modernism for the next fifty years. He insisted that literature had a duty to offer moral instruction to "the majority of people." Wilde countered that literature had a duty only to itself: to make a "beautiful thing" (81, 105). With his eye on the jury, Carson divided the world into those who candidly placed the "ordinary meaning" on *Dorian Gray*—by which he meant the true, immoral meaning, put there by the sodomitical poser—and those who boasted of reading an "artistic meaning" into the work; and he argued that Wilde's offense in publishing the novel could be excused only if the book "came into the hands" of a small artistic elite rather than the ordinary masses (261).

Carson's words echoed the test of obscenity that had been formulated in the 1868 case of *Regina v. Hicklin*: "whether the tendency of the matter charged as obscenity is to deprave and corrupt those whose minds are open to such immoral influences, and into whose hands a publication of this sort may fall" (369). The formula had a powerful effect on authors' conceptions of their readerships. When Walter Pater in 1888 published the second edition of his *Studies in the History of the Renaissance*—the work Wilde reverently called his "golden book" (Ellmann, *Oscar* 47)— he omitted its controversially hedonistic conclusion out of fear, he confessed, that "it might possibly mislead some of those young men into whose hands it might fall" (Pater 246 n). This *Hicklin*-inspired concern for a hypothetically corruptible class implied that a market for indecent literature, if allowed to exist at all, should be confined to a small group of professionals and connoisseurs whose morals the law need not bother to superintend. As we will see in Chapter 2, the dream of a divisible market insulated from obscenity prosecutions inspired the printing of deluxe and limited editions of transgressive modernist works.

If the impulse to censor derived from repression of desire, the search for the obscene was a crude kind of reader response that always revealed the limitations of the reader. "The books that the world calls immoral," Lord Henry remarks in *Dorian Gray*, "are books that show the world its own shame" (1891:163). In "The Soul of Man under Socialism," Wilde went further to say that when ordinary people find a work of art to be unintelligible, it is because the work is "a beautiful thing that is new"; and when they find a work to be immoral, it is because the work "is a beautiful thing that is true" (1092). It was this autotelic imperturbability of art, as much as the unspecified nature of Dorian Gray's corruption, that prompted Wilde to assert that readers who thought they had discovered Dorian's sins had actually "brought them" (*Complete Letters* 439). The self-righteous search for obscenity was, according to Wilde, an opportunistic prurience (a word he liked to half-rhyme with "Puritan") ("Critic" 1048), a form of projection that often revealed a lustful mind and always revealed a Philistine. He had long been familiar with the prude and the censor from his study of the trials of Gustave Flaubert and Charles Baudelaire for obscenity and immorality (Holland xxxv).

Several of Wilde's works were informally accused of immorality. His early *Poems*, which contained the narrative "Charmides" with its scandalous suggestions of fetishism and necrophilia, was requested for the library of the Oxford Union Society and then, by a divided vote of the members, rejected for supposed obscenity and plagiarism (Ellmann, *Oscar* 146–8). When Wilde was touring America, the minister Thomas Wentworth Higginson assailed *Poems* as reeking of "immorality" and "insulted innocence" (Lewis and Smith 118–19). Wilde repelled these attacks with his customary distinction between art and morality, but the charges continued to follow him about the country (Hofer and Scharnhorst, eds. 103). *Dorian Gray*, especially in its initial appearance in *Lippincott's Monthly Magazine* (1890), was attacked in the press as indecent, and the newsdealer W.H. Smith & Son pulled the issue from its bookstalls (Holland 310 n113).

Wilde also encountered accusations of blasphemy. In the 1880s, a "timorous editor" insisted that Wilde's sonnet on Keats's love letters be removed from a poetry anthology because of the perceived blasphemy of the sestet, which implies a comparison between the dead poet and the crucified Christ (Wilde, *Complete Letters* 445). When Edward Carson, cross-examining Wilde at the libel trial, assailed "The Priest and the Acolyte" as blasphemous, Wilde seemed for a moment to agree (he might actually have been disturbed by the story's irreverence), but he quickly recovered his poise and asserted that the story was aesthetically "disgusting" as distinct from "blasphemous" ("not my word") (Holland 70–1). In 1892, his drama *Salome* had been banned from the British stage, not ostensibly for its cruel, decadent eroticism, but because the Lord Chamberlain, the official licensor of plays, refused to allow the public representation of Biblical figures, although Wilde succeeded in printing the play in French and English (Ellmann, *Oscar* 372–4). He objected when his publisher mentioned the Lord Chamberlain's prohibition in advertisements for the book. The value of the drama, he said, lay in its "tragic beauty ... not a gross act of ignorance and impertinence on the part of the censor" (*Complete Letters* 547). As late as 1909, the Lord Chamberlain refused to license George Bernard Shaw's *The Shewing-Up of Blanco Posnet* because the protagonist makes irreverent statements about God (Marshik, *British* 61).

The Picture of Dorian Gray, one of Wilde's most transgressive works, escaped official prosecution for obscenity during his lifetime, but for years following his trials, the novel lay under unofficial ban in Britain. Carson had powerfully denounced the work as immoral and sodomitical in the libel trial, and Charles Gill, the prosecutor in Wilde's first criminal trial, had attempted to sway the jury by reading Carson's remarks into the court record. As Simon Stern has shown, Carson's dogged cross-examination concerning *Dorian Gray* essentially served the purpose of an obscenity prosecution and deterred republication of an authorized edition in England for nearly twenty years.

Yet many of Wilde's works, including *Dorian Gray*, continued to circulate in furtive pirated editions in Britain and France (Mason, *Bibliography* 543). Unauthorized American editions of *Dorian Gray* appeared for years after Wilde's death (Mason, *Oscar* 154–6). In 1910, guttermen in Fleet Street and the Strand sold crude reprints of *De Profundis* until these pirates, consisting of booksellers, printers, caterers, and hawkers, were arrested and sentenced to several months' imprisonment for criminal copyright infringement (Mason, *Bibliography* 532–3). (The prosecutor was C.F. Gill, presumably Charles Gill, who had been the prosecutor in Wilde's first criminal trial fifteen years before.) A structural antagonism existed between obscenity and copyright laws from the late nineteenth century through the rise of modernism. In banning controversial writings, censorship functioned as a sort of super-copyright, vesting the government or powerful purity groups with exclusive power to control publication, and making it difficult for anyone else, even authors, to print and disseminate suspect works. Copyright law, in perverse contrast, sometimes failed to protect allegedly immoral works at all. As we will see in Chapter 3, writings thought to be indecent could be poor candidates for copyright in Britain and the United States, chiefly because authors and publishers faced legal and practical obstacles to enforcing property rights in such writings. The mutually defeating ends of censorship and copyright produced an interactive emergency within the law—a juridical gap that spurred an underground market for unauthorized, experimental, and transgressive works.

* * *

The decade and a half that witnessed Wilde's celebrity also saw changes in the law that would trouble modernism well into the next century. Social transition and turbulence were making the law a difficult passage for what Wilde called the "new" and the "true" in literature: changing tests of obscenity; incipient but uncertain rights of privacy and publicity; the transatlantic copyright vacuum filling, slowly and unevenly, with onerous rules for protection. Wilde himself was an exception for whom legal rules were an alien alphabet; his "nemesis of character," he wrote, made him a "problem for which there was no solution"; he was a "perverse and impossible person," the "pariah-dog of the nineteenth century" (*Complete Letters* 995, 1006, 1079). It was not just the erasure of Wilde during his imprisonment that created his exceptional status. He had always embodied a kind of juridical void, a standstill or suspension of law (Agamben 48–9), which he expressed in the figure of the anomic, unassimilable dandy, the norm-dissolving individualist who represented "a disturbing and disintegrating force," and as a proud, homosexual Irishman who crossed class boundaries as a man and writer (Wilde, "Soul" 1091).

Law's passion for property amused and intrigued Wilde. He wrote paradoxically of serially held ideas and promoted an impossible commons owned separately by multiple investors. In his post-carceral vagabondage, he found new meanings for intellectual property, inventing stories, promising friends that he would write them down, but mostly keeping them to himself, fully formed "in [his] own mind," as a private public domain (qtd. in Ellmann, *Oscar* 571). Such mental hoarding allowed him to be a spendthrift of promises, an unselfish giant who had broken down the wall of his garden to let in his few remaining worshippers. In prison, he had observed the treatment of convicted children and noticed their bewilderment at the law's "strange abstract force," so unlike the comprehensible punishments administered by parents (Wilde, "Case" 960). Mourning and mourned as an outcast, he mocked and wept at the law's abstract force, fully inhabited by its past, present, and future—a complete man of law.

2

Obscenity and Censorship

The nervous paradox at the heart of obscenity law was that a crime that lacked identifiable victims could nonetheless inflict widespread social harm. Prosecutors in the nineteenth and early twentieth centuries were not required to offer evidence that indecency had actually injured consumers, yet vice crusaders were passionate about stamping out this "deadly poison, cast into the fountain of moral purity" (Comstock, *Frauds* 388). The nature of the poison was no easier to pinpoint than its claimed effects. The attorney Morris Ernst characterized obscenity as a crime in search of a definition, an offense floating on a sea of indignant adjectives: lewd, lascivious, filthy, disgusting (Ernst and Seagle vii). Obscenity law grew to be a tool of opportunistic moralism. The law could expand at need to punish ideas that simply offended accepted ideology. Radclyffe Hall's *The Well of Loneliness* (1928) and Norah James's *Sleeveless Errand* (1929) were suppressed in Britain partly because they were novels that threatened patriotic conceptions of women's work during the First World War. Censors were engaged in "a defense of the realm rather than a simple obscenity prosecution" (Marshik "History's" 152).

Obscenity laws punished thoughts that circulated in the form of words or pictures. The author usually sat in the eye of the regulatory storm, largely unmolested by official harassment, while the reader, occupying the endpoint of the communications circuit, also escaped sanction. It was the intermediaries connecting the acts of writing and reading that the law sought to discipline. When French authorities prosecuted Gustave Flaubert in 1857, his codefendants were the editor and the printer of the review that had serialized *Madame Bovary* (Haynes). As technologies of mechanical reproduction grew more efficient, forms of censorship, official and unofficial, proliferated. In the same year that Flaubert was charged with outraging public decency, the British Parliament passed the Obscene Publications Act, one of the most powerful weapons the law ever possessed for attacking obscenity. But the Act was not written for prosecuting persons; it was potent chiefly against things: books, prints, and pictures. Just as a defamatory libel requires an act of publication—some sharing of the injurious statement—so obscenity required an overt step toward transmission: publishing, printing, selling, or mailing.

The forces that sought to regulate what Rachel Potter calls "obscene modernism" were many and complex. This chapter offers an extensive, though inevitably incomplete, taxonomy of formal mechanisms of censorship—laws, courts, procedures, and sanctions—and of informal or quasi-official networks of censorship, such as purity groups and circulating libraries. I divide these mechanisms into two types: those that targeted persons or businesses and those that targeted books and other material embodiments of indecency. This will help bring us closer to the actual, material operations of the law as they shaped literary modernism. Multijurisdictional enforcement of obscenity laws created, particularly in America, a patchwork of overlapping regulation that thwarted access to modernist works. The emergence of a constitutional standard for testing obscenity in the United States—along with parallel innovations in Britain—in the late 1950s did much to unify the conditions that still hampered the historical development of modernism. At various points, I suggest that obscenity laws shared cultural and market effects with the scarcity-producing purposes of copyright laws.

Networks of censorship: Purity and prior restraint

In the late nineteenth century, purity groups and prosecutors in Britain and the United States increasingly targeted literary and artistic works after decades of focusing chiefly on pornography of "the grosser type" (Ernst and Seagle 107). As moral standards grew more rigid in the later Victorian period, progressive and unorthodox writers "became bolder and more adventurous," and a "wide breach" opened between unconventional literature and conventional morality (Manchester 234). The cleansing campaigns of vice crusaders ranged far beyond traditional pornographic materials to include books that earnestly discussed birth control, national poverty, and reproduction and population (235). In the late 1880s, the English publisher Henry Vizetelly came under attack by purity groups, politicians, and the press for issuing inexpensive translations of Émile Zola's novels depicting greed and brutality in French rural life, urban prostitution and erotic obsession, and bourgeois adultery and corruption (Mullin, *James* 6–7). The category of the obscene expanded as tolerance decreased for perceived ideological affronts to sexual modesty. Regulation became a weapon for attacking uncomfortable ideas as much as raw prurience.

The sanctioning force of censorship reached to almost everyone and everything in literature's communications circuit: publishers, printers, booksellers, sales clerks, and the book itself (Darnton). Potter argues that, in the early twentieth century, informal or quasi-institutional "networks of control operated in a space between state authorities and the spheres of business and literary exchange." Vice crusaders and circulating libraries, no less than customs officials and postmasters, "played their part in the censorship process" (1). Celia Marshik stresses the "repressive strategies" pursued, often collaboratively, by official and unofficial actors (*British* 3). As Katherine Mullin shows, purity groups in Britain and Ireland propagandized against indecent art and literature and often acted as complainants in prosecutions of obscene libels and in forfeiture actions against books (*James* 1–27). Britain's National Vigilance Association, which was founded in 1885, and the National Social Purity Crusade (1901), among other groups, succeeded the Society for the Suppression of Vice and the Pure Literature Society as private scourges of the purveyors of indecency.

In America, the New England Society for the Suppression of Vice (later called the Watch and Ward Society) was established in 1878. Early on, the Society pursued Walt Whitman's *Leaves of Grass*, and by the 1920s and 1930s its list of banned books included works by William Faulkner, Ernest Hemingway, D.H. Lawrence, James Farrell, and John O'Hara (Gertzman, *Bookleggers* 130–1).

In 1873, Anthony Comstock founded the New York Society for the Suppression of Vice as a successor to the Young Men's Christian Association's (YMCA's) Committee for the Suppression of Vice. The Society received quasi-governmental status under a special act of the New York state legislature that granted the Society's agents the powers of "search, seizure and arrest which had always been thought to belong exclusively to the publicly constituted police authorities" (Ernst and Seagle 11). Through formal prosecutions and informal intimidations, the Society worried publishers and booksellers and employed undercover agents who posed as smut-purchasers and wrote decoy letters to sellers and distributors. Under Comstock's successor, John Saxton Sumner, the Society sought to suppress the works of many controversial authors, including Joyce, Lawrence, Theodore Dreiser, Margaret Sanger, Oscar Wilde, and Frank Harris. After 1915, the Watch and Ward Society had a "gentleman's agreement" with the Boston Booksellers' Association to keep bookstore owners informed of works that the secret handshake deemed indecent. This collusive practice succeeded in coercing retailers and quietly censoring literature before it could reach consumers (Gertzman, *Bookleggers* 130).

The vice societies wielded something that the law typically denied to courts and prosecutors: the power of prior restraint. With their bullying prestige, the societies acted as pre-censors, persuading publishers and editors to submit material for their approval prior to publication, or sometimes to withdraw books and magazines freshly printed (Ernst and Schwartz 138). In 1927, the New York publisher Samuel Roth made two pilgrimages to obtain the smuthounds' blessing for his newsstand magazines (Gertzman, *Samuel* 92). In New York, he sought the Vice Society's approval of an excerpt from *Ulysses* reprinted in his *Two Worlds Monthly*. Sumner granted this request but disapproved of the inclusion of Benjamin Franklin's "Advice on Choosing a Mistress" (1745) in Roth's magazine *Beau*. In Boston, the president of the Watch and Ward Society gave bewildered approval to Roth's *Ulysses* extract—"this cubist Odyssey was entirely beyond my poor mental and imaginative powers"—but frowned on an article defending the morals of Charlie Chaplin, a man who had "violated even the most elementary principles of decency" (Calkins). The Watch and Ward president proposed this horse trade with a strange, paternal kindliness, as if he were protecting Roth's personal morals rather than rendering an unappealable decree that threatened a free press.

The vice societies routinely issued reports quantifying their seizures of indecent materials and their arrests of smut-dealers. In 1874, shortly after the founding of the New York Vice Society, the YMCA reported that Comstock had seized and destroyed 134,000 improper books, 194,000 pictures and photographs, 14,200 stereotype plates, and quantities of other forbidden materials (Broun and Leech 153). Near the end of his life, Comstock reckoned that he had "convicted persons enough to fill a passenger train of sixty-one coaches" (qtd. in Broun and Leech 15–16). Sumner continued his predecessor's statistical boasting. In the late 1920s when the prestige of purity groups was waning, the Vice Society continued to issue reports totting up its suppressions and even published tables showing the religious affiliations of offenders (Boyer 143). This numbers game strangely mirrored the incentive theory of Anglo-American copyright law. The copyright monopoly has traditionally been justified as a spur to creative output—a goal that, in the Anglo-American legal context, reflects a market-based "accumulationist model" of aesthetic progress (Beebe 346). Just as copyright law has operated to encourage individual authors by creating artificial scarcity in cultural goods, so obscenity laws produced an artificial scarcity of cultural goods in order to promote personal morality. Both sets of laws fostered the view that progress, ethical or aesthetic, could be measured by the quantity of cultural products demonstrably present or absent in the marketplace.

In the early decades of the twentieth century, forms of prior restraint operated powerfully in Britain. While the Lord Chamberlain determined which plays would be licensed for the public stage, private circulating libraries like Mudie's and W.H. Smith's effectively determined which books would reach large segments of the public (Potter 25–7). In the previous century, when middle-class literacy was rising, the high cost of books had confined most readers of fiction to the offerings of the circulating libraries (Ernst and Seagle 87–90). These offerings were prescreened to omit titles that had received complaints from subscribers or were otherwise reputed to be indecent—a process that George Moore ridiculed as "circulating morals." Even after books became more

affordable in the early twentieth century, the libraries continued
to limit readers' choices. In 1909, Mudie's and other libraries
organized the Circulating Libraries Association (CLA), vowing
to withhold any book that was "personally scandalous, libelous,
immoral or otherwise disagreeable ... to any considerable section
of our subscribers," and announcing that publishers would be
required to submit books before publication so that the libraries
could rate them "satisfactory," "doubtful," or "objectionable," and
decide whether to circulate them (Ernst and Seagle 96–7; Hynes,
Edwardian 296–8; Wilson 52–3). Urged by purity organizations, the
CLA restricted subscribers' access to books by many controversial
authors, including Dreiser, Joyce, Lawrence, Jean Rhys, and Upton
Sinclair (Marshik, *British* 177, 206).

The library censors were not always consistent—some of them
stocked *The Well of Loneliness* before the authorities moved
against it—but "the hidden nature of their decision-making"
created uncertainty for publishers and forced many readers to
seek fiction from other outlets (Potter 26–7). Virginia Woolf was
appalled by the degraded subservience of library subscribers,
observing on one occasion a "stout widow" who chose her books
"like a lapdog, only stipulating that she wanted no vulgarity, not
much description, but plenty of incident" (*Diary* 1:61). Although
Woolf herself borrowed from Mudie's, she was uncomfortably
aware of the homogenized quality of the experience. "I stood [in
queue]," she wrote in 1918, "with the pallid & respectable & got
my allowance" (1:166).

The networks of censorship were so finely meshed that they
snared even authors and editors in their reticulations. The forms of
suppression exercised by legal authorities, vice societies, circulating
libraries, and other forces—"the entire censorship apparatus"
(Marshik, *British* 205)—caused authors and editors to become
self-censors, an especially potent form of prior restraint. Harriet
Monroe deleted material from writings by T.S. Eliot and Ezra Pound
before allowing them to be printed in her Chicago-based magazine,
Poetry. As foreign editor of *The Little Review*, Pound himself
removed dangerous lines from installments of Joyce's *Ulysses*, as
on occasion did the general editor Margaret Anderson (Hassett
62; Potter 29). Eliot, as a director of Faber and Faber, published
Djuna Barnes's *Nightwood* (1936), but not before excising certain
strong references to homosexual sex (Potter 29–30). The Hogarth

Press, though a vehicle for Virginia and Leonard Woolf to exercise publishing autonomy, caused them "to police themselves lest the real police launch a prosecution for obscene libel" (Marshik, *British* 11).

In Britain, printers often played a pre-censorial role by refusing to set books until their authors agreed to omit material deemed libelous or immoral. Joyce's early stories remained unpublished for years while English printers, who were legally vulnerable along with publishers, anguished over an accusatory realism that insisted on naming actual public houses, describing women's legs, and employing words like "bloody" (Hynes, *Edwardian* 271–3). Potter notes the unpredictability of printers' squeamishness and points to the difficulties that Joyce's magazine publishers encountered in finding British and American printers who would set words like "piss," "fart," and "ballocks" (28).

Authorial self-censorship was sometimes legible. We can interpret the variance between the 1890 and 1891 texts of *The Picture of Dorian Gray* as a measure of the disciplining effect that press accusations of immorality had on Wilde's aesthetic craft. But often we are left to speculate about the roads not taken and the detours followed by modern authors in response to a repressive culture. Legal coercion may not always have resulted in debased periphrasis, however. Morris Ernst wondered if obscenity laws might have applied a beneficial "pressure for excellence of style" (Ernst and Seagle 205). More provocatively, Paul Vanderham speculates that the often impenetrable language of *Finnegans Wake* (1939) was partly Joyce's strategy for making obscenity safe for literature. Unlike *Ulysses*, which Joyce had published in France to avoid the strictures of English-speaking censors, *Finnegans Wake* contained "a language foreign enough to baffle any authorities," despite its motifs of sexuality and incest (59). Adam Parkes suggests that, even as *The Well of Loneliness* was being prosecuted for its direct intervention in the silencing of lesbianism, Woolf's *Orlando* (1928) offered modernist indirection and irony to "imply the possibility of illicit lesbian desires and quietly undermine censorious legal and sexological discourses" (*Modernism* 19). Marshik goes further to argue that the climate of regulation served as an enabling as well as a disabling condition for literary production, creating a "censorship dialectic" in which authors engaged in compliant or subversive forms of self-censorship and forged modernism's celebrated techniques of "self-reflexivity, fragmentation, and indirection" (*British* 6). More skeptically, Allison Pease contends that Joyce and other modernists often rendered subversive pornographic elements "impotent" by prioritizing literary form, "the high-art signifier of culture" (81).

Compelled creativity was another feature that obscenity laws shared with copyright laws. The minimal creativity required for securing copyright causes authors to introduce at least nontrivial variations in order to distinguish their writings from those of other authors. What indecent discourse was to obscenity law, an infringing copy was to copyright law. Virginia Woolf and other writers responded creatively to copyright's originality requirement, as we will see in Chapter 3. Both sets of laws inevitably compelled some degree of aesthetic innovation or compromise, for good or ill.

Mechanisms of censorship:
In rem and *in personam*

Censorship networks often acted in concert with legislatures and courts—the official mechanisms of censorship—but sometimes they saw their role as correcting or compensating for what they viewed as inadequate enforcement, essentially engaging in virtuous vigilantism (Ernst and Seagle 102). However, the mechanisms themselves—laws, courts, judgments, and sanctions—established the legal baseline of censorship from which all extralegal policing departed. It is critical to distinguish among the various mechanisms that implemented the law of obscenity, and to trace their historical development into the modernist period. Equally important is the distinction between mechanisms that operated *in personam*—against individuals or business entities—and those that acted *in rem*—against inanimate things. Specifically, some laws and procedures targeted the persons or businesses that produced, disseminated, or advertised offending content; others targeted books, magazines, prints, and other *res* that embodied offending content. The pursuit of books as corrupting things invited spectacles of public cleansing not unlike the popular images of federal agents smashing kegs of illegal beer during the Prohibition.

FIGURE 2.1 *John Sumner (hatted), New York Society for the Suppression of Vice, helping to incinerate objectionable materials.* From New York Journal American, *November 27, 1935. Courtesy Harry Ransom Center, University of Texas at Austin.*

When vice societies reported the quantities of objectionable books they had seized in the previous year, they were boasting *in rem*.

In Britain, the most basic *in personam* proceeding involved the common-law misdemeanor of publishing an obscene libel, punishable since the eighteenth century. A private individual or a vice society, or later a Crown prosecutor, typically initiated prosecution, and the defendant publisher or bookseller could be tried by summary process before a magistrate or by a jury in a crown court. If convicted in either venue, the defendant could be sentenced to a fine or imprisonment, or both (Potter 18). In 1888, the National Vigilance Association obtained an indictment for obscenity against Henry Vizetelly for publishing English translations of three novels by Zola: *Nana* (1880), *Pot-bouille* (1883), and *La Terre* (1887). After receiving a summons and appearing before a magistrate in a committal hearing, Vizetelly, aged sixty-eight, was tried in London's Old Bailey before a jury that begged the prosecutor (Sir Edward Clarke, who later served as Oscar Wilde's counsel) not to read out all twenty-one passages he had selected to establish Zola's "bestial obscenity" (De Grazia 40–6). Sensing the jury's disposition, Vizetelly changed his plea to one of guilty and was fined £100 and required to pay an additional £200 to secure an undertaking not to circulate any Zola books that were as objectionable as the three at bar (Hynes, *Edwardian* 259–60). Facing insolvency, the distinguished publisher tried to keep his promise by having his Zola titles revised to remove any chargeable indecency. As soon as he placed the expurgated books on the market, however, he was indicted again and haled into the Old Bailey. He once more pleaded guilty to publishing an obscene libel, forfeited his £200 bond, and was sentenced to three months in prison as a first-class misdemeanant. He died a few years later, a victim, George Moore felt certain, of "judicial murder" (qtd. in De Grazia 47–53).

The common law acted *in personam* when it convicted, fined, and imprisoned Vizetelly. Yet it is clear that the prosecutor and the jury, with an *in rem* instinct, directed much of their law-backed indignation at the publisher's stock: the books themselves that were purportedly poisoning the young and the susceptible. Indeed, the proceedings rendered Vizetelly insolvent and caused him to liquidate his publishing business for the benefit of creditors (Vizetelly 286–99). As Potter notes, early-twentieth-century British publishers and booksellers were often given a coercive choice between forfeiting controversial stock and risking a prison sentence—between their livelihood and their liberty (18). Various laws, such as the Post Office Acts of 1884 and 1908, the Vagrancy Acts of 1824 and 1838, and the Town Police Clauses Acts of 1847, continued to be employed in the twentieth century for *in rem* and *in personam* challenges to indecency (Cox 61–2). But the most formidable *in rem* mechanism was the Obscene Publications Act (or Lord Campbell's Act), enacted by Parliament in 1857 to permit what the common law's sensitivity for individual liberties made difficult: the search, seizure, and destruction of books deemed obscene by the authorities. In targeting books themselves, the statute hindered publishers and booksellers convicted under the common law from operating their businesses from prison by having family members or associates carry on the vending of stock (Ernst and Seagle 113–14).

Under Lord Campbell's Act, a magistrate, presented with a sworn complaint that obscene materials were being kept at a house or shop for sale, distribution, or exhibition, and persuaded that the materials were of the sort that would give rise to a misdemeanor conviction for an obscene libel at common law, would grant a special warrant empowering the police to search the place, by force if necessary, and to seize all accused materials and carry them back before the magistrate. Then, the magistrate would issue a summons requiring the occupant of the place to appear and show why the magistrate should not issue an order for destruction. The burden of proof was on the occupant; no other person—not even the author (if different from the occupant)—had standing to join the proceeding. Lord Campbell's Act was more of an *in rem* forfeiture provision than a strictly criminal statute (Gillers 225–6; Robertson 28). The famous 1868 case of *Regina v. Hicklin*, discussed below, was an appeal from a forfeiture order under Lord Campbell's Act. The case did not involve a full *in personam* prosecution of Henry Scott, the distributor of the obscene pamphlet, *The Confessional Unmasked* (1836). Although an order of forfeiture might lead to a separate common-law prosecution for an obscene libel, Lord Campbell's Act targeted things, not persons. It was an instrument for sanitizing the bookshelves.

The action taken against the first English edition of D.H. Lawrence's *The Rainbow* (1915) shows Lord Campbell's Act at work. In November 1915, after hostile reviews of the book had alerted authorities, a detective-inspector came to Lawrence's London publisher, Methuen, with a warrant to seize all copies and unbound sheets on the premises. A few days later, Methuen received a summons to appear before the Bow Street Magistrate to show cause why the books and sheets should not be destroyed as obscene. Told that Lawrence could have no voice in the proceedings, Methuen capitulated, offering no resistance to the prosecutor's arguments and abjectly apologizing for the indecent content (which Methuen blamed on Lawrence's refusal to allow revisions). In all, more than 1,000 copies and sets of sheets were ordered to be destroyed, and Methuen was taxed ten guineas as costs of the prosecution (not as a fine) (De Grazia 56–61; Kinkead-Weekes xlv–li).

Thirteen years later, Lord Campbell's Act was invoked against *The Well of Loneliness*, Radclyffe Hall's sincere, unsensational novel about "a woman who is a born invert" (qtd. in De Grazia 165). After the press denounced the work as loathsome and poisonous, the British Home Secretary advised the publisher, Jonathan Cape, to withdraw the novel or face legal proceedings. Cape ceased publishing the book but secretly had molds of the type flown to Paris so that copies could be produced there and shipped back to England for sale. The police promptly obtained warrants to seize copies from two London booksellers, and Cape received a summons to defend the book at Bow Street. Cape's attorneys persuaded forty prominent men and women—including Virginia and Leonard Woolf, E.M. Forster, and Rudyard Kipling—to be on hand to testify to the novel's seriousness and the importance of creative freedom. The magistrate, predictably for this period, rejected these witnesses and, after an adjournment to reread the novel, applied the *Hicklin* test (discussed below) to rule that the work plainly had a tendency to corrupt susceptible readers. He ordered all copies to be destroyed and assessed twenty guineas as costs against Cape. Unlike Methuen in 1915, Cape appealed the order to Quarter Sessions, but, after hearing arguments, the magistrates dismissed the appeal, with assessed costs (De Grazia 165–94). With the forfeiture order affirmed, both trial and appellate tribunals had acted against Hall's book.

In a draft of *A Room of One's Own* (1929), Virginia Woolf vividly depicted the *in rem* prosecution of an imaginary novel containing (like Hall's) references to lesbianism:

> [T]here flashed into my mind the inevitable policeman; the summons; the order to attend the court; the dreary waiting; the Magistrate coming in with a little bow; the glass of water; the counsel for the prosecution; for the defence; the verdict; this book is ... obscene; & flames rising, perhaps on Tower Hill, as they consumed ... masses ... of paper. (qtd. in Marshik, *British* 122)

Woolf's fearful fantasia precisely tracks the elements of Lord Campbell's Act: search and seizure by the police, a magistrate's summons requiring the publisher to appear in court, successful prosecution of the book, and incineration of the publisher's stock. With grim playfulness, Woolf figures the *in rem* destruction of books as an *in personam* execution on Tower Hill, the place in London where public beheadings of traitors and criminals of rank were traditionally carried out.

When the British common law—the body of judge-made precedent—crossed over to America, it brought along the misdemeanor of obscenity. In 1821, the printer Peter Holmes was tried in Massachusetts for the obscene libel of publishing an unedited version of John Cleland's *Memoirs of a Woman of Pleasure* (*Fanny Hill*) (1748–49), a work alleged to be "lewd, wicked, scandalous, infamous and obscene" (*Commonwealth v. Holmes* 336). This string of prosecutorial adjectives anticipated the clotted, repetitious language of later statutes, state and federal, that would define the obscene through lexical overchoice. A Massachusetts statute that prohibited books containing "obscene, indecent, or impure language, or manifestly tending to corrupt the morals of youth" was used to convict a Cambridge bookstore manager who in 1929 had sold a copy of Lawrence's *Lady Chatterley's Lover* (1928) to a Watch and Ward agent posing as an ordinary buyer (Mass. Gen. Laws, ch. 272, § 28). Tried without a jury and sentenced to a fine and imprisonment, the manager appealed, unsuccessfully, to Massachusetts' Supreme Judicial Court (*Commonwealth v. DeLacey* 328). Morris Ernst felt that the targeting of booksellers was especially unfair, since they could scarcely be familiar with all the items they stocked, or guess whether books might be found obscene (Ernst and Seagle 231). Donald Friede, a partner in the publishing firm of Boni and Liveright, was convicted under the same Massachusetts statute for selling a copy of Theodore Dreiser's *An American Tragedy* (1925) to a Boston police officer. A jury in the Superior Court convicted Friede without being allowed to hear or examine the entire book, and the Massachusetts high court upheld the verdict on appeal (*Commonwealth v. Friede* 322–3). The convictions of Friede and the bookstore manager resulted from *in personam* proceedings.

While the British attacked *The Well of Loneliness* in an *in rem* action, American authorities took an *in personam* approach. Section 1141 of the New York Penal Code made it a misdemeanor to sell, or possess with intent to sell, "any obscene, lewd, lascivious, filthy, indecent or disgusting book." Friede, now in partnership with Pascal Covici, published Hall's controversial novel and defiantly sold a copy to John Sumner of the New York Vice Society. Exercising his quasi-official powers, Sumner returned with police officers and seized more than 800 copies of the book (De Grazia 197–8). Friede, defended by Morris Ernst and Alexander Lindey (the team that would represent Random House in the *Ulysses* customs litigation three years later), moved to dismiss the complaint in the Magistrates' Court. Ernst characteristically loaded his brief with supporting comments by authors, critics, and publishers, and urged the court to assess the book according to contemporary social mores. Judge Hyman Bushel was not persuaded. He conceded that *The Well of Loneliness* showed "restraint" and "literary merit" but nevertheless found its theme to be "antisocial and offensive to public morals and decency," and bound Friede over for trial in the Court of Special Sessions (*People v. Friede* 614–15). Judge Bushel condemned the novel for its unsettling subject matter, not for any indecent language. The three judges in Special Sessions saw things differently, however, and dismissed the complaint. Friede was now exonerated in New York with respect to Hall's book, but a criminal offender in Massachusetts for selling a copy of Dreiser's novel.

The federal postal statute that criminalized the mailing of obscene matter—section 211 of the US Criminal Code—was originally enacted by Congress in 1873 as a result of Anthony Comstock's tireless lobbying (Ernst and Schwartz 31–2). Section 211, known as the Comstock Act, prohibited "[e]very obscene, lewd, or lascivious, and every filthy, book, pamphlet, picture, paper, letter, writing, print, or other publication of an indecent character, and every article or thing designed, adapted, or intended for preventing conception or producing abortion, or for any indecent or immoral use." Ezra Pound assailed the statute for "lump[ing] literature and instruments for abortion into one clause" (*Pound-Quinn* 132). Section 211 permitted obscene materials to be seized as "nonmailable matter" and imposed a fine, a prison term, or both, for the knowing use of the mails to transmit such matter. The statute thus had a dual punitive aspect, one *in rem*, the other *in personam*. The federal courts administered *in personam* criminal process to individuals charged with obscene mailings; the *in rem* power permitted postal appointees to engage in discretionary prior restraints without resorting to criminal prosecution. Section 211 allowed a faceless official to suppress books and magazines before they could ever reach retailers and consumers. The Comstock Act's *in rem* provision thus permitted broad prior restraints comparable in their social and cultural sweep to that of the circulating libraries at the height of their prestige in Britain (Ernest and Seagle 69–70, 85–6; Marshik, *British* 148).

Exercising his *in rem* discretion, the Postmaster of the City of New York, on the advice of the Solicitor of the Post Office Department, declared the October 1917 issue of *The Little Review* to be nonmailable on the ground that one of its items, Wyndham Lewis's story "Cantelman's Spring-Mate," was "obscene, lewd, or lascivious" within the meaning of section 211 (Vanderham 17–18). Margaret Anderson, editor of *The Little Review*, filed a motion in federal court to enjoin the Postmaster's exclusion of the issue from the mails, arguing that she and the magazine would be irreparably harmed and that Lewis's story was not obscene under the Comstock Act. Judge Augustus Hand, deferring to the broad discretion of the postal authorities, reluctantly upheld the suppression, ruling that the story, which recounted an English army officer's cynical seduction, impregnation, and abandonment of a young woman, arguably exhibited "a tendency to excite lust" that justified seizure (*Anderson v. Patten* 383).

The Comstock Act operated both *in rem* and *in personam* against *The Sex Side of Life* (1918), an educational pamphlet by Mary Ware Dennett, the suffragist and birth-control advocate. Postmasters suppressed the pamphlet as nonmailable in 1922 and 1925. In 1926, Dennett wanted to test the statute by attempting to enjoin another postal seizure, but the civil liberties lawyer Arthur Garfield Hays told her that no judge would declare a postal suppression invalid unless it was "arbitrary and wholly without foundation" (Ernst and Schwartz 80–2; Weinrib 351–2)—a difficult standard that Anderson had failed to meet in 1917 before the sympathetic Judge Hand. But what Dennett could not achieve in the *in rem* context she accomplished in the *in personam* context. In 1928, after mailing a copy of the pamphlet to a Post Office decoy, she was personally charged with violating section 211, convicted by an all-male federal jury in Brooklyn, and sentenced to a $300 fine. Represented by Ernst and Lindey, she appealed her conviction to the US Court of Appeals for the Second Circuit, which ruled, in an opinion by the same Judge Hand (now an appellate judge), that "an accurate exposition of the relevant facts of the sex side of life in decent language and in manifestly serious and disinterested spirit cannot ordinarily be regarded as obscene" (*United States v. Dennett* 569). The burden of proof to convict Dennett at trial had been guilt beyond a reasonable doubt, and Judge Hand ruled on appeal that the pamphlet was so clearly non-obscene that the trial judge should have dismissed the case without ever letting the question of guilt go to the jury. The *in rem* and *in personam* postal mechanisms could be as different on appeal as they were in substantive operation.

An *in rem* technique that had a significant impact on modernism was the obscenity provision of the US Tariff Act. In the late 1920s,

Morris Ernst interested Senator Bronson Cutting of New Mexico in reforming the arbitrariness of censorship by customs officials (Ernst 161–2). Up to that time, when a book was seized by customs as obscene, the person to whom the book had been addressed could, if he or she wished, challenge the seizure in the US Customs Court, but this was a weak safeguard. The addressee had the burden of proving that the book was not obscene; the Collector of Customs was not required to prove anything. Just as with *in rem* postal suppressions, the Collector's subjective decision to pounce on the book could not be overturned unless the Customs Court was persuaded that the official had substantially abused his discretion. In most cases, the seizure was upheld and the book was confiscated (Ernst and Lindey 14–16).

The Cutting amendment changed all that. The new statutory procedure, formulated by Ernst and codified in section 305 of the Tariff Act of 1930, established a coherent mechanism for testing the validity of seizures: promptly after a seizure, customs was required to inform the US Attorney of the district in which the book had been taken; the US Attorney was in turn required to initiate proceedings in the federal district court (not the Customs Court) for the book's forfeiture. The government had to make a reasoned case for forfeiture, and the book's addressee was entitled to intervene as claimant and demand a jury trial. Under the Cutting amendment, the confiscatory power of customs officials was subjected to meaningful judicial oversight.

The amendment also prevented the government from directing its power against the foreign sender or the domestic recipient of a seized book; those individuals were free from *in personam* prosecution under the revised Tariff Act (Ernst 161–2). Instead, the government was required to bring a civil forfeiture action directly against the accused book, the legal *res*. Tariff Act lawsuits directed against contraband imports were familiar during the Prohibition. *United States v. One Ford Truck* and *United States v. Approximately 126 Assorted Glasses, a quantity of intoxicating liquors, etc. found at Club La Lune* were just two of many actions brought against property involved in illegal alcohol trafficking. In the same spirit of protecting American purity, the US Attorney filed forfeiture actions against Marie Stopes's *Married Love* (1918) and *Contraception* (1923), books that discussed birth control, adult sexuality, and marriage equality. But the Tariff Act litigation that had the broadest implications for literary modernism was *United States v. One Book Entitled Ulysses by James Joyce*, discussed below.

Hicklin: Immoral tendencies and the law of the child

The test of obscenity that came to figure so prominently in British and American law was formulated in the 1868 English case of *Regina v. Hicklin*: "whether the tendency of the matter charged as obscenity is to deprave and corrupt those whose minds are open to such immoral influences, and into whose hands a publication of this sort may fall" (369). Construing Lord Campbell's Act, *Hicklin* offered a broad, elastic standard that tested for obscenity in terms of its purported effects on a vulnerable class of suggestible persons. Prosecutors could point to particular passages or lines in a text ("the matter charged") and argue that these fragments had a "tendency" to corrupt the young, the morbidly prudish, or the selectively salacious ("whose minds are open to such immoral influences") if there was any possibility of access ("into whose hands a publication of this sort may fall").

Hicklin made it difficult to know whether the whole of a book or only portions would be accused of obscenity. On the one hand, a trial court might refuse to consider anything but the passages charged by the prosecutor, and an appellate court might conclude (as the Massachusetts high court did in the *American Tragedy* case) that the harmful effects of "obnoxious passages" would not necessarily be cured even if children read the entire work (*Commonwealth v. Friede* 322–3). On the other hand, a court might base its ruling not on any particular passages but rather on objectionable themes or ideas, as Judge Bushel did in the *Well of Loneliness* case. The "matter charged" was often a moving target. Even if defense counsel was allowed to read the uncharged remainder of a book to the jury, the victory might be pyrrhic. "Jury antagonism is easily aroused by boredom," Ernst noted in 1928, "and the first duty of the defense is entertainment" (Ernst and Seagle 6). A jury might well vent its irritation by penalizing the defendant, regardless of the legal merits.

Moreover, *Hicklin* protected what Ernst called the "dullest-witted and most fallible"; its theory was that "if one libidinous man existed in an Anglo-Saxon community, then all its members would have to submit themselves to the inhibitions of the censorship" (Moscato and LeBlanc, eds. 249–50; Ernst and Seagle 192). Paternalistic, overbroad, often invoked to protect the young, *Hicklin* might be called the Law of the Child. Jane Heap, co-editor of *The Little Review*, complained that American obscenity law permitted "the mind of the young girl" to rule the country. "If there is anything I really fear," she wrote, "it is the mind of the young girl" (Heap 5–6). The *Hicklin* test had a devastating impact on adult Americans' access to serious reading matter (Paul and Schwartz 38; Rembar 20–2).

The speculative character of *Hicklin*'s effects test grew out of the ambiguous nature of obscenity itself. In the early eighteenth century, an obscene libel was thought to be less coherent as a common-law offense than blasphemous libel or seditious libel because obscenity "reflect[ed] on no person, and a libel must be against some particular person or persons, or against the Government" (*Regina v. Read* 777). Obscenity slowly emerged as an offense distinct from sedition and blasphemy, but it lacked the concreteness that sustained those theories of libel. Unlike political provocations or theological heterodoxies, obscenity seemed to exist "for its own sake, or for the sake of creating sensations" (Keymer 133). Autotelic and autoerotic, obscenity's elusive intransitiveness led courts to define it as a generally harmful tendency, "a penetrating poison in the air," thus relieving prosecutors of the burden of proving injury to any particular person ("Mr. Oscar Wilde's" 3; see also Stern). *Hicklin*'s formula, a "tendency ... to deprave and corrupt," assuaged a long-felt evidentiary anxiety by replacing particularized proof with a presumption of general harm to public morals.

Indiscriminate circulation and private editions

Obscenity's nebulous tendency to corrupt was paired with a hypothetical class of the susceptible "into whose hands [it] may fall." Such a class was plausible as long as an accused publication was available for general purchase or perusal. As Justice Blackburn put it in *Hicklin*, "the indiscriminate circulation of [an obscene work] must be calculated necessarily to prejudice the morals of the people" (375). The reverse proposition—that books confined to affluent or professional classes would not injure general morals— was a justification for the modernist institution of the private edition. American publishers often relied on pricey or limited editions to avoid action by the New York Society for the Suppression of Vice, which treated *Hicklin*'s principles as gospel. The New York publisher B.W. Huebsch cleverly employed scarcity tactics in publishing Lawrence's *The Rainbow*. Issuing an expurgated version just a few weeks after the novel's suppression in London in November 1915, Huebsch created a *de facto* limited edition by releasing copies to the trade slowly, "with a caution against talking too much about it" (qtd. in Roberts and Poplawski 32–3). By 1920, he was publishing a more expensive version, taking "refuge in the old trick of a limited edition ... at $5, which was pretty high for a novel in those days" (qtd. in Lawrence, *Letters* 3:457 n1). Thus, Huebsch achieved scarcity in two ways: by orchestrating timed-release distribution and by pricing books so that they would be purchased mainly by affluent readers.

Prosecutors and purity groups felt less anxiety for children and the working classes when a controversial book could be confined to aficionados or professional readers. In 1895, a few months after Oscar Wilde's trials, a British journalist wrote that Wilde had produced his "non-moral literature for the upper circles of the reading world," but the "penny dreadful" and the "shilling obscene" posed a greater danger to "the imagination of any boy, particularly in the lower classes" (Chisholm 765, 769). Lawrence published *Lady Chatterley's Lover* initially in an expensive edition through the Florentine bookseller Pino Orioli. Limited to 1,000 signed copies, the 1928 Florence edition sold for $10 to the American market and £2 (later £4) to the English market, nearly five times the usual price of a novel. After advancing the costs of production, Lawrence received 90 percent of the profits, more than £1,000 in all (Worthen 118–20). Although financial benefits were a large consideration, Lawrence welcomed the chance to publish his fictional polemic about war, class, and sexuality in a private, unexpurgated edition, and to scheme with Orioli to get copies past customs and postal authorities.

The "private edition" came to have a special meaning in modernism. As Lawrence Rainey shows, the term did not refer to a small print-run for the author's friends; rather, it denoted a marketing strategy for avoiding charges of indiscriminate circulation (48). Morris Ernst quipped that "cheapness of price" seemed to be "an integral part of obscenity," adding that a publisher of controversial books, "if he confines his advertising to 'Physicians, Clergymen, and Lawyers,' has not much to fear" (Ernst and Seagle 61). During the 1920–21 obscenity proceedings against the *Little Review* editors, the attorney John Quinn tried to get John Sumner of the New York Vice Society to drop the prosecution if Joyce would agree to withdraw *Ulysses* from magazine serialization and publish it in a private edition. The proposal intrigued Sumner, but Quinn did not get Joyce's approval (Quinn, Letter, April 13, 1921). Quinn had already been urging Huebsch to consider publishing a complete, unexpurgated *Ulysses* in a private edition of 1,000 or 1,250 copies priced at $8 or $10, although Huebsch in the end chose not to run the risk. Quinn also advised a private-edition solution for the publisher of James Branch Cabell's *Jurgen: A Comedy of Justice* (1919) after the Vice Society obtained an obscenity indictment under the New York Penal Code. As Quinn noted approvingly, the Irish author George Moore had avoided legal harassment by having Boni and Liveright of New York issue *A Story-Teller's Holiday* (1918) in a private edition, available to subscribers at $10 per copy (Quinn, Letter, August 15, 1920).

After many struggles, Joyce's *Ulysses* was published in 1922 by Shakespeare and Company of Paris in an edition of 1,000 copies priced from £3 3s. to £7 7s. Unlike the private edition urged by Quinn, this subscribed volume was a true deluxe edition, aimed at dealers and collectors as much as traditional purchasers. Joyce received 66 percent of the net profits, an arrangement that effectively turned "every purchaser of the edition into a quasi-patron, someone directly supporting the artist himself" (Rainey 53). Crucially, the volume was published in Paris, where the moral climate was far more accommodating than in the 1850s when the government of the Second Empire had prosecuted Flaubert, Baudelaire, and other writers for outrages against religion and public morality. France had signed the international Agreement for the Suppression of Obscene Publications (1910)—a treaty that coordinated multinational policing of indecent writings—but had attached reservations that allowed freer circulation of controversial books within its borders (Marshik, *British* 157–8). French authorities were little interested, moreover, in expending resources to prosecute an English-language work destined for transport to Britain and America anyway (Potter 65). In 1932, Joyce hoped that "a high priced private edition of *Ulysses*" might be published in Britain as a way of avoiding censorship under the Customs Consolidation Act (Joyce, *Letters* 316), but the book remained officially suppressed until 1936, not by any court ruling but as a result of the British Home Office's policy to seize any copy imported into the country (Medina Casado). France's unchallenged exports became England's contraband.

The price that Joyce and Lawrence paid for publishing their works in France and Italy was the loss of copyright protection in other parts of the world, notably the United States. As we will see in Chapter 3, copyright and censorship often worked in antagonism to each other; by withholding protection from works deemed immoral, copyright laws perversely encouraged an underground market for transgressive books. One such work was Gertrude Beasley's controversial memoir of her West Texas upbringing, *My First Thirty Years*, published in 1925 by Contact Editions of Paris. Barred by New York customs, Beasley's unsentimental picture of ignorance, poverty, and incest lost any chance of an American copyright and was soon serialized in Samuel Roth's *Casanova Jr's Tales* (Roth 105–6). Published for 1,000 subscribers, the quarterly sold for $5 a copy or $15 for a year. The hefty price, the small subscription base, and the label "privately printed" aimed the magazine at well-to-do seekers of titillation and kept vice crusaders from descending on the publication.

Obscenity, copyright, and mechanical reproduction

During the oral argument in *Hicklin*, the bookseller's attorney insisted that a person could not be convicted of publishing obscenity unless his actions had been accompanied by an obscene intent, and he illustrated his point by suggesting that a painting of Venus hanging in a gallery could not be obscene. Justice Lush interposed: "It does not follow that because such a picture is exhibited in a public gallery, photographs of it might be sold in the streets with impunity" (365). Anthony Comstock argued a similar point in 1883. With leaden sophistry, he contended that, just as a woman "in her proper womanly apparel" differed from a woman posing nude "in a lewd posture," so the indecency of a painted nude, tolerable perhaps in that unique format, was "unmasked in the [photographic] copy" (Comstock, *Traps* 171–2). Pursuing the parallel, he argued that Boccaccio's *Decameron*, though filled with indecency, might be acceptable if read by students in the original Italian, but when published and advertised as a cheap English translation, the book became "a corrupting element" in "the ever-ready hands of the youth" (176). Immodest canvases and medieval bawdy were infinitely more dangerous when made available in inexpensive copies sold indiscriminately, loosed "like a wild beast [on] the youth of the land" (173).

Thus, for vice crusaders, the already suspect aura of candid art grew far more poisonous and corrupting once it was widely disseminated by means of mechanical reproduction. I suggested in Chapter 1 that Dorian Gray, as he circulates in London society, might be viewed as a copyright-infringing photograph of the original painting that hangs, shrouded, in his attic. Just as the logic of copyright illuminates Wilde's strange tale, so does the logic of Comstockery. Dorian's painted portrait is a harmless, unique work, confined to a locked room; Dorian himself is a mass-produced copy that spreads indiscriminately through London, from afternoon teas to opium dens, and poses a moral danger to "young men" and "pure-minded girl[s]" alike (1890:79). His ageless allure is as inexhaustibly corrupting as the stock of cheap erotic pictures that vice societies carted away during repeated Sisyphean raids. Dorian is a poisonous copy in the age of infinite reproducibility.

Copyright laws and obscenity laws grew in response to printing technologies and fears of an ungovernable mass of readers. Copyrights are state-granted property rights that build invisible fences around infinitely reproducible public goods; they permit informational monopolists to reintroduce scarcity in a world where technology and markets have solved that problem. Whereas copyright induces artificial scarcity through legal monopoly, obscenity law does so through the threat of legal sanction. Copyrights seek to prevent the market failure that might result from unchecked freeriding; censorship seeks to prevent moral collapse from freely circulated indecency. Both produce scarcity in mass-reproducible cultural goods by applying rules that inhibit the instinct to imitate and consume. By condoning private editions of indecent works, prosecutors and purity groups helped create effects that mirrored those of copyright law: a reduced supply of works available at above-competition prices.

The classics escape

Much of the dispute in *Hicklin* centered on a clause in Lord Campbell's Act that stated that a warrant for the seizure of suspect books could issue only if a magistrate found that their publication would be an indictable misdemeanor at common law. Justice Blackburn ventured the opinion that the clause was intended "to guard against the vexatious prosecution of publishers of old and recognized standard works, in which there may be some obscene or mischievous matter" (372). Here was a familiar anxiety about how far purity reforms should go. Should they focus only on obvious, commercialized smut, or should they extend, for the sake of moral and legal consistency, to "the Bible, Shakespeare, Rabelais, Boccaccio, the Restoration dramatists, Fielding, Smollett, and Sterne and the rest of the 'obscene' classics" (Ernst and Seagle 53)? Morris Ernst framed the dilemma as a lawyer's question: did a different treatment for classic works show that there was some uncodified "statute of limitations on obscenity," and, if so, "when does a book become a classic?" (55).

The question haunted the litigation over the postal suppression of *The Little Review*, discussed above. In his brief to the court, Quinn, acting as Margaret Anderson's attorney, noted that the Bible, though it mentions many "lustful and lecherous acts," could not reasonably be found to be "obscene or lewd" (Quinn, Brief 17). Judge Augustus Hand, rejecting Anderson's motion to enjoin the Postmaster, responded that "numerous really great writings ... doubtless at times escape [the postal laws] only because they come within the term 'classics,' [and] have the sanction of age and fame, and usually appeal to a comparatively limited number of readers" (*Anderson v. Patten* 384). Hand thus offered two reasons for exceptional treatment of the classics: first, their venerable age did create a kind of statute of limitations, as Ernst supposed; second, they found so few readers that there was no possibility of the widespread corruption feared by vice crusaders and prosecutors. Pound—who never understood how difficult it was for a judge to overrule a Postmaster's decision—ridiculed Hand's dictum in essay after essay, as well as in his poem "Cantico del Sole," where he intoned, "The thought of what America would be like / If the Classics had a wide circulation / Troubles my sleep" (*Personae* 182).

The question continued to trouble Judge Hand as well. When in 1934 he authored the majority opinion affirming the lower court's finding that Joyce's *Ulysses* was not obscene under the US Tariff Act, he digressed to observe that "it may be questioned whether the obscene passages in *Romeo and Juliet* were as necessary to the development of the play as those in the monologue of Mrs. Bloom [in *Ulysses*] are to the depiction of the latter's tortured soul" (*United States v. One Book Entitled Ulysses* 707). Ernst, too, continued to mull the problem of the classics. The 1930 Tariff Act, which he helped to revise, contained a special provision that granted the Secretary of the Treasury discretion to "admit the so-called classics or books of recognized and established literary or scientific merit ... when imported for noncommercial purposes" (§ 305). While challenging the customs ban on *Ulysses* in federal court, Ernst's legal team also petitioned customs to admit a copy of *Ulysses* under this "literary merit" exemption. The petition was granted, but with the caveat that the Commissioner of Customs still regarded *Ulysses* as "obscene" (Vanderham 91–2). Of course, the Treasury provision was in the nature of an exemption, not an exoneration. It took the full litigation of the simultaneous customs action to prove the Commissioner wrong about *Ulysses*.

Wartime censorship

The repressive climate for modernism was exacerbated by wartime censorship. In Britain, the Defence of the Realm Act (DORA) was passed by Parliament four days after the declaration of war in August 1914. Amended and expanded frequently, DORA authorized the Crown to regulate many common activities and to punish violators with fines, confiscations, prison terms, and even death. The Act came to control numerous aspects of civilian life, including "the instruments of communication and the transmission of information" (Hynes, *A War* 79). In October 1918, the suffragist Sylvia Pankhurst was convicted under DORA for giving a Socialist speech accused of attempting "to cause mutiny, sedition or dissatisfaction among His Majesty's Forces or civilian population," and was fined £30 with costs (217). Two years earlier, the philosopher and pacifist Bertrand Russell, who had authored a pamphlet on conscientious objection, was found guilty of the DORA offense of prejudicing recruitment and military discipline, fined £100, and stripped of his Cambridge lectureship. In 1918, he was tried again and sentenced to six months in prison for an article on "The German Peace Offer" (147, 217).

DORA punished unpatriotic fictions as well. Rose Allatini's novel, *Despised and Rejected* (1918), about a young homosexual who is imprisoned and mistreated for being a conscientious objector, resulted in a fine for the publishers and forfeiture of all copies in their possession. The presiding magistrate criticized the book for immorality and pacifism, though only the latter gave the court jurisdiction under DORA (Hynes, *A War* 232–4). Virginia Woolf observed that the novel had been "burnt by the hangman" (*Diary* 1:246). Miles Malleson's *Two Short Plays: Patriotic and Unpatriotic* (1916) was confiscated under DORA as "a deliberate calumny on the British soldier," according to the War Office (Hynes, *A War* 151). Even D.H. Lawrence may have suffered, indirectly, from DORA. After the prosecution of *The Rainbow*, officially under the Obscene Publications Act, a question was asked in the House of Commons whether proceedings had been taken under DORA. The Home Secretary answered in the negative, but it is possible that Lawrence was being targeted for anti-war attitudes registered in his other writings of the period (60–2). The Lawrence and Allatini cases show that censorship was richly overdetermined during the war years: overlapping laws gave courts, martial and civilian, ample power to suppress and punish.

In the United States, the Espionage Act of 1917 and the Sedition Act of 1918 combined with obscenity laws to authorize comparable disciplinary overchoice. While these wartime measures punished individuals such as Socialist Party leader Eugene Debs and anarchist Emma Goldman as threats to national security, they also suppressed politically progressive periodicals such as *The Masses*, which had its second-class mailing privileges revoked under the Espionage Act (Morrisson 177). The US Court of Appeals for the Second Circuit upheld the New York Postmaster's revocation in a decision handed down on November 2, 1917 (*Masses Publishing Co. v. Patten*)— four weeks before Judge Hand, in the trial court, sustained the same

Postmaster's denial of mailing privileges to the October 1917 issue of *The Little Review*.

In upholding the Postmaster's suppression of *The Little Review*, Judge Hand stressed that his ruling was based on the salaciousness of "Cantelman's Spring-Mate," but he also mentioned another item from the same issue: a purported translation of an official German document "containing instructions to [a German soldier] to beget children of all women available in a designated district" (*Anderson v. Patten* 383). This anonymous commission was in fact an invention of Ezra Pound, who later regretted his "squib on the Hun" ("This Approaches Literature!"; *Pound-Quinn* 132, 134). Judge Hand pointed out that this item, too, might reasonably be thought to have immoral tendencies, but he denied that it could be considered "a publication giving information [or teaching] the reader how dangerous or demoralizing is the Teutonic foe" (*Anderson v. Patten* 384). He meant that he was not assessing Pound's bagatelle or Lewis's story under the Espionage Act. Yet the Postmaster himself may have done so. Margaret Anderson had a reputation as a political radical that made *The Little Review* "suspect to official eyes" (*Pound-Quinn* 92), and Post Office records referred to the magazine as a "Publication of Anarchistic tendency" and cited the Espionage Act as a basis for suppressing it (Vanderham 18, 28–9; Potter 75). Just as with DORA in Britain, the Espionage Act could mingle with obscenity laws as an additional, interchangeable ground for attacking transgressive texts.

Patchwork regulation of the obscene: *Ulysses* in America

Ulysses was officially suppressed in Britain from 1922 to 1936. In December 1922, the Home Office banned the volume from the mails, and the first of many seizures was executed by officials at Croydon Aerodrome under the Customs Consolidation Act, with the approval of the Assistant Undersecretary of State and the Director of Public Prosecutions. Chief constables in major cities required booksellers to notify them of orders placed for *Ulysses*, and public libraries were asked to report patrons who requested copies (Houston). This panoptic pursuit of *Ulysses*, emanating from the sovereign command of the Home Office, represented one model of governmental suppression. The official war on obscenity was less centralized in the United States but equally difficult to resist.

American federalism, which permits federal and state laws to operate independently and concurrently in many instances, led to uncoordinated regulation of indecency. The case of *Ulysses* illustrates this jurisdictional atomizing of the obscene. We typically think of Joyce's novel as having suffered under a unitary legal ban until federal Judge John M. Woolsey liberated it in 1933, but in fact *Ulysses* was neither comprehensively banned nor fully exonerated in the United States at any point up to or even after Woolsey's famous ruling. Instead, *Ulysses* was subjected to a series of sporadic suppressions and piecemeal adjudications—to the uncoordinated, capillary assaults of the law. Between January 1919 and January 1920, the US Post Office acted *in rem* against three different issues of *The Little Review*, each containing a portion of Joyce's novel, by revoking the magazine's second-class mailing privileges (Vanderham 1–2, 28–36). This mailing rate was critical to the survival of little magazines. It permitted, for example, some three thousand copies of *The Little Review* to be mailed for four dollars or less (Quinn, Brief 3; Anderson, Affidavit 2). The three *Little Review* issues were probably deemed nonmailable because of the perceived indecency of the *Ulysses* segments, but the Post Office may also have disapproved of some material on political grounds, such as the satirical treatment of English royalty in the "Cyclops" episode of *Ulysses* (Vanderham 34–5).

After the Post Office, it was the New York courts' turn to condemn *Ulysses*. In the autumn of 1920, John Sumner of the New York Vice Society swore out a complaint against the editors of *The Little Review* for publishing the section of *Ulysses* in which Leopold Bloom masturbates while observing a young woman on the seashore. In early 1921, after a defense by John Quinn that Joseph Hassett has criticized as halfhearted and ineffective (94–112), the New York Court of Special Sessions found the editors guilty of publishing obscenity under section 1141 of the Penal Code and fined them $50 each (Ellmann, *James* 502–4; Vanderham 41–53). Whereas the postal seizures under the Comstock Act had acted *in rem*, directly against Joyce's text, the New York law acted *in personam*, against the text's disseminators. Under this combined assault, the circulation of *Ulysses* came to a halt.

Once *Ulysses* appeared in unexpurgated form in Paris in 1922, it became a book that British and American travelers, collectors, and booksellers schemed to import and that officials in those countries vowed to intercept. Harriet Shaw Weaver, who arranged for *Ulysses* to be specially printed in France for her London-based Egoist Press, claimed that as many as 500 copies had been held up at US post offices and later destroyed. Nearly 500 more were reportedly seized and confiscated in 1923 by English customs authorities at Folkestone (Slocum and Cahoon 26–7). US customs also intercepted *Ulysses*. In 1928, the US Customs Court upheld the seizure of seven copies, along with Pierre Louÿs' novel *Aphrodite* (1896) and other titles, at the port of Minneapolis under the Tariff Act of 1922 (*Heymoolen v. United States*).

As noted previously, the US Tariff Act was amended in 1930 to provide a fairer mechanism for testing the validity of customs seizures. It was under this procedure that Random House and its attorneys Ernst and Lindey orchestrated the seizure of a copy of *Ulysses* imported from Paris in 1932. That copy was the sole defendant in the federal *in rem* action, *United States v. One Book Entitled Ulysses*, in which Judge Woolsey implicitly rejected *Hicklin*'s Law of the Child and ruled that the net effect of *Ulysses* would not lead to lustful thoughts in a person with average sex instincts. In all, between 1919 and 1934, *Ulysses* was the subject of numerous official seizures and suppressions, multiple state and federal court adjudications, and a criminal fine, in the United States (Gertzman, *Bookleggers* 15–48). There was also at least one incarceration: Samuel Roth was imprisoned in 1929 for violating parole after vice crusaders seized warehoused copies of *Ulysses, Lady Chatterley's Lover, Fanny Hill*, and other titles (16–17). None of these events definitively settled the legal status of *Ulysses* in America.

Even after the US Court of Appeals for the Second Circuit affirmed Judge Woolsey's decision in 1934, *Ulysses* was still vulnerable to attack by postal authorities, state prosecutors, and vigilant vice societies. Just a few months after Woolsey issued his decree, an Episcopal clergyman learned that the US Post Office had seized a copy of the Random House *Ulysses,* which he had mailed to himself along with *Lives of the Saints* and Richard Maurice Bucke's *Cosmic Consciousness* (1901). When the clergyman protested, the Post Office stated that it planned to hold the book until the appeal of Woolsey's decree was decided; in the meantime, the good pastor could consider himself technically

FIGURE 2.2 *John Munro Woolsey, US District Court for the Southern District of New York, 1931. Courtesy John Woolsey III.*

charged under the Comstock Act with sending obscenity through the mails (Brainard). After the Second Circuit pronounced in favor of *Ulysses*, the government decided not to seek review of that appellate ruling in the US Supreme Court. Thus, there was never a last legal word on *Ulysses* in America. Instead, the passage of time has acted as the court of last resort, conferring an informal immunity on Joyce's masterpiece.

Modernism constitutionalized

The Second Circuit panel that upheld Judge Woolsey's decree was deeply divided. Judges Learned and Augustus Hand voted to affirm Woolsey, but Judge Martin Manton vehemently dissented. Manton suggested that in passing the Tariff Act, Congress had implicitly adopted the strict *Hicklin* test as the definition of "obscene" (Paul and Schwartz 65 n6). "The statute is designed to protect society at large," he wrote, "notwithstanding the deprivation of benefits to a few" (*United States v. One Book Entitled Ulysses* 711). Manton faulted Judge Woolsey for ignoring the popular will and favoring a hyper-educated elite at the expense of the young and the vulnerable. "If we disregard the protection of the morals of the susceptible," he worried, "are we to consider merely the benefits and pleasures derived from letters by those who pose as the more highly developed and intelligent?" (711). Manton's use of the word "pose" to characterize pretentious devotees of modernism recalls the derisive suggestion of Edward Carson during his cross-examination of Oscar Wilde that "the majority of people" would not be able to "live up to the pose" that Wilde and other artists had adopted (Holland 81).

Judges in other obscenity cases implied the same ironic contrast between "the reading public" and "literary artistry," and argued, as Manton did, that the voice of the moral majority, speaking through legislators, should not be silenced by judges setting themselves up as advocates of literary progress (see, for example, *People v. Seltzer* 333–4; *People v. Friede* 615). The perceived gulf between the artist and the people polarized the obscenity debate in the early twentieth century. Charged with publishing an obscene extract from *Ulysses* in *The Little Review*, Jane Heap denounced vice crusaders, judges, and laws as incompetent before a true work of art: "The heavy farce and sad futility of trying a creative work in a court of law appalls me. Was there ever a judge qualified to judge even the simplest psychic outburst? How then a work of Art?" (5). Wilde, too, had argued that law's writ did not run far enough to justify any regulatory interference with the sovereignty of literature.

The federal civil forfeiture action did much more than simply open American ports to *Ulysses*; it helped stabilize the legal standards for measuring obscenity in the United States and Britain. Up to that time, lawyers and judges often seemed to be groping for a coherent vocabulary with which to fix the meaning of the obscene. Quinn had cited a mass of conflicting legal standards in his effort to enjoin the New York Postmaster in 1917. Parts of his brief listed cases that applied some version of the *Hicklin* rule; other parts contended that literature was not written "for babies or for young girls' seminaries" and that the proper test of Wyndham Lewis's story was whether it was "likely to corrupt the morals of the average reader" (Quinn, Brief 8, 13–14, 20). The *Ulysses* opinions of Judges Woolsey and Hand could not, as a legal matter, command nationwide obedience, but their cogent eloquence and judicial prestige helped clarify and standardize several concepts as applied to obscenity: average or normal sex instincts, serious literary value, dominant literary effect, the relevance of objectionable passages to a work's theme, the validity of expert opinion on a work's reputation, and the inappropriateness of the *Hicklin* test in modern society. These ingredients would later be fused and constitutionalized in obscenity rulings of the US Supreme Court (Hassett 166–7). The *Ulysses* customs case also helped change the legal climate in Britain: Woolsey's opinion influenced the Home Office's decision to lift the ban on Joyce's book in 1936 (Birmingham 332–36; Marshik, *British* 163–4; Medina Casado 499–502).

Recent scholars of modernism have properly cautioned that court battles were only part of the war against censorship and obscenity laws. Potter, for example, identifies informal or quasi-official networks that resisted censorship in the first half of the twentieth century, including groups such as Britain's Incorporated Society of Authors, Playwrights and Composers, and the English and international P.E.N. (Poets, Playwrights, Editors, Essayists, Novelists)—collectives that fostered an international awareness of authors' rights to literary property and free expression (Potter 34–40, 153–67). Nevertheless, courts and legislatures, under pressure from changing mores, undoubtedly transformed the mechanisms and networks of censorship in the twentieth century. In America, the watershed case was *Roth v. United States* (1957). In *Roth*, the US Supreme Court considered a challenge by Samuel Roth, under the free-speech and due-process clauses of the US Constitution, to the federal Comstock Act, under which he had been convicted of mailing obscene circulars for his periodicals *Good Times* and *American Aphrodite*. Despite the arguments of counsel and *amici curiae*, the Court upheld Roth's conviction by a 6–3 vote. The lawful pirate of Joyce and other modernists, now in his sixties, entered a federal penitentiary and remained there until 1961 (De Grazia 273–326).

Yet the *Roth* majority, expressly rejecting *Hicklin*, established a new test of obscenity. Under this test, a work was obscene, and therefore unprotected as free speech, if, to the average person applying contemporary community standards, the dominant theme of the work, taken as a whole, appealed to prurient interest. Such a work was "utterly without redeeming social importance" (*Roth v. United States* 488–9). The Court had reached back into the *Ulysses* opinions and extracted some of their critical components, adding a new emphasis on community standards and social value. Yet the presence of the First Amendment—the principle of free speech—is what really distinguished *Roth* from earlier obscenity rulings. It was not that lawyers had never argued the constitutional question before. More than a quarter of a century earlier, Ernst had challenged the obscenity provisions of the Comstock Act and the Tariff Act as inconsistent with the First Amendment, but even judges as progressive as John Woolsey and Augustus Hand had given him no hearing (*United States v. Dennett* 569; *United States v. One Obscene Book Entitled "Married Love"* 822). As late as 1950, the Massachusetts high court, ruling in an *in rem* action filed against Erskine Caldwell's *God's Little Acre* (1933), brushed off constitutional issues as "requir[ing] no discussion" in an obscenity case (*Attorney General v. Book Named "God's Little Acre"* 285). The law was not ready to entertain such novelties.

In previous decades, before censorship was tested by a constitutional standard, American courts had confined themselves to assessing obscenity as a mixed question of fact and law, weighing a work's offensiveness against its isolable virtues, its salaciousness against its moral message. After *Roth* and similar cases, judges could put aside the quantifying of smut and decide the question as a matter of First Amendment law, inquiring whether a work had serious social or literary importance despite its full-throated indecency. This approach, growing out of the "qualified immunity from the law of obscenity" established in the *Ulysses* customs case (Hassett 152–3), allowed courts to do what even socially progressive jurists of earlier decades could not: openly concede a book's offensiveness yet rule that inherent free-speech values forbade suppression. Now the classics could escape, not because of age or obscurity, but because the law deferred to their intrinsic merit. In a sense, the law was restoring to art the sovereignty that Jane Heap had accused the law of usurping.

The Supreme Court extended the principles of *Roth* when it declared in 1964 that Henry Miller's *Tropic of Cancer*—originally published in Paris in 1934 but banned by US customs and later subjected to dozens of prosecutions around the country—was protected by the First Amendment (*Grove Press v. Gerstein*). Under the *Roth* test, regional moralism was giving way to a nationwide standard for assessing indecency; federalism's uncoordinated regulation of art and literature was being replaced by a unified constitutional test of social value. The literary was becoming the legal. In contrast, pre-*Roth* litigations had rendered controversial works vulnerable to the patchwork of laws and parochial mores of many jurisdictions, and often made victory in one court merely a prelude to litigation in another. The legal had fragmented the literary by subjecting texts to the reader response of geographically and culturally diverse judges and juries. *Roth* promised to relieve this legal and moral gridlock.

The significance of *Roth* was clear in *Grove Press v. Christenberry*, a 1959 litigation in which the publisher Barney Rosset sued to restrain the Postmaster of New York from barring the unexpurgated *Lady Chatterley's Lover* from the mails. The Post Office had declared copies of the book and advertisements for it nonmailable under 18 USC § 1461 (the amended Comstock Act). Like Margaret Anderson forty years before, Rosset sought relief in the federal district court, but, unlike Judge Hand in *Anderson v. Patten*, the judge in *Christenberry* felt no need to defer to the Postmaster's discretion. In 1917, the Postmaster had concluded that "Cantelman's Spring-Mate" was obscene after examining the story's language and themes in light of the Comstock Act and judicial definitions of obscenity. Judge Hand would not overturn the Postmaster's factual conclusions for anything less than an abuse of discretion. But in 1959 the question was less a factual than a legal one: whether *Lady Chatterley's Lover*, for all its shocking candor, embodied social and literary value and was therefore protected as free speech. The Postmaster no longer had the last word on the legality of texts; the courts had greater competence in constitutional questions and would decide them *de novo*. The judge in *Christenberry* concluded that Lawrence's novel did not "exceed the outer limits of the tolerance which the community as a whole gives to writing about sex and sex relations" and was therefore entitled to the protection of the First Amendment (502–3; see also De Grazia 338–42; Glass,

Counterculture 101–44). The US Court of Appeals for the Second Circuit agreed that the Post Office had applied the *in rem* provision unconstitutionally to *Lady Chatterley's Lover*.

In America, modernism was becoming constitutionalized. A similar process, led by statutory change, was taking place in Britain, where the Obscene Publications Act of 1959, while retaining a few elements of *Hicklin*, liberalized the test of obscenity by requiring that accused works be considered as a whole; giving authors standing in forfeiture proceedings; making expert opinion admissible; and creating a "public good" defense that brought the interests of science, literature, art, and learning to bear on challenged works. The US Supreme Court's doctrine of "redeeming social importance" had influenced the statute's "public good" defense (De Grazia 190 n). The 1959 Act was applied in 1960 when Penguin Books was summoned to the Old Bailey to defend against *in personam* charges that its unexpurgated edition of *Lady Chatterley's Lover*, freshly printed and ready for sale at 3s. 6d., was obscene. After a trial during which numerous experts, including E.M. Forster and Rebecca West, testified to the value of the novel, a jury of three women and nine men returned a unanimous verdict of not guilty (Rolph, ed.). Penguin sold 2 million copies of the book by the end of 1960; within the next few years, the novel was lawfully available in Canada, Australia, New Zealand, and other countries (McCleery 36–43). Lawrence's modernism had finally arrived.

Censorship had the effect of inhibiting modernism well after its commonly recognized terminus. As long as laws forbade the circulation of controversial texts, modernism remained partly latent as a sociohistorical phenomenon. By suppressing texts or driving them underground, restrictive laws created an artificial scarcity that only liberalized laws could remove. Modernism could not fully inhabit its own history until this law-induced scarcity was eliminated. Again, obscenity law appears as the dark twin of copyright law. As I will suggest in the next chapter, copyright laws have stunted the development of modernism by prolonging monopoly control, and therefore forms of textual scarcity, many decades beyond any accepted endpoint for the period. Private control by copyright owners ensures that the history of modernism will remain in progress for years to come. The growth of modernism's public domain through expired copyrights has proven to be an even slower process than the expansion of modernism's freedom of expression through enlightened judging and legislating.

3

Copyright, Patronage, and Courtesy

Copyrights are scarecrows. They discourage free riders from descending on authors' creative efforts and usurping their hard-won markets through the production of unauthorized copies. According to economic theory, unless there is a prospect of financial reward—difficult to extract from vaporous intellectual creations unless they can be owned and allocated through legal monopoly—authors will have no incentive to create, and the storehouse of culture will remain an empty barn. In 1710, Daniel Defoe urged statutory protection for "the Author's Property ... the Child of his Inventions, the Brat of his Brain" (qtd. in Rose, *Authors and Owners* 39). Already the idea of copyright was inspiring a profusion of polemical tropes: authors' works were owned, invented, born, kidnapped, and always filiated. Yet the protection conferred by Britain's Statute of Anne (1710) was not without limit. Statutory copyrights were to last no longer than a total of twenty-eight years. Later copyright statutes, including the first US copyright act of 1790, also granted rights for limited times. In making copyrights perishable, these laws effectively decreed a public domain. The end of copyright was the beginning of the commons. Authors and publishers enjoyed exclusive rights in their intellectual creations for a time, whereupon those creations were to pass into a legislatively demarcated public domain for anyone to use without permission or fear of liability.

That, anyway, is the Anglo-American theory of copyright, briefly summarized. But modernist authors were witnesses to the beginning of copyright's proprietary turn—a transition from the bounded, incentive-based monopoly described above to an ideology of absolute ownership. In this transitional moment, modernists could still rely on unchallenged norms of borrowing, allusion, and bricolage in pursuing their mythical methods and ideas of order. Writers such as Ezra Pound, James Joyce, Marianne Moore, and T.S. Eliot adapted and quoted freely from texts that were copyrighted at the time. As Leonard Diepeveen has noted, "appropriation of previously existing material may well be *the* aesthetic of [the twentieth] century" (viii; italics in original).

But copyright law was already changing from a regulatory regime to a propertized one, from a source of limited exclusive rights to a warrant for claiming broad authorial entitlements (Patterson and Lindberg 77; Saint-Amour, "Introduction" 10). With this change came a reimagining of the public domain. Increasingly unlikely to arrive during an author's lifetime, the commons was coming to be viewed as a distant, inequitable event, something to be resented as a deprivation of property and dreaded as a *memento mori*. Modernists were historically positioned to glimpse what copyright laws were becoming, and what only the *rentier* class of their heirs and transferees would see face to face: the "maximalist or 'thick' copyright constraints" that make up today's rights-cluttered culture (Saint-Amour, *Copywrights* 199).

Modernists not only generated and husbanded copyrights; they also produced texts that internalized a "proprietary self-consciousness" about copyright as a formation of modernity—a "copyright metadiscourse" through which these texts "internally engaged with [their] legal status as property, and therefore with [their] economic status as commodity" (Saint-Amour, *Copywrights* 13). Paul Saint-Amour reads Oscar Wilde's "The Portrait of Mr. W.H." (1889) as a parable of copyright's proprietary turn, George Sylvester Viereck's *The House of the Vampire* (1907) as a novel that broods on plagiarism and postmortem copyright through motifs of haunting and vampirism, and the "Oxen of the Sun" episode of Joyce's *Ulysses* (1922) as a parodic performance of copyright and fair use culminating in "a celebratory portrait of public domain discourse" (18). Attending to copyright's textual and intertextual voices, Celia Marshik shows that in *A Room of One's Own* (1929), Virginia Woolf drew freely on public domain works for much of her discussion of women writers but, as she approached her own moment, veered prudently from quoting copyrighted texts to "*inventing* contemporary novelists and their writings" (Marshik, "Thinking" 72; italics in original). Caren Irr examines later fiction writers such as Leslie Marmon Silko,

Ursula K. Le Guin, and Kathy Acker who have gone beyond modernism's copyright metadiscourse to navigate between "the language of the commons and vigorously individualist versions of property rights in culture, reading the latter through a critical, feminist lens" (11).

Yet the proprietary turn was only part of modernism's encounter with copyright. Before copyright law became propertized, it was porous and unreliable, especially in the transatlantic setting. What Pound decried as America's cultural provincialism in the early twentieth century resulted partly from its economic protectionism. The insulation of America's book-manufacturing industries—typesetters, printers, binders—from foreign competition, along with popular hunger for cheap foreign literature, led to copyright isolationism, a rejection of broad international agreements that were unifying markets for cultural goods throughout Europe (Spoo, *Without* 65–89). Transatlantic copyright asymmetries—aggravated by statutory conditions and formalities that could defeat US copyright protection—hindered the authorized dissemination of modernist texts; obscenity laws and censorship made it difficult to secure and enforce copyrights for controversial or experimental works. The problem was viciously circular: censorship impeded the ability to comply with statutory requirements for copyright (especially in the United States), and the inability to secure or enforce copyrights fueled the work of lawful pirates who sometimes bowdlerized their reprints in order to avoid conflicts with censors. Transatlantic modernism was shaped by the mutually destructive embrace of copyright and obscenity laws, and by three contiguous institutions: copyright, trade courtesy, and patronage.

Patronage or copyright?

Patronage and copyright are often viewed as distinct moments, historically and conceptually. Until 1710, writes Mark Rose, "authors' primary economic relations were still typically with patrons rather than with booksellers" (*Authors and Owners* 4). In that year, the Statute of Anne enabled authors to secure the exclusive right to print and reprint their books, in contrast to earlier grants and privileges enjoyed by the Stationers' Company, a printing monopoly that also acted as a censor of writings offensive to church and state authority (Rose, *Authors in Court* 8–9). Once possessed of remunerative copyrights, authors increasingly came to rely on a public market economy that offered independence from private patronage. By 1760, Oliver Goldsmith could declare that "[English poets] have now no other patrons but the public ... a good and a generous master" (qtd. in Taylor 102). A century later, Charles Dickens, who owed much of his success to mass literacy on both sides of the Atlantic, toasted "the great compact phalanx of the people" as true benefactors of literature, in contrast to "individual patrons—sometimes munificent, often sordid, always few" (*Speeches* 140–1).

Neil Netanel has argued that the Framers of the American Constitution, with its clause empowering Congress to enact copyright and patent laws, deeply distrusted the corrupting influence of "government and elite patronage" and viewed copyrights as enhancing "the diffusion of knowledge" and fostering "an autonomous sphere of print-mediated citizen deliberation and public education" (89, 92). Copyright law in the United States thus had both a productive function that spurred creativity and a structural function that shielded deliberative democracy from private economic capture (84–92). Similarly, when Thomas Macaulay rose in the British House of Commons in 1841 to oppose a bill for longer copyrights, he treated it as a truism that patronage and copyright were "the only two ways" in which authors could be remunerated. Although copyright was a "tax on readers for the purpose of giving a bounty to writers," Macaulay was willing to tolerate a limited copyright tax because all forms of patronage were, he declared, "fatal to the integrity and independence of literary men" (198, 201).

Virginia Woolf also distrusted patronage. Like Oliver Goldsmith, she viewed the public as a patron-paymaster, but she warned that this paymaster was "in a very subtle and insidious way the instigator and inspirer of what is written" ("Patron" 211). For Woolf, there was no unitary patronage, only a collection of assorted micro-patrons—the press in its many forms, English and American readerships, highbrow and bestseller markets—that clamored for authors' attention and obedience. Success or failure depended on a writer's choice of patron; the "desirable" patron was one who would "cajole the best out of the writer's brain" without distorting her medium or message (211). The danger of modern micro-patronage was not that a government or an aristocracy would purchase the writer's intellectual freedom, but that she might produce for a public that would deform her aesthetic product.

Woolf's modern patron was a cluster of public institutions that exerted "potentially harmful pressure at the most crucial moment—the moment of composition" (Collier 370). According to Marshik, Woolf conceived of female authorship as empowered by material independence—a locked room to write in and exclusive copyrights or other financial resources to live on—and nourished by a vast, often anonymous tradition of "communal, populous authorship" that escaped all intellectual property, "a room of *our* own" to balance the narrow, solitary room of copyright ("Thinking" 65–86, 80, 84; italics in original). For Woolf, authorial freedom perched precariously between two shaping collectivities: the voices of the past that supplied inspiration and the paymasters of the present who induced or coerced creativity. Patronage threatened compromise with the public taste.

Yet public patronage was only part of the picture. Private donors directly or indirectly supported many modernist authors (Delany 335–51; Rainey; Wexler). Djuna Barnes, Hart Crane, H.D. (Hilda Doolittle), Langston Hughes, Zora Neale Hurston, D.H. Lawrence, and W.B. Yeats enjoyed private patronage for long or short periods of time. Beginning in 1917, James Joyce received substantial sums from the English editor and publisher Harriet Shaw Weaver; by 1923, his annual income from her gift had risen above £1,000. Joyce also benefited from Sylvia Beach, the American bookstore owner in Paris, who worked tirelessly to publish *Ulysses* under her own imprint, assisted him in his fight against Samuel Roth's unauthorized reprintings, and provided countless loans and advances. Lady Rothermere, the wife of a London newspaper magnate, financed T.S. Eliot's magazine *Criterion* for several years beginning in 1922. Early in his career, Pound was gifted $1,000 a year by the American expatriate musician, Margaret Cravens (*Pound-Cravens* 6). He later received support from John Quinn, the New York attorney and art patron, who underwrote his editorial work for *The Little Review* and made it possible for him to pay authors who appeared in its pages (Hassett 17, 30, 57). Quinn's patronage was multifaceted, often taking the form of investments or purchases (Delany 347–8; *Pound-Quinn* 1–18). He spent many

thousands of dollars on contemporary art and bought manuscripts
from Joyce, Eliot, and other writers. He worked to get books by
Pound, Yeats, and John M. Synge published in trade or private
editions, sometimes to secure US copyright (Spoo, *Without* 91–4,
104). He also represented authors in court, as when he defended the
Little Review editors against obscenity charges in connection with
their serialization of *Ulysses* (see Chapter 2). Perhaps his largest
benefaction was the varied law-related work he performed, mostly
without fee, for modernism.

These private supporters were, according to Lawrence Rainey,
a facet of modernism's "strange and perhaps unprecedented
withdrawal from the public sphere of cultural production and debate
... into a divided world of patronage, investment, and collecting" (75).
Rainey argues that, until the Great Depression, private patronage
served as the economic infrastructure of the literary avant-garde,
"an essentially premodern form of social exchange" that reflected a
profound distrust of impersonal, bureaucratized forms of cultural
production but also made authors perhaps "too dependent on the
goodwill and good fortune of a tiny elite" (108). Such a regression
to pre-capitalist modes of gifting should, in theory, have eliminated
the need for copyright, the historical alternative to patronage. If
authors could look to donors for financial support, what need
had they for the economic incentives offered by copyright law?
Copyrights, with their gray, uncertain promise of future income,
could scarcely compete with the vivid, tangible benefactions of a
modern Maecenas.

Yet many patronized modernists guarded their copyrights
jealously and sought to enforce them as they could. This both/and
approach to economics was partly a desire to multiply sources
of income and facilitate dealings with publishers and editors, but
it also reflected a tenacious sense of authorial dignity, a belief
that literary property was somehow a badge of true authorship.
Dependence on both private and public paymasters was a symptom
of the divided world of economic exchange that Rainey identifies as
characterizing the institutions of modernism. Saint-Amour locates
a metadiscourse of this division in *Ulysses* where Stephen Dedalus
holds forth on Shakespeare and paternity—a faint mapping of
Joyce's own "bizarre itinerary between two historically discrete
regimes of authorial inducement: the Scylla of patronage and the
Charybdis of copyright" (*Copywrights* 166).

Transatlantic copyright

Modernists' copyrights often suffered from transatlantic bifurcation. While authors could be reasonably certain of legal protection in Europe, their literary rights were far more precarious in the United States where, until the 1950s and even later, foreign authors could lose protection to the bewildering technicalities of US copyright law. In Britain, the 1911 Copyright Act conferred protection on an author's work from the moment she created it and for fifty years after her death. No formalities, apart from deposit of copies in certain libraries, had to be observed; and, because Britain in 1886 had joined the international Berne Convention for the Protection of Literary and Artistic Works, British authors could expect fair treatment from other Berne countries. In the United States, by contrast, copyright protection could exist only if authors satisfied certain rigid conditions, notably the requirement that books be manufactured on US soil (discussed below). And because America did not accede to the Berne Convention until 1989, its copyright isolationism often made domestic authors unsure of their rights in foreign countries. Transatlantic modernism thus enjoyed no unified literary property regime.

As an American living abroad, Pound experienced all the difficulties of a foreign author attempting to obtain copyright protection in the United States. Several of his early books lacked US copyrights, including *A Lume Spento* (1908), *A Quinzaine for This Yule* (1908), *Personae* (1909), and *Exultations* (1909). But after encountering John Quinn, who became his copyright mentor, Pound learned to comply with legal formalities and obtained protection in America for *Lustra* (1916), *Pavannes and Divisions* (1918), and *Instigations* (1920). Under Quinn's tutelage, Pound grew obsessed about copyrights. In 1923, he complained that the failure of the magazine *The Dial* to help coordinate simultaneous publication of his writings in Britain and the United States had jeopardized his US copyrights and caused him "financial loss (admittedly problematical)" (*Pound*-Dial 278–9). He viewed magazine publication not only as a vehicle for establishing modernism as a movement, but also as a strategy for securing intellectual property. He used his role as foreign editor or correspondent for the US-based magazines *Poetry, The Little Review*, and *The Dial* to help transatlantic authors obtain US copyrights for their contributions. He planned to make

The Little Review, he told Quinn in 1918, a vehicle for "hold[ing] down American copyrights" for Yeats, Joyce, and others (*Pound-Quinn* 164). While Quinn's financial support of *The Little Review* allowed for modest payment of contributors, Pound hoped to secure their copyrights as well. Copyright and patronage thus coexisted in modernism's signature institution—the little magazine—mixing public and private incentives and complicating any narrative of modernism's full retreat into a specialized economy.

In 1928, Virginia Woolf wrote to Vita Sackville-West after learning that the latter wanted to translate Rainer Maria Rilke's *Duino Elegies* (1923) for Woolf's Hogarth Press: "For God's sake, translate Rilke: only be sure of your rights" (*Letters* 3:469). As an author and publisher, Woolf had learned to care for her own and others' copyrights. She had also learned, as Pound had, to play the transatlantic copyright game. In 1919, with her reputation rising, she had been approached by the New York publisher George H. Doran about reissuing her first two novels, *The Voyage Out* (1915) and *Night and Day* (1919), in the United States. The first English editions had lost any chance of protection in America when she published them without complying with US copyright formalities. Doran wanted Woolf to revise the texts so as to justify a new claim of copyright in the United States. "I have to send the books off on Monday," she wrote Lytton Strachey, "and they say the more alterations the better—because of copyright" (*Letters* 2:401). Here was an instance, far from uncommon, of copyright needs compelling creativity—revision as a matter of law. Scholars have noted the extensive deletions and alterations Woolf made in the American edition of *The Voyage Out* (Briggs 24–8; DeSalvo 110–25). Later, Woolf would regularly provide variant texts of her writings for American publishers and issue palpably different versions on either side of the Atlantic. Her apprenticeship in designing around the obstacles of American copyright law may have helped her to develop, for her later works, an expressive craft of transatlantic differences.

T.S. Eliot also kept a close watch on his copyrights. When Samuel Roth discovered that two pieces by Eliot—"Fragment of a Prologue" and "Wanna Go Home, Baby? (Fragment of an Agon),"—later to be published as scenes from his unfinished verse drama, *Sweeney Agonistes* (1932)—lacked US copyright, he reprinted them without permission in 1927 in his New York magazine, *Two Worlds Monthly*, and then aggravated the offense by dedicating an issue to Eliot. When

Eliot expressed his annoyance publicly, Roth pleaded the freedom of the American public domain and cheekily mailed the poet a check for $25 as a formality. Eliot would have no part of the lawful pirate's game and haughtily spurned the payment as a form of "bribery or hush money" (qtd. in Spoo, *Without* 197). He no doubt wished to avoid the appearance of having sold his right to denounce Roth as a thief operating under the shelter of law, but he was also repudiating Roth's parody of patronage. Roth's proffered gift, uncompelled by law, impudently mimicked the graces of true patronage, and Eliot, who had known genuine benefactions, stood on his dignity. If American law had stripped him of his copyrights, he could live with that loss. But bandits should not play at being patrons or paymasters.

Roth's boldest act of lawful piracy was his unauthorized serialization of *Ulysses* in *Two Worlds Monthly* from 1926 to 1927. Sylvia Beach had published the complete, unexpurgated *Ulysses* in 1922 under her Paris imprint, Shakespeare and Company. As I noted in Chapter 2, there had been earlier ideas for issuing *Ulysses* in a private edition—largely to avoid obscenity challenges—but the Paris *Ulysses* was a true deluxe rarity, an expensive edition of 1,000 copies. By publishing a limited, instantly collectible edition from which Joyce received most of the net profits, and making herself the sole source of the book (she dissuaded Harriet Shaw Weaver from issuing a cheaper English edition), Beach created a market that was, in Rainey's words, "inherently monopolistic," the result of aggressively manipulated supply and demand (56). Here, patronage and copyright converged again in the modernist moment. Beach essentially dedicated her life, as a patron in kind, to maximizing the monopoly that European copyright conferred on *Ulysses*. Not content with a slow, modest return on a large stock of affordable copies, Beach tightened the circle of monopoly to a small supply of expensive books, only later issuing less expensive printings. Joyce was the double beneficiary of patronage and copyright. On top of earnings from *Ulysses*, he continued to receive his large annual income from Weaver's gift.

Enter Samuel Roth. Beach had not extended her *Ulysses* monopoly to the United States (apart from copies of the Paris edition that slipped past customs or through the mails) because another kind of monopoly—the scarcity-producing monopoly of obscenity laws—effectively vested title to the book in the state and federal authorities that controlled lawful access. Alert to the fact that *Ulysses* lacked copyright protection in the United States, Roth serialized an expurgated version in *Two Worlds Monthly*, thus circumventing both the copyright monopoly, nonexistent in America, and the holders of the obscenity monopoly, apparently indifferent to Roth's fig-leafed *Ulysses*. Fearing that Roth was capturing the American market, Joyce, with Beach's help, cabled an international protest, signed by more than 160 recognized authors and intellectuals, to hundreds of American newspapers and magazines for publication in February 1927 (Spoo, *Without* 153–92). He followed up this informal protest with a lawsuit filed against Roth in a New York state court, though not for copyright infringement, as we will see in Chapter 4. Despite his patron-supplied income and five years of earnings from the Paris *Ulysses*, Joyce was unwilling to give up the American public-as-paymaster.

From the start, the Paris *Ulysses* had been a product of both copyright and patronage. The edition, printed by Maurice Darantiere of Dijon, contained in its front matter two paratexts that signaled the presence of these adjacent institutions of modernism. On one page, a limitation notice announced an edition of "1000 copies: 100 copies (signed) on Dutch handmade paper numbered from 1 to 100; 150 copies on vergé d'Arches numbered from 101 to 250; 750 copies on handmade paper numbered from 251 to 1000." On the facing page, a copyright notice barked its no-trespass warning in two languages: "Tous droits de reproduction, de traduction et d'adaptation réservés pour tous les pays y compris la Russie. Copyright by James Joyce." The first notice signaled a private, collectible artifact whose royalty structure rendered purchasers "quasi-patrons" (Rainey 53); the second spoke the language of public markets and exclusive rights to reproduce, translate, and adapt in all countries, including Russia.

In contrast, a paratext in H.D.'s *Kora and Ka* (1934), a book of short fictions also printed by Darantiere, was cast almost entirely in the idiom of patronage: "This edition of one hundred copies has been privately printed for the author's friends. No copies are for sale. All rights reserved." H.D.'s resort to small, private editions underwritten by her wealthy companion Bryher (Annie Winifred Ellerman) was not a strategy for escaping the censor, but rather "a mechanism to avoid the public sphere altogether" and to appeal to "a minute coterie" (Rainey 154). H.D.'s paratext signaled a form of private patronage undiluted by the public markets that modernism had ambivalently entered by the 1930s. The tag "All Rights Reserved"—an old formula that gained new currency with the Buenos Aires Convention, which governed copyright relations between the United States and Latin American countries—was only a printer's reflex; the "author's friends" were unlikely to turn pirate. Although she would become a much more public author in later years, H.D. had scant need for copyrights at this point in her career.

Despite the ruthlessness of the American public domain, some authors persisted in believing they had not lost all literary rights, as a point of dignity no less than proprietorship. Gertrude Beasley, like Beach, clung to the erroneous notion that US copyright could somehow survive the failure to comply with American legal formalities (Spoo, *Without* 87). Pound held a more radical and antiquated opinion. He had heard, he wrote *The New Statesman* in 1927, that "in England, copyright or no copyright, an author has a common law right to his work," and he wondered at what point "the decay of American life" had allowed this right to disappear ("American" 383). Joyce, too, hoped that his New York lawyers might be able to enforce some "law of property" against Roth, despite the lack of federal copyright protection for *Ulysses* (*Letters* 266–7). Nine years later, he was still arguing that "a work belongs to its author by virtue of a natural right" ("Communication" 274–5). The belief that statutory protections were only a supplement to deep-running, perpetual common-law rights was an old and resilient one, but courts had settled the point in Britain in 1774 and in the United States in 1834: when authors obtained statutory copyright for their published works, common-law rights were to that extent extinguished (*Donaldson v. Beckett; Wheaton v. Peters*). As we will see in Chapter 5, Pound went so far as to propose a law that would have made even statutory copyrights perpetual. The modernist dream of inalienable rights was not easily dispelled by courts or lawmakers, or satisfied by patrons.

Manufacturing piracy

There has always existed a tension between copyright laws and obscenity laws. The same government that granted a property right in creative products could ban those products if they violated laws against immorality. The nice legal question was whether a work that had been deemed obscene lost copyright protection automatically, or whether literary rights existed independently of any judicial finding of obscenity. Did property require propriety? Or did any advancement of learning, however objectionable under present community standards, deserve protection from piracy? In English judicial practice of the early 1800s, an equity court would decline to issue an injunction against proven piracy if the court considered the plaintiff's work to be of questionable morality. The court would instead direct the plaintiff to establish his literary property in a successful damages action in a law court, and then return to the equity court for an injunction. Because an action at law was costly and, if unsuccessful, could trigger criminal prosecution for obscenity, many authors simply dropped the matter. Robert Southey, Lord Byron, and Percy Bysshe Shelley each suffered ongoing piracies because equity courts required copyrights in potentially scandalous narratives to be tested first in a law court. The unintended result, as James R. Alexander shows, was that judicially unchecked piracies proliferated, and morally suspect works enjoyed a wider and cheaper circulation than they would have had under monopoly conditions. As Lord Eldon remarked in 1817, "It is very true that, in some cases, [equity procedure] may operate so as to multiply copies of mischievous publications by the refusal of the Court to interfere by restraining them" (*Southey v. Sherwood* 1008).

This functional antagonism between obscenity and copyright laws continued through the period of modernism. Writings thought to be indecent were poor candidates for copyright protection in Britain and the United States, not because they were typically incapable of enjoying copyright but because authors and publishers faced legal and practical obstacles to securing or enforcing copyright (as was true of the equity suitors of the nineteenth century). Notably, the US copyright acts of 1891 and 1909 granted protection to non-US authors only if they managed to have their works printed from type set within the United States—and, later, printed and bound there—simultaneously with or shortly after publication in their home country. This requirement came to be known as the manufacturing clause, a transparently protectionist measure that favored American book manufacturers at the expense of authors. Failure to comply with the manufacturing clause resulted in the loss of US copyright for many foreign works. Pound, who bitterly resented the manufacturing requirements, complained that in America "any, absolutely *any*, material gain to no matter whom is of more importance than clarity of thought, enlightenment, or any possible property of the mind" ("American" 383; italics in original).

For him, US copyright laws, like book tariffs, perverted the order of things, ranking articles of manufacture above intellectual creation.

The US copyrights of many works first published abroad were lost for noncompliance with the manufacturing clause: W.H. Hudson's *Green Mansions* (1904); Arnold Bennett's *The Old Wives' Tale* (1908); Woolf's *The Voyage Out* (1915) and *Night and Day* (1919); Joyce's *Ulysses* (1922); Lawrence's *Lady Chatterley's Lover* (1928); Terry Southern and Mason Hoffenberg's *Candy* (1958); and Sylvia Plath's *The Bell Jar* (1963), to name only a few. Various obstacles—reputed literary indecency, limited authorial fame, privacy concerns—delayed the reprinting of these works in America until it was too late to salvage their US copyrights. The manufacturing clause had claimed them. The suggestion, made by some scholars, that an obscene work could never be copyrighted is misleading shorthand. The manufacturing clause, operating on works that could not be promptly reprinted in the United States, was the proximate cause of lost copyright (Spoo, *Without* 65–75).

FIGURE 3.1 *Workers, Riverside Press, New York City, February 1917. Photograph L.W. Hine. Courtesy Library of Congress Prints and Photographs Division.*

In the eyes of many foreign observers, the manufacturing clause was little more than a continuation of pre-1891 US policies that had withheld copyright protection from foreign authors and encouraged American publishers to flood the market with cheap reprints of Dickens, Sir Walter Scott, George Eliot, and other writers who appealed to an increasingly literate populace. A parallel form of lawful piracy had earlier plagued Samuel Richardson and other English authors whose writings were unable to enjoy copyright protection in pre-Union Ireland (Fysh 100–23). When notorious works like *Lady Chatterley's Lover* and *Ulysses* lacked enforceable rights, pirated editions proliferated, sometimes in expurgated form, sometimes sold clandestinely without changes. Here, those antagonistic secret sharers—obscenity law and copyright law—converged in what Saint-Amour refers to as "the disciplinary and the biopolitical aspects ... of the censorship-copyright system" ("Introduction" 27).

Lawrence recounted his struggles with copyright, obscenity, and piracy in "A Propos of *Lady Chatterley's Lover*" (1929). Soon after his novel had appeared in the expensive Florence edition of 1928, unauthorized facsimiles came on the market in the United States, selling for as much as $50 per copy, and a "European pirated edition" of 1,500 copies followed shortly from Paris, priced as high as 500 francs (327–8). Lawrence tried to fight the pirates with predatory pricing, first issuing a small second printing of the Florence edition priced at a guinea and then a "cheap popular edition, produced in France and offered to the public at sixty francs" (327). Having lost any chance of US copyright for the Florence edition, Lawrence, at the urging of his authorized publishers, tried to produce an expurgated version that, like Woolf's revised text of *The Voyage Out*, might justify a claim to copyright protection, but he found the task of revising impossible. "I might as well try to clip my own nose into shape with scissors" (329). In fact, he did attempt to expurgate, but his English and American publishers feared that he had not sanitized sufficiently. Shortly after Lawrence's death, Roth published his own expurgated and unauthorized *Lady Chatterley's Lover* in New York, grandly naming it "the Samuel Roth Edition." This was a safe text that "titillated the general reader, but that he or she was not ashamed to keep in the parlor" (Gertzman, *Bookleggers* 234). Because Lawrence could not or would not play the censor's game, and so vouchsafed no version that could acquire copyright in the United States, a lawful pirate stepped in and did his own bowdlerizing.

The pattern was the same for *Ulysses*—a transgressive text, an intransigent author, a failure to obtain US copyright, a lawful pirate keen to expurgate. Joyce was faced with a choice of modernist institutions: should he allow a copyrighted but expurgated text to enter the public marketplace at affordable prices, or should he opt for a private, deluxe edition, complete but uncopyrighted (in the United States at least) and sold at steep prices to quasi-patrons in a limited market? By taking the latter course, he invited lawful pirates, trolling "the contraband public domain" (Saint-Amour, *Copywrights* 168), to supply the public markets he had spurned in his distaste for legally compelled expurgation. Like Lawrence, he could only hope that substantial profits from his pricey edition would compensate him for all the revenue lost to piracy.

Roth built his career on repackaging experimental modern writing, much of it uncopyrighted, as titillating entertainment for men, filling his magazines with bits of modernism caught in an amber of transatlantic decadence, mild eroticism, and international realism. In addition to Joyce and Lawrence, he reissued fiction and prose experiments by Djuna Barnes, Frank Harris, and Catulle Mendès; the ghost stories of Richard Middleton; and the Welsh realism of Caradoc Evans. He reprinted poems by Eliot, Synge, Carl Sandburg, Emanuel Carnevali, Lawrence, and Pound, together with verse by Richard Le Gallienne and risqué translations of Arabic poems by E. Powys Mathers. He ran a serialized translation of Octave Mirbeau's *A Chambermaid's Diary*—an account of sexual manipulation and ruined innocence—in the same magazine that contained his bowdlerized *Ulysses*, advertising them together as "great suppressed novels" (qtd. in Spoo, *Without* 179). His business model was simple: purported or adjudicated obscenity paved the way, via the unsatisfied manufacturing clause, for the loss of American copyright, and lost copyright smoothed the waters for lawful piracy, one body of law in effect subverting the purpose of the other. Lawmakers were sometimes the booklegger's best friend.

Courtesy

Copyright-free foreign works were a mixed blessing in nineteenth-century America. Although gifted a commons brimming with popular foreign fiction, publishers realized by the 1850s that they had to impose some kind of order on unrestrained reprinting if they hoped to control the price of books and sustain their lists of foreign titles. Free resources could be lucrative only if they were somehow allocated, not promiscuously fought over, so publishers adopted a form of self-regulation called the courtesy of the trade, or trade courtesy—an informal, norms-based practice that imitated the main features of copyright law and permitted both publishers and authors to benefit from the extralegal rights that courtesy recognized. Publishers respected each other's claims to particular foreign authors or titles and paid the authors or their original publishers sometimes handsome honoraria or royalties. Dickens, for example, received £1,000 each for the uncopyrighted *Our Mutual Friend* and *A Tale of Two Cities* (Madison 26). To be a courtesy publisher was to agree to participate in a communal fiction that the publisher Henry Holt proudly referred to as a form of "philosophical anarchism—self-regulation without law" (Holt 522–3). Those who defied the fiction, who insisted on taking the public domain literally, were viewed as unregenerate pirates by the courtesy fraternity. It made no difference that courtesy-flouting pirates were law-abiding reprinters.

Trade courtesy arose as an informal surrogate for international copyright protection in America and as a way for American publishers to insulate themselves from injurious competition for free resources. The copyright law that provided a windfall of foreign materials failed to create artificial scarcity in those materials. Therefore, publishers developed the system of courtesy to fill the legal vacuum, salve their consciences, and install a signaling system by which good players could be distinguished from bad players—courtesy publishers from so-called pirates. Courtesy privatized a plentiful commons that, had it not been collusively enclosed, might have been lost or severely eroded as a profitable resource for publishers (Spoo, "Courtesy"). Whether a monopolistic practice, an ethical improvisation of conscientious businessmen, or both, trade courtesy bears out the scholarly thesis—advanced by Kal Raustiala and Christopher Sprigman—that informal, extralegal practices may sometimes avert, or at least mitigate, a kind of market failure for unprotected or underprotected intellectual creations (see also the essays in Darling and Perzanowski, eds.).

Largely because of the strict manufacturing requirements, the American public domain continued to be an aggressive acquirer of new foreign works even after the 1891 and 1909 US copyright acts made it possible for foreign authors to obtain copyrights in America. For foreign authors and publishers who could not satisfy its rigors, the manufacturing clause raised barriers similar to those created by the affirmative withholding of copyrights in earlier US statutes. Yet vulnerable authors were not always exploited after 1891 because a sense of honor and propriety still underlay the practices of many American publishers. Even after the Sherman Antitrust Act of 1890 and other developments rendered the anticompetitive practice of trade courtesy less systematic and overt, the old informal equities continued to shape respectable publishing, often with as keen a sensitivity for foreign authors' rights as before (Spoo, *Without* 107–15). The "ghost of courtesy," as Jeffrey Groves calls it (147–8), persisted well into the twentieth century and played a significant role in transatlantic modernism.

Courtesy quietly tempered sharp practices among publishers of modernism. When Bennett Cerf, cofounder of Random House, purchased the Modern Library from Horace Liveright in 1925, Alfred Knopf complained that Liveright had been a "crook" to include in the Library W.H. Hudson's strong-selling romance novel *Green Mansions* (1904), which Knopf had helped introduce in America. Although the novel lacked US copyright, Cerf offered to pay Knopf a courtesy royalty of six cents on each copy, an arrangement Knopf thought "very fair, since legally he had no case" (Cerf 57). Liveright himself was no stranger to the graces of courtesy. When in 1922 he offered Yeats $25 for certain reprint rights, the poet urged his agent to agree to the proposal, "as [Liveright's] term 'courtesy fee' suggests that he has found out that those very early poems of mine are not copyright in U.S.A." (qtd. in Spoo, *Without* 109).

B.W. Huebsch combined courtesy's fair-play principles with a canny business sense. He was willing to pay Joyce royalties on reprints of two works unprotected in America—*Chamber Music* (1907) and *Dubliners* (1914)—in part because he was able to publish *A Portrait of the Artist as a Young Man* (1916) and *Exiles* (1918) in accordance with US copyright law. Huebsch therefore mixed courtesy with copyright in building his Joyce list. His dutiful negotiations for the "American rights" in *Chamber Music* and *Dubliners* were essentially ceremonial, a courtly bow to Joyce and his English publishers. When he learned that the Cornhill Company of Boston was planning to beat him out with an unauthorized version of *Chamber Music*, he urged that firm not to "violate the moral right of the author to his property" but instead to "withdraw the volumes that you've announced" (Fargnoli, ed. 214). The plea had no effect, so Huebsch resorted to the traditional courtesy punishment of publicly shaming the norm-scoffer. He wrote *The Nation* that his was "the only authorized American edition of the book" and that Cornhill had unfairly exploited Joyce's legal disability in the United States ("Unfair Enterprise" 7). Pirates like Cornhill and Roth were not outlaws; they were moral outcasts, deviants from the canons of courtesy.

Some American publishers dealt courteously with D.H. Lawrence and his estate. Although the 1928 Florence edition of *Lady Chatterley's Lover* had lost its chance for US copyright, Knopf issued an authorized expurgated edition in 1932 at $2.50 per copy, to compete with the unauthorized Roth edition (Roberts and Poplawski 140–1). *Sons and Lovers*—unprotected in America since 1913—received fair treatment from publishers. Although Boni and Liveright had begun by putting out an unauthorized edition in 1922, the firm later issued authorized printings until the early 1930s (21). Roth himself attempted to pay for proposed adaptations of *Lady Chatterley's Lover* until Frieda Lawrence rebuffed the "awful man" and sent him back to lawful piracy (qtd. in Gertzman, *Bookleggers* 234–5). Booksellers, too, practiced courtesy. Lawrence was surprised to learn that certain bookstore owners would "not handle the pirated edition [of *Lady Chatterley's Lover*] at all," out of "sentimental and business scruples" ("A Propos" 328–9). A "semi-repentant bookseller of New York" even sent him a sum of money as a royalty on all unauthorized copies of the novel sold in his shop (329).

Courtesy proved its potency again in the aftermath of the federal customs litigation in which Joyce's *Ulysses* was judicially declared to be nonobscene under the US Tariff Act. Cerf had invited the lawsuit in the hope of becoming the first authorized publisher of a lawful American edition of the book. But *Ulysses* was troubled by two sets of laws that operated at cross-purposes: obscenity and copyright. After Judge John M. Woolsey issued his decree in favor of *Ulysses* in 1933 (see Chapter 2), Cerf was reasonably worried that American pirates would reprint the uncopyrighted book with their greatest legal fear much allayed: prosecution for publishing obscenity. Yet the publishing world welcomed the 1934 Random

House edition *en masse*. Cerf received letters of congratulation from various houses—Horace Liveright, Inc., Farrar and Rinehart, Houghton Mifflin, and Knopf—some of which had vied for *Ulysses* in the past (Spoo, *Without* 255–6). Cerf had doubly earned the courteous treatment of his peers. Not only did he have a contract with Joyce; he had also spent time and money on a high-profile litigation—in trial and appellate courts—that made the legal climate safer for all venturesome publishers. It would be decades before anyone dared to trespass on Random House's courtesy claim. For transatlantic authors, trade courtesy was an improvised, second-best form of intellectual property, an imperfect but tangible consolation for a hyper-technical, discriminatory copyright law.

Modernism propertized

Of the three paymasters of modernism discussed in this chapter—patronage, copyright, and courtesy—none was permanent or infallible. Private patronage declined with the coming of the Great Depression and in any case rarely outlasted the lives of individual donors, as Pound learned with the untimely deaths of Margaret Cravens and John Quinn, or their whims, as Eliot discovered when Lady Rothermere withdrew her capital from *The Criterion*. Trade courtesy, too, was unpredictable. It survived on legally unenforceable handshakes and was ever vulnerable to defection and retaliation among participating publishers, and to competition from nonparticipating upstarts and outsiders. Although it mimicked other elements of copyright law, courtesy established no precise term of protection for the informal entitlements it allocated. Courtesy rights lasted only as long as claimants practically needed or desired them, or the collective memory of publishers remained cooperative and unclouded. Trade courtesy was a strategy for solving a public-goods problem in the near term, not a system for conferring durable property rights.

Unlike courtesy and patronage, copyright law did have a fixed duration. Under Britain's Copyright Act of 1842, copyright in a published work lasted for the author's life plus seven years, or for forty-two years from first publication, whichever period was longer

(§ 3). The 1911 Act extended that term to the author's life plus fifty years (§ 3). For many years prior to the 1909 US Copyright Act, the term of copyright in the United States had been twenty-eight years from first publication, with a right of renewal for an additional fourteen years. The 1909 Act increased that term to twenty-eight years from first publication, with a right of renewal for another twenty-eight years (§ 23). Renewal thus gave authors a chance to enjoy a total of fifty-six years of protection for published works in America, but renewal was not automatic; and if authors or publishers bungled the paperwork or missed a deadline, they relinquished their work to the public domain. A venial sin against other formalities—such as the omission of copyright notices from published copies—could also result in the loss of protection. As we saw earlier, the manufacturing clause, when unpropitiated, swept new foreign works prematurely into the American public domain. US copyright law was thus precarious and permeable, in contrast to the more stable, mostly unconditional British law. Transatlantic copyright, uncoordinated and asymmetrical, was a leaky ship that might not land its cultural cargo safely.

By the mid-twentieth century, the United States had begun a rapprochement with international copyright law, notably by joining, in 1952, the Universal Copyright Convention (UCC), along with a bloc of nations that included the United Kingdom, Australia, and Canada. America's adherence to the UCC meant, among other moderations, that the manufacturing clause would no longer apply to works first published abroad by UCC nationals (Act of August 31, 1954). In 1976, Congress enacted a massive revision of the law that increased copyright terms to the author's life plus fifty years for works created after 1977, and seventy-five years from the year of first publication for works published before 1978. These terms were extended again, in 1998, to the author's life plus seventy years, and ninety-five years from the year of first publication, respectively, in an effort to harmonize US copyright law with that of the European Union (Sonny Bono Act). By then, the United States had at last joined the international Berne Convention, repealed the last vestiges of the manufacturing clause, and enacted a law that restored copyright protection to foreign works that had suffered under US formalities (Uruguay Round Agreements Act; Saint-Amour, "Introduction" 1–12; Spoo, "Copyright"). By 2000, copyrights were longer and stronger than ever before in the United States and Europe.

The half-century after 1950 thus saw a change from transatlantic copyright asymmetry to a rights-race for harmonization. American copyright law lurched from exceptionalism to internationalism not long after modernism's putative terminus. US copyrights eventually grew to the length of their counterparts in Europe, and works that had once been free resources for Samuel Roth and his contemporaries returned to private hands. Indeed, the law that had invented Roth as the fulfillment of its protectionist logic now followed Europe down the path of maximal protection for authors and owners.

In one respect, however, America has not tried to match Europe right for right. Various European countries recognize additional protections known as authors' moral rights (Shloss). Moral rights, which are distinct from the economic rights conferred by copyright law, safeguard authorial reputation and dignity and include the right to be named the author of a work (attribution), the right against mutilation of the work (integrity), and the right to choose when and how to disclose the work to the public (divulgation) (Baldwin 28–37). In France, moral rights exist perpetually and are passed down through families (Code arts. L.L 121–1 to 121–2). The divulgation right, in particular, has proved to be an obstacle for researchers. A planned edition of the unpublished letters of René Char to his mistress ran aground on the divulgation right when lengthy litigation with the French poet's widow ended in a court injunction (Lefebvre). Some French repositories, citing the divulgation right, have refused to allow scholars to obtain research copies of, or even to view, Joyce's letters without his estate's permission, despite the fact that the letters are no longer protected by French copyright (Spoo, "Uncoordinated" 139–44). Moral rights "give [an author's] descendants especially powerful tools," as Peter Baldwin notes (38). That power can turn repositories into archival tombs.

In addition, the European Union adopted laws in the 1990s that grant twenty-five years of new copyright protection to any person who first publishes or makes available a work that has never before been published and whose copyright has expired (Council Directive art. 4). A kind of first-come-first-served monopoly, this post-copyright copyright purports to offer incentives for making older works available for the first time and to reward the disseminator's effort and investment. There is a significant difference between these after-rights and other revived or restored copyrights: an unpublished work no sooner enters the public domains of the European Union than it can be restored to copyright by the first industrious disseminator, not as an entitlement of the original author's estate, but as a new right vested in the disseminator. This finders-keepers copyright has already impacted the study of modernism. Soon after Joyce's unpublished writings entered the EU public domains at the end of 2011, they became the subject of controversy when two small presses announced the publication of some of these materials and claimed new EU copyrights in them, despite the protests of the archives that owned the physical documents. It is not entirely clear who, if anyone, owns post-copyright copyrights in these writings, and scholars are predictably wary of copying or quoting from materials they had believed, until recently, would be freely available seventy years after Joyce's death (Spoo, *Without* 270–3).

Upward harmonization of authors' rights has produced a downward fragmentation of users' privileges; the touted unity of international law has created an uncoordinated global public domain that renders works freely available for use in some countries while subjecting them to copyright or moral rights protection in others. The fragmented world commons shares certain features with the property problem known as an anticommons—notably, ownership gridlock and resource stagnation (Heller; Spoo, "Uncoordinated" 108–19; see also Chapter 1). This contradictory commons has fractured many modernist works, rendering them half owned, half free to common use. *The Waste Land*, for example, entered the American public domain at the end of 1997, seventy-five years after its first publication in 1922 (just missing the twenty-year copyright extension granted by the Sonny Bono Act of 1998). In Canada, the poem's copyright expired at the end of 2015, fifty years after Eliot's death. But in Britain, Australia, and most of the European Union, where copyrights run for seventy years from the author's death, it will remain protected until the end of 2035. Copyright's dividing line in the United States is modernism's *annus mirabilis*: everything published through the end of 1922 is in the American public domain, while many works published afterward enjoy Bono-enhanced protection (until the end of 2018, when, absent further extensions, US copyrights in those works will once again begin to expire annually). As Saint-Amour notes, US law has "effectively cut modernism in half at its wonder year, partitioning it into a freely accessible early modernism and a heavily protected later one" ("Introduction" 2). Transnational copyright fragmentation produces inhibiting checkerboard effects for scholarship.

Fragmentation is one stint on the public domain; length is another. In his meditation on the public domain, James Boyle observes that "because the copyright term is now so long, in many cases extending well over a century, most of twentieth-century culture is still under copyright—copyrighted but unavailable" (9). Boyle refers here to the problem of "orphan works"—works protected by copyright but lacking identifiable owners—but his larger point concerns the cultural pathologies traceable to the extreme longevity of copyrights. The anthropomorphism implicit in the word "longevity" is richly explored by Saint-Amour in his study of mourning and commemoration in modern copyright culture. By treating copyright protection as a form of veneration of dead authors, this culture figures the public domain—the absence of protection—as a kind of ancestral desecration. Because it "survives the author-owner, copyright plays a role in the work of personal and collective mourning," allowing the dead to "remain present despite their absence, spectrally exerting their influence through copyright estates" (Saint-Amour, *Copywrights* 154).

Once again, censorship and copyright reveal their kinship. I suggested in Chapter 2 that censorship sought to make transgressive modernism scarce, to remove it from bookstores, warehouses, and the mails, as if its physical disappearance from public life could somehow be a measure of moral growth in the population. Copyright's paradox involves a related fantasy. By giving authors the power to create scarcity through legal monopoly, copyright promises to expand the great "storehouse" of creative works—achieving more through less (Beckerman-Rodau 88). Just as obscenity law's vision of moral progress demanded a dearth of cultural products, so copyright has sought to realize its accumulationist dream through induced scarcity. The long copyrights of modernism extend these forms of scarcity into the present, making the dysfunctions of orphan works, permissions stalemates, and publishers' fears a frequent concern for scholars and creative adapters. Long-lived copyrights allow choices concerning cultural scarcity to pass to the descendants and transferees of modernist authors, remote chronologically and sometimes temperamentally from those forebears. The aggressive control—viewed by some as arbitrary and capricious—of the literary estates of Joyce, Marianne Moore, Samuel Beckett, and others continues to enforce a scarcity of creative adaptations, revisionary performances, and innovative scholarship nearly a century after copyright or patronage cajoled the best from those authors' brains (Max; Rimmer). Much of modernism—unpublished letters, diaries, drafts—remains legally confined to repositories, helpless to increase the celebrated storehouse of culture.

Copyright's longevity has thus distorted the history of modernism. Just as censorship slowed the unfolding of modernism, postponing its full, unexpurgated arrival (in works by Lawrence, Henry Miller, and others) until the 1950s and 1960s, so copyright's monopolizing of historical space has far exceeded canonical estimates of modernism's endpoint, forcing modernism to inhabit an ever-receding future presided over by legislative extensions of property rights. If, as Saint-Amour suggests, modernism is "that which is still propertized" (Review 511), it is also true that in the hands of remote, unsympathetic owners, this property lacks one of property's traditional characteristics: social utility. Unpublished writings become sentimentally hoarded, signifiers for the sacredness of family privacy, heirlooms to be taken from a drawer for an occasional memorial caress.

This is all the more ironic in that, as Mark Lemley notes, the idea of copyright as property is grounded in economic rationality, which holds that dividing the commons into private entitlements allows intellectual creations to be put to their highest and best use—"if one assumes that efficient transactions will always occur" ("Romantic" 897). And there is the sticking point. Modernist copyrights do not unfailingly circulate in efficient markets that benefit owners and users. Often, they are orphaned children, markers for mourning and melancholia, fetishized bulwarks against the invasion of privacy. The privacy of the dead is a strange, perhaps lawless notion, and the attempt to use copyrights as a shield for defunct ancestors is quixotic (Spoo, "Three" 105–10). But modern authors themselves knew the uses and abuses of privacy. It is to their anxious relationship to privacy, publicity, and reputation—as proprietary and dignitary concerns—that I now turn.

4

Privacy, Publicity, Defamation, and Blackmail

By the late nineteenth century, the conditions of modernity had made privacy a preoccupation, a sacred space of selfhood that, as its moral and monetary value grew, attracted the coercions of blackmailers and the assaults of tabloid journalism and instant photography. Blackmailers illegally promised to conceal injurious truths; libel and slander doctrines legally redressed injurious falsehoods. Reputation could thus be preserved through costly back-alley agreements or rehabilitated in expensive courtroom proceedings. Privacy laws as we know them today were still largely notional constructs, urged as remedies for outrageously invaded personal space; much later, publicity rights, breaking from the husk of privacy, would permit the monetizing of disseminated personality (Bartholomew). These forces and intuitions converged in the divided modern self that looks to the law to uphold its ambitious regimen: its domain of secrecy, its policy of selective disclosure, its carefully managed reputation.

This chapter explores what might be called the reputational cluster: the modern expectation that the law will guarantee a person's domestic privacy and intimate secrets, her freedom from false imputations, and her exclusive right to exploit her name and likeness. Legal protections for these features of private and public life were incomplete and in disarray in the transatlantic setting of the late nineteenth and early twentieth centuries. The absence of strong privacy laws in what Henry James called "this age of advertisement and newspaperism" (*Notebooks* 148) led legal scholars to propose new common-law theories and compelled James himself to engage in anxious forms of self-help. On the one hand, he took pains to ensure his own privacy by destroying materials that might fall into biographers' hands; on the other, he made the crisis of authorial privacy a motif of his later fiction.

Blackmail—another extralegal mechanism—offered privacy for purchase or lease. Arthur Conan Doyle's story, "The Adventure of Charles Augustus Milverton" (1904), portrays the terrors of extortion but also suggests the strange proximity between privacy and publicity at the turn of the century. Incipient celebrity culture, presciently glimpsed in Conan Doyle's tale of professional blackmail, fostered a paradox of privacy that led Judge Richard Posner to observe, "Very few people want to be let alone. They want to manipulate the world around them by selective disclosure of facts about themselves" ("Right" 400). Victims paid blackmailers to assist them with their fictions of self.

Defamation

The law of defamation protects personal reputation by combating harmful falsehoods. A civil action for libel or slander imposes liability for a false communication, published or publicly spoken, that injures another's reputation or good name (*Black's* 417). This theory of tort holds that a distortion of the truth, not the truth itself, may cause reputational harm. By contrast, criminal libel prosecutions—rare today but familiar enough in Britain in the late nineteenth and early twentieth centuries—targeted the publication of scandalous or embarrassing truths no less than of falsehoods, on the theory that even true statements could disturb the public peace (Latham 75–6). The law of criminal libel sought to substitute controlled courtroom battle for the brawling and feuding that often broke out over exposed secrets or wounded honor. The escalating physical threats exchanged among the Marquess of Queensberry, Lord Alfred Douglas, and Oscar Wilde ended—logically, in the law's eyes—in Wilde's summoning Queensberry to criminal court, where a jury took the place of a bullet as decision maker.

Yet the fierce culture of honor among literary men, which intensified during the nineteenth century, ensured that the épée would sometimes seem mightier than the pen. Marcel Proust, who challenged several men to duels for impugning his writing or his sexuality, actually fought one with the author and dandy Jean Lorrain, who had attacked Proust's *Les Plaisirs et les jours* (1896) as "elegiac mawkishness" and implied that he was a homosexual. Proust and Lorrain met by arrangement in the Bois de Meudon, accompanied by writers, painters, and art critics acting as seconds, and fired pistols harmlessly at each other (Painter 207–10). Two years earlier in the wake of Wilde's arrest on charges of committing indecent acts, the French authors Marcel Schwob and Catulle Mendès threatened or fought duels with a journalist who had named them in print as close friends of the tainted Irish wit (Ellmann, *Oscar* 458). Such feigned or real violence among artists and intellectuals continued into the twentieth century. James Joyce narrowly escaped a duel in 1903 when a literary dispute in a Paris café grew passionate (Ellmann, *James* 123). Ezra Pound reportedly challenged the Georgian versifier Lascelles Abercrombie to a duel for giving retrograde advice to young poets (*Pound-Joyce* 48 n6). In Wyndham Lewis's novel *Tarr* (1918), the "libelled and outraged" painter Otto Kreisler provokes a farcically abortive duel in prewar Paris's Bourgeois-Bohemia (315).

Libel claims and the fear of them have shaped literature, from the political use of libel for patrolling the border between fact and fiction in the eighteenth century (Davis), to the private policing of reputational and commercial harm in later periods. In 1930, George Bernard Shaw wrote witty but firm letters to Frank Harris, threatening libel and copyright actions if Harris published a biography that took Shaw's name "in vain" or reproduced so much as "a word" of his texts (Harris 27–30). Shaw was protecting both his honor as an author and his monetizable celebrity. As Sean Latham has shown, libel lawsuits—feared, threatened, or actually filed—dogged the writings of D.H. Lawrence, Wyndham Lewis, George Orwell, and other writers in the early decades of the twentieth century (86, 105–23). In 1921, Philip Heseltine ("Peter Warlock") threatened a libel action against Lawrence's London publisher, Martin Secker, for what he claimed was a damaging portrait of himself and his wife in *Women in Love* (1920). Lawrence hotly dismissed the claim as "blackmail," but Secker, fearing a costly wrangle, settled the matter out of court for £50 and an additional £10 10s. in legal costs, and agreed to reissue the book with modifications by Lawrence to pixelate the offending likenesses (Lawrence, *Letters* 4:113 n2).

Lewis saw several of his works, including his novel *The Roaring Queen* (1936), withdrawn from publication or abandoned at the proof stage to appease complainants who had recognized themselves in his satirical portraits (Latham 105). Drawing on the roman à clef's "anarchic powers to savage the realist novel by extending fiction into the historical world" (91), Lewis published one of his most aggressive satires, *The Apes of God* (1930), in a signed, limited edition of 750 copies priced expensively at £3 3s. Lewis's resort to private subscription suggests that defamation law was shaping the market for modernist fiction in ways analogous to the pressures of obscenity law. Just as Joyce and Lawrence produced limited, pricey editions to avoid rousing public prosecutors and semi-official smuthounds, so Lewis availed himself of a small luxury market after his trade publisher, fearing private lawsuits for defamation, refused to issue the novel without substantial changes (116).

James Joyce's collection of stories, *Dubliners* (1914), languished for years in unpublished limbo as publishers and printers objected to his naming of actual persons and businesses. The gamut of historical forms of libel—obscene, blasphemous, seditious, and reputational—seemed to pursue Joyce's stories, as intermediaries in the communications circuit raised objection after objection. Maunsel and Company, the Dublin publisher that had signed a contract for the collection, insisted that Joyce remove potentially libelous and unpatriotic references to the deceased King Edward VII in "Ivy Day in the Committee Room," and required other deletions. When lengthy negotiations fell through in 1912, Maunsel's printer, John Falconer, destroyed the sheets, and the volume remained unpublished for another two years (Ellmann, *James* 328–35). Furious, Joyce wrote a satirical broadside called "Gas from a Burner." Initially he had titled it "Mr Falconer Addresses the Vigilance Committee," suspecting that organized purity groups had fed the printer's fears (Mullin, *James* 15; see also the discussion of purity groups in Chapter 2).

Joyce's long self-exile from Ireland may have been prompted as much by fear of libel suits as by loftier questions of art, religion, and politics. More than a dozen years after Joyce's death, an old schoolmate who is mentioned in *Ulysses* sued the BBC for broadcasting a reading of the allegedly defamatory book and collected a substantial settlement (Latham 98–9, 104). When Richard Aldington referred to *Ulysses* as a "libel on humanity," T.S. Eliot questioned the legal and literary accuracy of the phrase, pointing out that the book was no "powerless fraud" but rather a potent indictment of and remedy for "the immense panorama of futility and anarchy which is contemporary history" (*"Ulysses"*

176–7). Yet the book's penetrating diagnosis of modern culture did not stop individuals from resenting their impressment as characters in a fiction they thought injured their good names.

Authors, publishers, printers, and even broadcasters lived in fear of hawkeyed, hypersensitive, or opportunistic readers who peered through the keyholes of fiction and claimed to glimpse their maligned selves. Modernist writers like Joyce and Lewis produced "defamatory works lightly cloaked in the roman à clef's 'conditional fictionality,'" exploiting that subgenre's potential "to disrupt the legal, moral, and aesthetic compromises that underwrote the novel's rise in the eighteenth century" (Latham 86). Fear of libel actions encouraged authors to conceal or obscure scandalous referentiality and to retreat into aesthetic postures. Like obscenity law, actions for libel, though filed against individuals and business entities, often had the *in rem* effect of targeting the tangible vehicles of damaging messages: books. Judgments and settlements resulted in books being revised, withdrawn, suppressed, or even destroyed. Compensatory payments were not enough for many plaintiffs; the book itself— the offending *res*—had to be visited with righteous punishment and removed from commerce.

Menaced with legal liability, the novel's troubled relationship to external fact has generated a familiar paratext, encountered at the start of many books: "All characters appearing in this work are fictitious. Any resemblance to real persons, living or dead, is purely coincidental." This disabusing incantation appeals to the reasonableness of readers in the text's vestibule (Genette 2), asking them to respect the difference between imagination and life and to avoid crude roman à clef assumptions. It urges the deluded, the literal-minded, and the thin-skinned to put aside their instinct to sue for libel or privacy invasion and to play the author's game of fictiveness in a sporting spirit. With the growth of celebrity culture, modernist authors resorted to this defensive paratext as a charm against libel actions. The Scribner editions of Ernest Hemingway's *In Our Time* (1930) and *To Have and Have Not* (1937) contained the irritable, lawyerly caveat: "In view of a recent tendency to identify characters in fiction with real people, it seems proper to state that there are no real people in this volume: both the characters and their names are fictitious" (*In Our* 6).

Paratexts in Radclyffe Hall's *The Well of Loneliness* (1928) mostly sought to ward off obscenity charges, but one addressed the easily defamed: "All the characters in this book are purely imaginary, and if the author in any instance has used names that may suggest a reference to living persons, she has done so inadvertently." This paratext went on to praise a British women's ambulance unit during the First World War and to distinguish it from the unit joined by Hall's main character Stephen Gordon, which "never had any existence save in the author's imagination." The dual purpose of such disclaimers was to assert the primacy of the imagination and to discourage legal disputes, to make aesthetic autonomy double as a shield against legal harassment. The modern novel's ritual inclusion of these threshold paratexts served both to prepare the literary experience of readers and to steer them away from the courthouse doors. These disclaimers reinforce Latham's thesis that "Modernism's sudden return to the roman à clef as part of its campaign against Victorian realism led ... not to aesthetic autonomization, but to a turbulent encounter between literature and the law" (73).

Blackmail

Libel law acts on published communications and therefore intervenes, typically, only after harm has been done. Plaintiffs must try to salve their emotional wounds with the legal metonymy of money damages and the satisfaction of future deterrence. In contrast, blackmail offers protection from injurious communications before they have entered the public arena, and thus acts as a prior restraint on scandalous truth-telling. An extortionist enters her victim's life by vowing to play one of two roles: if paid, she promises to preserve the victim's reputation; if unpaid, she winkingly disclaims responsibility for the consequences. She offers her services as protection from a danger she has created. The victim has no choice but to live with the blackmailer on some terms. A third option—life without the blackmailer—is existentially barred. Libel could inflict great personal damage by circulating its falsehoods, but the divided modern self, coveting and cultivating reputational hygiene, feared blackmail the most.

Blackmail spares reputation by means of illegal, menacing promises—a forced partnership in secrecy. Essentially an agreement to keep quiet in exchange for cash or other consideration, blackmail converts a former transgression into a trade secret and compels the transgressor to finance the new partnership built on this asset. In the late nineteenth and early twentieth centuries, criminals preyed on those who led double lives or sought to protect old secrets. As Angus McLaren shows in his detailed study, blackmailers found a particularly rich resource in sexual respectability and asked casuistically whether a lifelong practice of smug hypocrisy was really any better than the blackmailer's dishonest day's work of threatening to unmask hypocrites (5).

The paradox of blackmail was that its basic ingredients were innocuous: a threat to disclose the truth about a person's past and a request for money (Christopher 2). Lawful in its separate components, blackmail became unlawful as a coercive ensemble. Statutes such as the Libel Act of 1843 and the Larceny Acts of 1861 and 1916 made extortionate practices a crime punishable by sometimes lengthy imprisonment in Britain. Robert Clibborn, the young man whom Oscar Wilde dubbed "the panther," was sentenced to seven years' penal servitude for blackmailing offenses (Ellmann, *Oscar* 454; Wilde, *Complete Letters* 759 n1). At the same time, laws against sexual deviancy—products of a society that prized respectability as a middle-class virtue and proprietary good—created a black market for preserving reputations. The Labouchere Amendment of 1885, which made it a misdemeanor for any male to commit "any act of gross indecency with another male person," came to be known as the blackmailer's charter. As Wilde learned, those who were prepared to practice gross indecency sometimes doubled down on delinquency by becoming practitioners of blackmail as well. "Renting," the slang term for blackmail, hinted that bedding a panther might be foreplay to extortion (Holland 55). A consensual partnership in sex could evolve into a coerced partnership in secrecy, payment for pleasure effectively being a first installment of blackmail.

Within and outside of fiction, blackmail straddled private and public life. In Henrik Ibsen's plays, the pressures of social conformity make former transgressions intolerable for middle-class women. Ibsen's zero-sum moral economies turn the past and the present into transactional nightmares. Just as the financial or sexual sins of parents impose transgenerational debts on children, love and marriage become implied bargains in which complex women exchange their freedom for unions with complacent, obtuse males. The logic of blackmail suffuses these respectable lives. The only escape from the extortionate economy is an abrupt "closing out [of] accounts," as Nora Helmer informs her husband in *A Doll's House* (1879) after deciding to leave him and their children (Ibsen, *Four* 108). Nora has become the victim of explicit blackmail for having forged her father's name on a loan to help her husband through financial straits. Her benign act—the law forbade women to borrow funds without a male co-signor—turned a simple contract into a crime that the lender now threatens to expose unless Nora persuades her husband to employ and promote him. Suffocated by the legal and ethical rules fashioned by men, Nora walks out of her doll-house domesticity to recover the authenticity that she, like "millions of women," traded for marriage (112). Hedda Gabler achieves a more violent closing of accounts. Finding herself in the power of Judge Brack, who has learned that she played a role in her former lover's accidental death, Hedda commits suicide with her father's pistol, escaping the amorous, blackmailing Brack as well as her vapid husband. In Ibsen, blackmail is a figure for unequal bargaining power in sexual and marital relationships.

Sexual indiscretion created a reliable market for blackmail. The bear-baiting gangs that worried Wilde and other homosexual men preyed on those who led, in Elaine Showalter's words, "a double life, in which a respectable daytime world, often involving marriage and family, existed alongside a night world of homoeroticism" (106). In Robert Louis Stevenson's *Strange Case of Dr. Jekyll and Mr. Hyde* (1886), the chemical division of a man into proper citizen and uninhibited monster offers a parable of late Victorian hypocrisy. Jekyll's serum-induced alter ego, Edward Hyde, is described as a "young" ruffian, not unlike the renters who hustled and then blackmailed older, respectable men like Wilde (32). Unaware of the truth, Jekyll's lawyer, Gabriel Utterson, fears that young Hyde has been blackmailing his client over "the ghost of some old sin, the cancer of some concealed disgrace," and Utterson's friend Richard Enfield refers to Jekyll's dwelling as "Black Mail House" (10, 28). Earlier, Hyde himself is blackmailed after Enfield sees him brutally trample a young girl in the street. By threatening to expose Hyde's cruelty, Enfield makes "capital out of this accident," but instead of keeping the payment for himself, he passes it on to the girl's distraught family (8).

As we saw in Chapter 1, blackmail motifs pervade Wilde's *The Picture of Dorian Gray* (1890–91), climaxing in Dorian's murder of the painter Basil Hallward, who, having learned the secret of the changing portrait, poses a threat to Dorian's safe segregation of outward appearance from true self (Goldman 34). When Dorian slashes at the painting in a desperate attempt to expunge all evidence of his private sins, he winds up turning the knife on himself, revealing in death that the public dandy and the secret sinner were one and the same, just as Henry Jekyll's "profound duplicity of life" ends when the repressed doctor commits double suicide (Stevenson 107). According to Showalter and Wayne Koestenbaum, Stevenson employed uncanny doubleness and polarity to probe the margins of homosexual panic and desire in fin-de-siècle Britain. The homoerotic duality hinted at in the sinister Jekyll-Hyde pairing becomes comic inversion in Wilde's *The Importance of Being Earnest* (1895), where John Worthing maintains separate lives by being "Ernest in town and Jack in the country," and Algernon Moncrieff splits his existence by inventing a chronic invalid named Bunbury whom he pretends to visit in the country (325–7). In a gothic register, Henry James's "The Private Life" (1892) depicts an author, Clare Vawdrey, whose "second-rate" public persona corresponds to a ghostly double who privately writes his masterpieces (220). Conversely, Lord Mellifont's triumphant social self dwindles to literally nothing, a frightening absence like a vampire in a mirror, in private.

Blackmail, in life and literature, often transgressed class boundaries. E.M. Forster's novel *Maurice* (written in 1913–14 but not published until 1971) is a homosexual *bildungsroman* in which the hero finds love with a young gamekeeper, but not before he is tormented by fears and threats of blackmail. Forster's tragicomedy avoids a plunge into cross-class extortion by making Maurice's relationship with Alec very different from Wildean dalliance with dangerous renters. As with many blackmail plots, the power to hurt across class lines builds the narrative tension. Henry James's tale "In the Cage" (1898) explores this theme through modern communication technology. A young London telegraphist with a novel-fed imagination becomes obsessed with the romantic intrigues of wealthy customers whose encoded transmissions she processes in her barred work cage. Treated as a messaging machine rather than a knowing, feeling subject, she has fantasies of "mastery and ease, a sense of carrying [her customers'] silly, guilty secrets in her pocket, her small retentive brain, and thereby knowing so much more about them than they suspected or would care to think" (387). Katherine Mullin argues that the story links telegraphy and sexual blackmail as "invisible, insubstantial forms of knowledge" (*Working* 64). Yet James's telegraphist remains a reader rather than an exploiter of the secrets of the rich, and in the end reconciles herself to marrying a grocer and being confined to the cage of ordinary class aspirations. In making the reluctant blackmailer a telegraphist, James ingeniously transposed the theme of the all-knowing servant from the domestic setting to an information network. The dangerous power of James's "obscure little public servant," like that of the blackmailing butler, lies in her invisibility to her wealthy clientele, her role as a faceless means to a pleasurable end. She is presumed to be an unthinking transmitter who neither retains nor cares. Yet because she does care, she recognizes that, just as her customers lead two lives, so her eavesdropping has given her a "double life ... in the cage" ("In the Cage" 86). Her pathetic gratitude for the privileged glimpse is partly what keeps her from becoming a blackmailing machine.

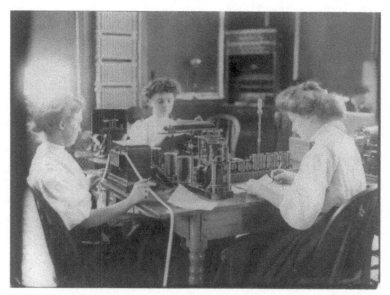

FIGURE 4.1 *Telegraph operators, 1908. Photograph John Robert Schmidt. Courtesy Library of Congress Prints and Photographs Division.*

All the motifs of blackmail—power, class, gender, ruthless professionalism—come together in Conan Doyle's "The Adventure of Charles Augustus Milverton." Sherlock Holmes regards Milverton, who has turned blackmail into a thriving business, as "the worst man in London." No murderer has ever given Holmes the "repulsion" he feels for this extortionist "who methodically and at his leisure tortures the soul and wrings the nerves in order to add to his already swollen money-bags" (373). This was typical rhetoric of the period. A British judge in 1923 referred to blackmail as "moral murder"; another, a few years later, found it "morally indistinguishable from murder" (qtd. in McLaren 78). A middle-class man in a contemporaneous story by John Galsworthy reflects that "[n]o other human act was so cold-blooded, spider-like, and slimy; none plunged so deadly a dagger into the bowels of compassion, so eviscerated humanity, so murdered faith!" ("Blackmail" 131). This hyperbole was a measure of the value that had come to be placed on reputation and privacy, as well as of the loathing that respectable society felt for coercive parasites who made others' secrets their income stream.

Holmes's revulsion is also rooted in the difficulty of enforcing blackmail laws. Extortion represented a negative space within the law, a suspension of the juridical brought about not by law's absence but by its impotence. The British Larceny Act of 1916 made reputational blackmail a distinct offense punishable as a misdemeanor or a felony, but prosecution often resulted in the very disclosure the blackmailer had threatened, despite judicial refusal to allow a blackmailer to defend himself by pointing to the victim's actual immorality (in contrast to civil actions for defamation) (McLaren 21, 28, 60, 122). Moreover, blackmail was the crime that kept on giving. Although blackmail poses as a contract—an exchange of silence for cash or other consideration—such bargains are often tainted by fraudulent promises, as Stephen Galoob has argued. "The victim," according to Ronald Coase, "once he succumbs to the blackmailer, remains in his grip for an indefinite period" (675). Serial squeezing resembled another common fin-de-siècle figure for the continuity of evil: the vampire. A British judge remarked in a 1933 case that if the victim had paid his blackmailer, "he might as well have cut his [own] throat, as he would have been bled and bled and bled" (qtd. in McLaren 78). Blackmail's tendency to peddle illusory peace shows the aptness of the slang

term "renters" for professional extortionists. Victims who thought
they were purchasing silence in fee simple often found they were
merely leasing it for a term of months or years, with an option to
renew.

Conan Doyle's story cleverly varies the theme of the blackmailing
servant. Certain innocuous but "imprudent" letters written by
Holmes's client, Lady Eva Brackwell, have come into the possession
of Milverton, who threatens to turn them over to her morally rigid
fiancé, the Earl of Dovercourt, unless she comes up with £7,000 in
a few days (374). Since the sum is impossible, Holmes hits on the
bold stratagem of disguising himself as a plumber, falsely offering
marriage to Milverton's housemaid, and obtaining from her the
information he needs to enter her master's house and recover Lady
Eva's letters. One night, he and Watson sneak into the house and are
on the point of securing the letters when Milverton unexpectedly
steps into the room. As Holmes and Watson hide behind a curtain,
a veiled woman arrives by appointment, purporting to be a servant
offering to sell compromising letters of her mistress. Suddenly she
raises her veil and shows herself to be one of Milverton's wealthy
victims who, like Lady Eva, did not pay the blackmailer's price,
with the result that her husband, an aristocrat and statesman, died
from the shock of the revelations. The widow draws a revolver from
her cloak, empties it into Milverton's chest, and then grinds her heel
into his face as Holmes and Watson watch approvingly from their
hiding place.

Holmes's disgust for blackmail is underscored by the crimes he
has committed or condoned in order to defeat it. In the course of
the story, he engages in attempted assault and robbery, burglary,
theft, breach of promise, and destruction of property and evidence,
and he refuses to report a murder to which he and Watson are
material witnesses. He defends his lawless chivalry by remarking
that "there are certain crimes which the law cannot touch, and
which therefore, to some extent, justify private revenge" (Conan
Doyle 383). The vacuum created by the juridical exception of
blackmail may legitimately be filled, Holmes believes, by informal
vigilantism. Moreover, the insatiability of blackmail can only end,
the story suggests, in someone's death. The predatory cycle might
conclude with the victim's suicide (as in *Hedda Gabler*) or the death
of the person from whom the scandalous truth must be kept. But
the most complete solution is to drive a stake through the heart of

the extortionate vampire. Law's slow, unsatisfying process would only allow the undead to continue to batten on old transgressions.

In their efforts to combat blackmail, Holmes and the avenging widow disguise themselves, respectively, as a common workman and a maidservant, precisely the figures so often feared as the domestically embedded agents of extortion. Holmes—whose genius for solving crimes owes in part to his strange attraction to criminality—commits many crimes in the course of the story, but he halts short of the offense of blackmail. Capable of threatening to expose the widow's act of premeditated murder (he has learned her identity), he chooses to make a sympathetic gift of his silence instead of selling it to her, as Milverton would have done. Discreet silence operates on the narrative level as well: Watson promises to tell the story "with due suppression" and to conceal "the date or any other fact by which [the reader] might trace the actual occurrence" (373). Watson's storytelling thus participates in the gift economy that Holmes has substituted for blackmail's business model, and recalls the generosity of the telegraphist of "In the Cage," who, like Watson, would rather construct and savor narratives from the clues she encounters in her work than use them to coerce benefits from misbehaving clients.

"Milverton" concludes with a glimpse of privacy's ambiguities at the turn of the century. Having guessed the identity of the avenging widow, Holmes takes Watson to an Oxford Street shop window "filled with photographs of the celebrities and beauties of the day," and they gaze at the image of "the regal and stately lady in Court dress" whom they lately saw gun down the blackmailer (383). Privacy and publicity converge in this Edwardian anagnorisis. Holmes gallantly "put[s] his finger to his lips" to signal that his gift of silence will end the harassing pattern of humiliation, but the narrative has already passed beyond the moment of blackmail (383). Blackmail, with its threat to turn private facts into unwanted publicity, has receded into the sepia-toned background, for now. The photograph of the lady points ahead to modernity's twin imperatives of privacy and publicity, presided over by technologies of mass reproduction and image peddling. Henceforth, men and women will cheerfully part with portions of their privacy in the interests of selective public display, but they will want the law to back them in their self-serving discriminations. It is the uneasy relationship between privacy and

FIGURE 4.2 *Illustration by Sidney Paget for "The Adventure of Charles Augustus Milverton,"* Strand Magazine, *April 1904. Image reproduction courtesy Gina Bradley.*

publicity, and the legal doctrines that were beginning to coalesce around them, that I examine next.

Privacy

Privacy is a physical need before it is a dignitary status protected by law. Modern authors required spatial privacy as a condition of productivity. For women especially, privacy in its simple, nonlegal sense was often hard to come by. The domestic responsibilities of wives and daughters demanded dutiful interaction even when they preferred aloneness. Virginia Woolf's call for a room of her own began early in life, not as a space for professional self-fulfillment but as a simple retreat from the claims of family and friends. In 1904, she confessed that when traveling to visit friends she would like to have "2 rooms of my own [for] greater freedom" (Letters 1:162). For Katharine Hilbery, who feels stifled by her family in Woolf's novel *Night and Day* (1919), solitary spaces seem rare and magical. Standing in the chambers of Mary Datchet, the professional suffrage campaigner, Katharine realizes that "in such a room one could work—one could have a life of one's own" (272). Even in *A Room of One's Own* (1929), this primary, visceral meaning of privacy remains strong: "a separate lodging" to be "sheltered ... from the claims and tyrannies of ... families" (54). Privacy in the legal sense of a reputational right to be let alone is not the immediate value for which Woolf argues.

Yet writers desired legal privacy as well. Blackmail's potency at the turn of the century stemmed partly from the dearth of legal protections for the private lives of persons. Civil defamation required an injurious falsehood before the law could act, and even a criminal libel prosecution could be defeated if the defendant was able to show, as Queensberry did in response to Wilde's charges, that the libel was true and had been published for the public benefit (Libel Act 1843 § 6). Legal protections for privacy were diffuse and undeveloped in the transatlantic setting, often confined to contractual understandings or expectations of trust within defined relationships. The English tort of confidentiality was gradually unfolding through judicial decisions, beginning with *Prince Albert v. Strange* (1849) in which the courts ruled that the unauthorized circulation of Royal Family etchings along with a catalogue describing them could be enjoined on the basis of confidentiality. Britain's privacy protections remained rooted in relationships of trust for much of the twentieth century and have only recently expanded with the infusion of European human rights principles and Parliament's passage of the Human Rights Act in 1998 (Richards and Solove 160–73). Continental concepts of privacy have been more philosophically grounded. German law, influenced by Kantian notions of non-instrumental personhood, enforces a unitary right of personality that holds that "each person, as a unique and self-determining entity, is due certain kinds of protection" (Schwartz and Peifer 1927).

In the United States, privacy law did not follow the British path of confidentiality and trust. In 1890, two Boston lawyers, Samuel D. Warren and Louis D. Brandeis, published in the *Harvard Law Review* a groundbreaking article entitled "The Right to Privacy." In it, they contended that "the right to enjoy life" in the modern era must include "the right to be let alone." "The press," they wrote, "is overstepping in every direction the obvious bounds of propriety and of decency. Gossip is no longer the resource of the idle and the vicious, but has become a trade which is pursued with industry as well as effrontery" (196). The authors argued that the common law should acknowledge the sacredness of human privacy by making violators liable for damages in tort. Drawing on an aspect of *Prince Albert v. Strange* that British confidentiality law largely ignored (Richards and Solove 158–9), they reasoned that a right to privacy could be inferred from the law of literary property, which had long recognized a person's right to withhold private documents from publication (Warren and Brandeis 205). But the law's protection of unpublished papers was only superficially a concern for property, they suggested; in truth, it was an acknowledgment of the sacred space of individuality under threat from "the too enterprising press, the photographer, or the possessor of any other modern device for recording or reproducing scenes or sounds" (206). In the twentieth century, American law came to recognize a cluster of distinct, loosely related privacy torts. By the 1960s, state statutes and common law provided remedies for four harm-based wrongs: intrusion upon a person's solitude; public disclosure of embarrassing private facts; publicity that placed a person in a false light; and appropriation of a person's name, likeness, or other personal indicia (Prosser).

But when Warren and Brandeis issued their call in 1890, the law offered little redress for emotional harm caused by invasions of privacy. Without a clear cause of action—apart from weak approximations in contract, confidentiality, and defamation—authors resorted to two homemade remedies: self-help and literary representation. They took pains to destroy or conceal external sources of private information, or they internalized the problem of privacy in their fictions, or both. Anxious to shield his privacy from the scrutiny of biographers, Henry James notoriously made a bonfire of his accumulated manuscripts, notebooks, and letters (Edel 664). Authors such as Franz Kafka, Samuel Beckett, and H.D. (Hilda Doolittle) also destroyed or urged destruction of their drafts, typescripts, and private letters (Friedman 44; Sax 45–7). Availing himself of the second remedy, James made privacy and celebrity the central themes of *The Bostonians* (1886), *The Reverberator* (1888), and "The Aspern Papers" (1888). With an intensity that was "admonitory" and "sternly didactic" (Salmon 2), James decried what he called "the devouring publicity of life" at a time when gossip journalism and celebrity culture were rapidly eroding the ability of authors and other figures to conceal their private lives and control their public images, and when copyright laws and embryonic privacy rights gave scant hope of keeping inquiring minds at bay (*Notebooks* 82).

James's fictions record the rising tide of commercialized gossip and offer images of individual resistance to the modern assault on privacy. *The Bostonians* dramatizes a fierce struggle between domestic privacy and "the great arts of publicity" that render personal experience "food for newsboys" and the subject of "infinite reporting" (122–3). The novel traces the spectacular rise of Verena Tarrant, whose magnetic oratory makes her a popular figure in the women's movement. Her mentor, Olive Chancellor, seeks both to promote her public image and to build a private domestic life with her, even as Basil Ransom, a Southerner with dogmatic conservative views, fiercely battles Olive for control of Verena's mind and body. In the end, Basil forcibly abducts Verena just before her most highly publicized lecture, convinced that she is meant not for "the public mind" but "for something divinely different—for privacy, for him, for love" (268–9). Basil's victory over "the great public" requires the sacrifice of Verena's career to his private desire and rigid ideology. The novel ends ironically, with Verena captive in Basil's arms, telling him how "glad" she is and unable to suppress her tears—perhaps "not the last she was destined to shed" (449). The novel's concluding image of vindicated companionate privacy comes at a price: the triumph of heterosexual domestic norms is brought about by the loss of Verena's public voice and the destruction of her private life with Olive.

James reserved his most withering attacks on publicity for his fictions about authorship. Among his psychological and moral chillers is a short story called "The Real Right Thing" (1899). It opens with the recent untimely death of a celebrated author, Ashton Doyne, and the plight of his grieving widow. The Doynes' marriage had lacked something. James, in his portentously teasing way, offers little elaboration, but he hints that Mrs. Doyne had never fully appreciated her husband's genius, and now, in an "attitude of reparation," she hopes to make up for it by authorizing a multivolume biography of the great man—a life amply written as atonement for a life incompletely lived (411). She chooses for the job an acquaintance of his, a young writer named George Withermore, talented but still rising, who is dazzled by the offer. Mrs. Doyne is completely "free" to do as she likes in assigning the task of biography: all the materials of Doyne's life—his "diaries, letters, memoranda, notes, documents of many sorts—were her property and wholly in her control, no conditions at all attaching to any portion of her heritage" (411–12). As owner in fee simple of her husband's past, she alone can authorize access to his buried life and supervise its excavation. Her choice of the obscure, malleable Withermore is calculated to maximize her control.

Given the run of the great man's study, Withermore sets to work every evening unlocking drawers and poring over papers, mysteriously aided, he feels, by Doyne's approving presence. When on occasion Withermore mislays a document, it suddenly turns up as if restored by an invisible hand. When he happens upon some of Doyne's "secrets" while "drawing many curtains, forcing many doors, reading many riddles," he senses that he has the blessing of the departed author, "his mystic assistant." For Withermore, the experience is "an intercourse closer than that of life" (420, 422). This unexpected intimacy with the obliging ghost leads him to look forward to "the growth of dusk very much as one of a pair of lovers might wait for the hour of their appointment" (419). Strangely, in this process of uncovering and assembling a life, both biographer and widow feel closer to Doyne than they did when he lived. The work of biography becomes both an active search for a personality taken for granted in life and a passive surrender to a subjectivity that is being painstakingly conjured from private documents.

Withermore's work moves along swiftly and satisfyingly for a time. Then something happens; the mood of spectral collaboration changes. He feels suddenly that Doyne has left him, that the phantom's approval has been withdrawn. Withermore recalls that in life Doyne had doubted the value of biography and had asserted that "[t]he artist was what he *did*—he was nothing else" (415; italics in original). Awakened to the possible impropriety of his commission, the young man explains to Mrs. Doyne that "[t]here are natures, there are lives, that shrink" from public scrutiny (427–8). The phantom "strains forward out of his darkness, he reaches toward us out of his mystery, he makes us dim signs out of his horror." The "horror," Withermore adds, is the ghost's alarm "[a]t what we're doing." Doyne has given signs that he opposes a three-decker monument. "He's there to be let alone" (428). At the end of the story, both Withermore and Mrs. Doyne "give up," convinced that Doyne's perturbed spirit has barred the way to biographical reparations. Although she had thought she was doing the right thing by commemorating her husband in leather-bound detail, Mrs. Doyne realizes that she must do "the real right thing" by respecting his right to be let alone (426). The best life, it seems, is the unrecorded life.

James was preoccupied with the privacy of the dead. Earlier, in "The Aspern Papers," he had offered a portrait of the degraded deviousness to which an obsession with the secrets of a great writer might lead. The narrator of the tale, a writer himself, ingratiates himself with Juliana, an elderly woman who had once been the lover of the famous poet Jeffrey Aspern, and becomes a lodger in her decaying palazzo in Venice, all in order to be near a virgin cache of Aspern's letters. Carried away by lust for hidden knowledge, the narrator one night furtively rifles Juliana's desk, only to be caught in the act and branded by her a "publishing scoundrel" (118). Later, on the brink of contracting a loveless marriage with Juliana's niece and heir—among the tale's morally perverse fungibilities is the narrator's readiness to exchange his ethical being for access to the coveted papers—it is only the niece's revelation that she has burned the papers "one by one" that restores the narrator to humiliated sobriety (142–3).

In a different key, Morris Gedge in James's tale "The Birthplace" (1903) grows obsessed with a famous unnamed poet—obviously

Shakespeare—after Gedge and his wife become custodians of the bard's much-visited birthplace. Distressed over tourists' uncritical voracity for rank legend, and desiring only "to let the author alone," Gedge takes to prowling about at midnight and communing with the poet's spirit in the darkness of "the sublime Chamber of Birth" (153, 180). Nocturnal encounters with an elusive biographical subject in a small, sacred room are a regular ghostly motif in James's fictions, but none of his treatments brings together as succinctly as does "The Real Right Thing" the themes of privacy, unpublished documents, and literary property rights. The story's legal *donnée* is Mrs. Doyne's unchallenged ownership of these rights and her consequent ability to "control" all biographical revelations. She is "free to do as she liked—free in particular to do nothing" (412). As the inheritor of her husband's copyrights, she has stepped into his vacated sovereignty and assumed his power to publish or suppress— the very prerogatives of the possessive authorial self.

As we saw earlier, Warren and Brandeis grounded a right of privacy in copyright's control over the publication of private papers. For them, the law, in its fumbling, case-bound fashion, had pointed the way to the real right thing by recognizing perpetual rights in unpublished writings. Mrs. Doyne likewise bases her power over her husband's private life on her ownership of the rights in his papers. But the great irony is that her unassailable property right does not, in the end, allow her to divulge her husband's secrets—he continues to hold a veto power from the grave. Doyne, though defunct, remains stronger than the bundle of rights that the law recognizes in the unpublished witnesses to his earthly existence. Warren and Brandeis had contended for a privacy right of living persons, and today in the United States the right of privacy is largely confined to the living (although various states now recognize publicity rights for deceased personalities, discussed below). James took the matter much further by writing an amicus brief for the right of the dead to be let alone. And yet Doyne's postmortem resistance, his determination to haunt his widow's commemorative enterprise, is consistent with Warren and Brandeis's claim that literary rights in unpublished documents are only an outward and visible sign of the larger sacrality of personality. Personality, like its crude signifier, the ghost, can be thought of as surviving death and transcending a mere right to damages. In "The Real Right Thing," James makes just that argument by closing the story with the ghost triumphant in its preserved privacy.

The proprietary connection between literary rights and authorial privacy—between copyrights and confidentiality—has remained a persistent belief of authors and their estates up to the present. Copyrights have been used for authorial image-crafting and as a stick for beating back the curious public. T.S. Eliot's estate opposed biographies of the poet for decades after his death, and slowed the publication of his letters to a trickle (Max 36). The family of Marianne Moore has been difficult about permissions, and denied a biographer permission to quote from her unpublished archive (Leavell xvi). Ted Hughes claimed to have destroyed Sylvia Plath's journal containing entries made just before her death (Plath, *Unabridged* ix), and Plath's literary estate sought to prevent the posthumous release of her semi-autobiographical novel *The Bell Jar* (1963) in the United States, relenting only when it became clear that the novel's failed US copyright would permit anyone to issue it there (*Bell Jar* xii–xiv). In the 1980s, the reclusive author J.D. Salinger sued Random House to enjoin the release of an unauthorized account of his life, alleging that the biography infringed his copyrights in unpublished personal letters, even though the letters were available to the public in libraries (*Salinger v. Random House*).

The James Joyce estate, which once warned that the private lives of Joyce and his family, living and dead, were "no one's fucking business," has notoriously brandished its copyrights, existent and nonexistent, to discourage scholars and others from pursuing disapproved biographies, critical studies, digital and analog editions of Joyce's works, dramatic performances, musical compositions and recordings, and internet celebrations of Bloomsday (Spoo, "Three" 89–105). So aggressive had the Joyce estate's behavior become by 2006 that a group of American lawyers agreed to represent a scholar pro bono in a lawsuit that charged the estate with misusing its copyrights to silence discussion of Joyce's life, family, and writings (*Shloss v. Sweeney*). One of the scholar's allegations was that the estate had asserted a US copyright for the first Paris edition of *Ulysses* (1922) long after the claim was shown to be baseless (Spoo, "Three" 100–5). For decades, the Joyce estate has sought, through intellectual property, to realize Henry James's ideal of protecting the author in "the tower of art, the invulnerable granite," free from the taint of revealed secrets and meddling biographers (James, "She" 23).

Publicity

Legal strategies for preserving authors' privacy have the reciprocal effect of shaping their public image: to control privacy is to superintend publicity. While copyrights have often been invoked to preserve authorial privacy, James Joyce conversely used privacy law as an indirect means to enforce an uncertain copyright. In 1926, Samuel Roth began reprinting *Ulysses* in his magazine *Two Worlds Monthly*, without permission from or payment to Joyce. Joyce hired a New York law firm to try to halt Roth's serialization and obtain monetary damages from him. Realizing that courts might not enforce rights in *Ulysses*—a book that suffered from a questionable US copyright and bore the stigma of an earlier obscenity prosecution—Joyce's lawyers chose to sue Roth under section 51 of the New York Civil Rights Law, which forbade the commercial appropriation of an individual's name or likeness. Essentially a statutory right of privacy, section 51 allowed the attorneys to attack Roth for using Joyce's name without authorization, even though Roth had done little more than designate Joyce as the author of *Ulysses* in his magazine and advertisements (Spoo, *Without* 202–4).

Joyce's lawsuit demanded $500,000 in damages, a sum meant to compensate him not for injured feelings (the usual harm alleged in privacy litigation) but rather for what he claimed were his lost profits from Roth's magazine sales. *Joyce v. Roth* was a backdoor copyright action that sought to reverse the logic of Warren and Brandeis's theory by making privacy a predicate for securing literary property. Shaky though Joyce's name-theft claim was, his attorneys managed to extract a consensual injunction that prohibited Roth from making use of Joyce's name in connection with *Ulysses* or any other work. (Joyce received no damages at all.) The injunction had the strange effect of reviving the defunct or doubtful US copyright in *Ulysses* to the extent of making it enforceable against one person: Samuel Roth. As a property right, a copyright is normally an *in rem* right against the entire world. In America, the *Ulysses* copyright had become, through the alchemy of privacy litigation, a kind of *in personam* right against one pirate-pornographer, who soon issued an underground forgery of *Ulysses* anyway.

Joyce also used his privacy lawsuit, quite consciously, as a vehicle for spreading his fame in the United States and fashioning himself as an embattled, violated artist. Several weeks before filing his action in New York, he had set the stage by issuing an international protest against Roth's *Ulysses* piracy (see Chapter 3). The lawsuit quickly followed as phase two of Joyce's campaign to crush Roth and conquer America. Nor was Joyce the only noted figure in this period to use a right of privacy to enhance celebrity and seek copyright-like benefits. In 1922, Douglas Fairbanks had invoked section 51 to sue a movie company that proposed to reedit his motion pictures in ways he found objectionable (*Fairbanks v. Winik*). Increasingly, however, celebrities would avoid the fiction of privacy altogether and treat their public personas as legally enforceable property, or argue that unauthorized imitators were creating consumer confusion through unfair competition. Charlie Chaplin, for example, vigorously sought to enforce proprietary rights in his Little Tramp character (Decherney 67–76).

Modernist authors knew that names had monetary worth in proportion to celebrity. Keenly aware of his bankable fame, Shaw wrote Frank Harris in 1921 that he could get £10,000 for allowing his name to be associated with a film about Oscar Wilde then being contemplated (Harris 208–11). Joyce, undaunted by the meager results of his litigation against Roth, considered launching another lawsuit in 1931 over an innocent misattribution to "James Joyce" of a crime story authored by one Michael Joyce and published in the *Frankfurter Zeitung* (Ellmann, *James* 639–40). Celebrated names plainly could be monetized; what was missing was a reliable legal theory undiluted by notions of contract, privacy, or defamation. Britain recognized no publicity rights, apart from second-best protections found in the law of trademark or passing off (Leaffer 1367). From the start, the American tort of name appropriation had been "[not] so much a mental [tort] as a proprietary one" (Prosser 406), but courts were only gradually shifting the "targeted harm from one of appropriation to one of intellectual property" (Solove 543–4).

Joyce's pursuit of Roth under the New York Civil Rights Law in 1927–28 showed publicity rights struggling to emerge from the formal rubric of privacy. At last in 1953, a US court acknowledged that, "independent of [the] right of privacy ... a man has a right in the publicity value of his photograph" (*Haelan Laboratories v. Topps Chewing Gum*). Later in the century, publicity rights expanded under state statutes and common law, protecting not only living persons but also in some cases deceased personalities (Bartholomew 315–20). In Oklahoma, a descendible right of publicity lasts for 100 years after the death of a personality; in Tennessee, publicity rights are potentially perpetual. Numerous lawsuits have sought redress for the unauthorized exploitation of the names, likenesses, or voices of famous persons: Bela Lugosi, Groucho Marx, Elvis Presley, Clint Eastwood, and Janis Joplin, to name only a few (Spoo, *Without* 227). Joyce was a precursor of these outraged personalities; like them, he sought through litigation to propertize his public image.

In some respects, Joyce was treating his name as if it were a trademark—a signifier that, in addition to naming a living individual, had acquired a secondary meaning that designated a commercial source. When Wilde toured America as a flesh-and-blood marquee for the authorized production of Gilbert and Sullivan's *Patience, or Bunthorne's Bride*, he was lending the power of his name and persona to authenticate an opera that lacked secure copyright protection (see Chapter 1). Joyce, too, used a legal amalgam of publicity and privacy to shore up an uncertain copyright in America. Just as Wilde's personal success caused his name and likeness to detach themselves from the comic opera and reappear as markers of his own brand of wit, so Joyce's lawsuit against Roth came to exceed its original purpose. Officially an action to restore Joyce's appropriated name, the suit and its publicity caused his name and fame to overflow any boundaries that could have been secured by legal process.

The "right to be let alone"—that resonant phrase and modern desideratum—echoes through the writings of Warren and Brandeis, Judge Thomas Cooley (29), Wilde, and Henry James, and is perfectly pantomimed when Sherlock Holmes puts his finger to his lips as a pledge that he will keep the secret of Charles Augustus Milverton's slayer and never place her in any public light, false or true. Only her photographed image "in Court dress, with a high diamond tiara upon her noble head," will be turned toward the public gaze, a careful selection of personal facts for general consumption (Conan Doyle 383). Like modernism, the unnamed lady has passed from blackmail and privacy to the moment of publicity. In a few more decades, blackmail itself would give way to the tabloid journalism that James so feared and loathed. Checkbook journalism—the selling of secrets (including one's own) to scandalmongering magazines—would become safer than the old renter's game of selling secrets back to those who had been indiscreet (McLaren 260–3). Modernity wants to be let alone, up to a point. Privacy is simply that part of publicity that has not yet been offered to the consuming public.

5

Ezra Pound, Man of War

In 1956, BBC producer D.G. Bridson visited St. Elizabeths Hospital to tape-record Ezra Pound reading from his poems. Pound had been confined to the Washington, DC, psychiatric hospital in 1946 after a federal jury found him mentally unfit to defend himself against charges of having broadcast treasonous tirades from Benito Mussolini's Rome radio division during the Second World War. Pound began one of Bridson's taping sessions with a monologue in which he described the "four steps" that had led to his conflict with American authorities. The first step in his "pilgrimage" had been his quarrel with an American consular official in Paris who tried to block his return to London in 1919. The second was learning what an American judge had told a man who was claiming his rights as a naturalized citizen: "[I]n this country there ain't nobody has got any goddamned rights whatsoever." The third was the boast of a prosecuting attorney in one of America's largest cities: "All that I'm interested in is ... seeing what you can put over." The fourth and final step was learning that President Franklin D. Roosevelt (FDR) had planned to "pack" the US Supreme Court by adding Justices who would rule favorably on New Deal legislation. That was where Pound "took off from." "When the [legislature] is unable to prevent breaches of the Constitution ... the duty ... falls back onto the individual citizen. And that is why ... when I got hold of a microphone in Rome, I used it" ("Four" 192–3).

The "four steps," with their fairy-tale causality, are a distilled chronicle of Pound's disenchantment with America and liberal democracies. Like his encapsulation of economic wisdom in the slim pamphlet he called *Introductory Text Book* (1939), his "four steps" seek to elucidate a world of complexity with the simplicity of a village explainer. Each of the "steps" purports to document a perversion of law by a tainted official: a consular desk jockey for whom red tape was a religion; a judge whose sense of legal realism had declined into cynicism; a district attorney who flaunted prosecutorial indiscretion; a ruthlessly pragmatic chief executive keen to abuse his power of judicial appointment. In contrast to this rogues' gallery, Pound paints himself as a reluctant hero compelled to take up vigilante justice after legal officialdom had abdicated its responsibilities. One can almost hear the music of the Declaration of Independence swelling in the background: "[W]henever any Form of Government becomes destructive of [inalienable rights], it is the Right of the People to alter or to abolish it, and to institute new Government." The difference is that Pound describes his seizing the reins of justice as not merely a right but a "duty." In doing so, he sketches a defense to the treason charges he never had a chance to combat in the courtroom: he had been forced to pour his righteous rage into a Roman microphone in order to prevent a greater harm at the hands of lawless leaders.

Pound was essentially a moralist crying in the wilderness of modernity. His indictments of grasping financiers, corrupt politicians, and pandering publishers were rarely grounded in a specific idea of legal culpability. His classification of villains was more Dantesque than juridical. His famous definition of usury—a "charge for the use of purchasing power, levied without regard to production" (*Cantos* 230)—offered moral generalization but no precise legal framework for determining impermissible exactions of interest (in the manner, say, of usury statutes). Pound's fury was often too capacious to be bothered with the sort of detail that engrosses lawyers, judges, and legislators.

Law as historical theme or morality tale emerges often in Pound's writings, particularly his epic poem, *The Cantos*. From the decrees of the Chinese emperors (Cantos LII–LXI [1940]), to the lawyerly and constitutional preoccupations of John Adams (LXII–LXXI [1940]), to the meditations on the common law set down by the early modern jurist Sir Edward Coke (CVII–CIX [1959]), law plays a role in adumbrating Pound's typological vision of moral heroism in history. Yet it was in his engagement with contemporary laws and legal problems, often as letter-writer or journalist, that he recorded some of his most revealing attitudes toward art and society. Here, Pound did grapple tangibly with the details of law's coercive power. Like Oscar Wilde whose life condensed many of the legal forces of the late nineteenth century, Pound embodied a sociopolitical militancy that made him a penetrating if eccentric critic of restrictive laws during the first half of the twentieth century. Like Wilde, he began as an aesthete and *épateur* and made his way inexorably toward personal confrontation with the law by acts that would have been avoidable by someone less haunted by a sense of virtuous singularity. Both men were flamboyant outsiders, at odds with country and convention, self-doomed to disgrace and incarceration. Wilde launched litigation to defy the bullying aristocrat, Marquess of Queensberry; Pound unleashed his anti-Semitic rants against figures who had assumed a comparable mythic largeness: FDR, Winston Churchill, international bankers, all bureaucrats. Along the way, he made war on passport regulations, book tariffs, copyright statutes, and obscenity laws. In the end, he was left with a conception of the US Constitution that was both resonant and empty.

Between 1915 and 1935, Pound repeatedly inveighed against laws—largely operative in the United States—that he regarded as meddlesome interferences with the ability of writers and their works to gain free passage across national borders. In 1927, he wrote:

> For next President I want no man who is not lucidly and clearly and with no trace or shadow of ambiguity against the following abuses: (1) Bureaucratic encroachment on the individual, as [in] the asinine Eighteenth Amendment [prohibiting the manufacture, sale, and transportation of intoxicating liquors], passport and visa stupidities, arbitrary injustice from customs officials; (2) Article 211 of the Penal Code [the Comstock Act, banning obscene materials from the mails], and all such muddle-headedness in any laws whatsoever; (3) the thieving copyright law. ("Pound" 393)

For Pound, an indispensable condition of creativity was the artist's ability to move freely in time and space—to have access to unfamiliar ideas and *moeurs*. Defending his preoccupation with medieval poetry, he wrote in 1912, "I have not been penned up within the borders of one country and I am not minded to be penned into any set period of years" (qtd. in Spoo, *Without* 117). But travel in time and space could occur only to the extent permitted by law. In Pound's view, laws that mandated passport controls, literary purity, book tariffs, and discriminatory copyright conditions were essentially restraints on the body and mind of the individual. In 1917, he denounced the barriers to international understanding that had been erected by America's book tariff and copyright laws, declaring that "[t]ransportation is civilization." Laws that hinder "the free circulation of thought," he added, "*must* be done away with" ("Things" 190; italics in original). Abolishing such obstructive laws would serve the same goal as learning a foreign language or publishing works in translation: a broadening of the mind through international and transhistorical travel.

Passports

Pound's hatred of passport restrictions was indelibly fixed in 1919 when an official in the American consulate in Paris, announcing that all Americans should go back to the United States, tried to prevent him from returning to his expatriate domicile in England. The "whippersnapper" vanished behind an office "partition" to confirm this anti-mobility policy with a colleague ("Four" 192). "Damn the partition!" Pound exclaims in Canto VII, written that same year. "Paper, dark brown and stretched, / Flimsy and damned partition" (*Cantos* 25). So upset had he been over this incident (from his first visit to France since the war) that he included the flimsy partition among the signs of postwar decay chronicled in Canto VII, where it grew from a mere division of office space into an emblem of geographic and cultural impassability (Farley 36–43). Pound idealized the prewar norm of fluid movement across national borders, when he "wandered around Europe … with nothing … except an unstamped membership ticket in the Touring Club de France" ("Four" 193). If transportation was civilization, then passports, visas, and other restrictions were barbarous confinements of the body and mind to a rigid conception of isolated nationalism.

Passports and visas became requirements for international travel during the First World War. The "modern mobility regime," Mark B. Salter explains, arose in the aftermath of the war as the League of Nations sought to reconcile "the liberal desire for travel and trade" with "skepticism displayed toward foreigners, spies, and the fifth column" (77). Beginning in 1915, the British Nationality and Status of Aliens Act increased regulations concerning passports. In December 1915, President Woodrow Wilson issued Executive Order No. 2285, which required American citizens traveling abroad to obtain passports. For much of US history, passports had been optional, but the outbreak of European war in 1914 sealed their importance in controlling the movements of "hostile aliens, suspicious neutrals, potential spies, and displaced populations" (*Pound-Cutting* 29). A federal law enacted on May 22, 1918, provided that, upon presidential wartime proclamation, "it shall ... be unlawful for any citizen of the United States to depart from or enter or attempt to depart from or enter the United States unless he bears a valid passport" (§§ 1–2). The statute imposed heavy fines and imprisonment for violations. The Passport Act of 1926 enlarged the power of the Secretary of State to issue passports to American citizens in foreign countries, subject to rules prescribed by the President.

Pound never tired of attacking what he viewed as Wilson's attempt to use passports "to tie all serfs to the soil" (*Pound-Quinn* 181). He raged at "Woodie Wilsi's rough necks," the petty bureaucrats who were permitted by law to tyrannize over travelers (*Pound-Cutting* 50). For Pound, the fact that hired officials could enforce a "closed frontier" meant that "free lines of communication between one country and another" depended on the whim of a "pie faced Y.M.C.A. clerk" (*Pound*-Dial 329; *Pound-Quinn* 180). Underlying Pound's theories of economic and cultural health was a vision of "unobstructed circulation within and among national communities—circulation of ideas, publications, works of art, consumer goods, money, and people" (*Pound-Cutting* 23). The "flimsy and damned partition" of 1919 became for him a symbol of thwarted international communication—an evil he thought he could overcome when the Italian Ministry of Popular Culture made the airwaves available to him in 1940.

Book tariffs

What passports were to the body in transit, book tariffs were to the mind migrating in textual form. From 1864 to 1913, federal law imposed a 25-percent tariff on books entering the United States (Act of June 30, 1864 § 13; Payne-Aldrich Tariff Act § 416). In 1913, the tariff was reduced to 15 percent, still an obstacle for ordinary book purchasers (Underwood Tariff Act § 329). By then, an import duty was levied only on books published in English; foreign-language works had been on the free list since at least 1890 (Act of October 1, 1890 § 513). Even English texts came in duty-free if they were more than twenty years old or were imported for limited use by public libraries or educational institutions (Underwood Tariff Act §§ 425, 427; Anderson, "Tax"). It was widely recognized that this "tax on knowledge" protected the interests of American printers and bookbinders. Bible manufacturers protested that without a tariff on imported Bibles, their industry would be destroyed. One commentator retorted, "The price of Bibles to a hundred million people is to be maintained in the interest of a few hundred people engaged in their manufacture!" (qtd. in Anderson, "Tax" 75). By 1914, the United States and Russia were the only major powers that still levied a tariff on books published abroad.

In 1918, Pound described the book tariff as a "hindrance to international communication." He noted that books have "an immaterial as well as a material component, and because of this immaterial component they should circulate free from needless impediment." It was a category error, he insisted, to treat literature "as a commerce or as manufacturing." The real harm fell on American writers, who as a result of the high cost of imported books came to innovations in foreign literature too late. The tariff thus contributed to "a provincial tone in American literature to its invalidation" ("Tariff" 227). American publishing became debased as well. Instead of expanding their lists of classical reprints, firms would compete cheaply with foreign publishers by selling the same titles at sub-tariff prices. The book tariff thus encouraged redundancy rather than variety of knowledge. In the absence of law-inflated prices, American firms would have an incentive, Pound thought, to vie with foreign publishers by diversifying stocks of older works. If that were to happen, he would have "two chances of getting a cheap issue of Golding's *Ovid*, or Gavin Douglas' *Virgil*, which now I can not get save by sheer luck in finding a 1719 issue of one and a three dollar reprint of the other" (228).

Pound believed that all books should be exempt from tariffs, but especially those by "living authors, and of those the non-commercial books, scholarship and belles lettres most certainly" (*Pound-Quinn* 22). One reason for the growing number of American expatriates, Pound suspected, was the high cost of books imported into the United States. He admired John Quinn who in 1913 had labored on an amendment of the Tariff Act that removed the 15-percent duty on paintings and sculpture less than twenty years old (Payne-Aldrich Tariff Act § 470). Acting as legal counsel for the Association of American Painters and Sculptors, Quinn helped forge a bill that extended duty-free status to all imported original art, new as well as old (Underwood Tariff Act § 652; "Praises" 10). He argued before the House Ways and Means Committee that the art tariff should be removed because American artists needed no protection from competition, and the tariff hindered persons of moderate means from purchasing artworks before they rose in value and became "merely the hobby or exclusive possession of the rich" ("Testimony" 5696). Above all, contemporary art should come in duty-free, Quinn argued, so that American artists would not have to go abroad to find "stimulus to their work" (5703). Because only original artwork could come in free under Quinn's revised law, the amendment had the added virtue, he boasted, of turning back many fake Old Masters, which were taxed at the usual rate as copies (Reid 159; *Pound-Quinn* 19).

Pound urged a comparable reform of the book tariff: "AT LEAST the first 3000 copies of ANY book of which there is no American edition should go in free. After that there may be some question of favoring the printer at the expense of the public" ("Tariff" 228). Such a compromise would allow the most deserving readers—students, scholars, young authors—to obtain new foreign works at competitive prices without having to travel abroad for them. Only by such a measure, Pound thought, could America be raised up from the medieval "atavism" that Paris had shaken off in the sixteenth century when Henry IV removed the "octroi"—or tax—from books entering the city (*Pound-Quinn* 22). And books would be largely restored to their true identity as bearers of disembodied knowledge rather than mundane articles of commerce lumped together by law with wood pulp, labels, playing cards, and cigar bands (Underwood Tariff Act §§ 325, 329, 331). Despite Pound's campaigning, however, a US book tariff would remain in place for years to come.

Although inexpensive paperbacks were not new during the Second World War, Pound felt that cheap books had truly arrived with the wide circulation of Armed Services Editions. Between 1943 and 1947, nearly 123 million copies of 1,322 titles were distributed to US troops overseas; the books were sold to the army and navy at cost (six cents per volume) plus a small percentage for overhead, with a royalty of one-half cent per copy to authors and publishers (Cole 3–4). The list contained many modern authors, including Willa Cather, F. Scott Fitzgerald, Ernest Hemingway, Carl Sandburg, and John Steinbeck. Writing to his wife Dorothy from the US Army Disciplinary Training Center (DTC) outside Pisa where he was being held on charges of treason, Pound crowed about the Armed Services Editions: "AT LAST cheap books as I have been wailing for for past 30 years" (*Ezra and Dorothy* 131). Yet even here forms of censorship operated. Initially approved, George Santayana's *Persons and Places: The Background of My Life* (1944) was later vetoed by the army as "brilliant [but] dubious as to democracy" (Cole 6). An amendment in the Soldier Voting Act of 1944, supported by New Deal opponents, prohibited the executive branch from disseminating to American troops books, periodicals, or other materials paid for by the government, out of fear that "political argument or political propaganda" would favor the reelection of FDR (§ 22). Under this law, the army vetoed a book that Pound particularly admired—Charles A. Beard's *The Republic: Conversations on Fundamentals* (1943), an analysis of the US Constitution and government—until strong protests led to a reversal of the ban (Cole 7). It took a world war to make books cheap and borderless.

Patronage

A patron's generosity surprised Pound early in his career. Margaret Cravens, an American musician living in Paris, gifted him approximately $1,000 per year, attaching no conditions except that he not reveal her identity; her payments continued for two years, until her death in 1912. Cravens's spontaneous benefactions convinced Pound that private, individual gifts were superior to the subsidies of governments and foundations, and he made her patronage a model for fostering an "American Risorgimento," a renaissance of art, culture, and politics: "an endowment of 1,000 dollars per year, settled on any artist whose work was recognized as being of value to the community ... provided it were left to develop unhampered by the commercial demand" ("Patria" 140). Pound believed that patronage should be bestowed on writers and artists when they were still struggling to establish themselves, as sustenance and incentive rather than retrospective reward for achievement. Both patron and artist should remain outside of commerce, he argued—a sentiment resembling Virginia Woolf's fear that the public, as patron-paymaster, would distort the writer's craft (see Chapter 3). When individual largesse nurtured artistic growth, the patron and the artist became equal partners. "[W]e both work together," he wrote Cravens, "for the art which is bigger & outside of us" (*Pound-Cravens* 11).

Pound conceived of patronage as an ideal collaboration insulated from capitalist markets, a bond of trust operating in a private gift economy. When a writer no longer needed the patron's benefaction, there should be no hoarding or investing. Instead, "he would pass it on to the man who, in his opinion was most likely to use his time for the greatest benefit of the art" ("Patria" 140). For Pound, patronage was a private exchange based on real artistic merit, an open-ended, iterative gift circulating freely—like books and bodies liberated from tariffs and passports—among the needy and deserving. As foreign editor of *The Little Review*, he insisted on spreading most of Quinn's annual subsidy of £150 among the authors who contributed to the magazine, remarking that it would have "spoiled the spirit of the thing if I had taken more than £60 [for myself]" (*Pound-Quinn* 165). He considered the magazine's readers to be beneficiaries of Quinn's largesse as well. Each volume year, Pound made "the limited public an annual present of the sum," a "donation ... willingly made" (*Pound-Anderson* 213). True patronage was fertile, unconfined, and dynamic. He refused to internalize all the benefits of Quinn's gift, insisting that it create what IP scholars call "spillovers": "uncompensated benefits that one person's activity provides to another" (Frischmann and Lemley 258). Private patronage was a public good, a social dividend.

Pound revisited the idea of spillover patronage a few years later in his abortive scheme, Bel Esprit, to assemble thirty private donors who would give an average of £10 per year to enable T.S. Eliot to leave Lloyds Bank and devote himself to writing. In part, Bel Esprit was an effort to build syndicated patronage at a time when Pound felt that "the individual patron [was] nearly extinct" (*Pound-Quinn* 11). According to Lawrence Rainey, he hoped to "institutionalize the community forged by the deluxe edition of *Ulysses*"—the "quasi-patrons" who had purchased Joyce's expensive volume (53, 65). Pound insisted that Bel Esprit was not to be a "pension" for Eliot, who had recently published *The Waste Land* (1922), because pensions were for "taking care of old crocks." Instead, he regarded his own £10 donation as "an investment" in Eliot's creative future. "I put this money into him, as I wd. put it ... into a shipping company, of say small pearl-fishing ships, some scheme where there was a great deal of risk but a chance of infinite profit" (*Pound-Quinn* 213). Pound's simile echoed the economic amnesia intimated in *The Waste Land*: "Those are pearls that were his eyes ... Phlebas the Phoenician, a fortnight dead ... [f]orgot ... the profit and loss" (57, 65). Like the drowned sailor who is past caring for capital, the patron participates in a sea change that may result in unimagined profit.

But profit to whom? The author? The patron? Rainey suggests that Pound's pearl-fishing image incongruously straddles two forms of private property—an investor's cash speculation and an author's intellectual property—while treating both as things to be dedicated to the public (74). Yet this was precisely Pound's notion of patronage: a gift through which the donor sought not to capture private benefits but rather to create spillovers that would build culture. He subordinated risk-and-return to the patron–artist collaboration, imagining a balance sheet where black ink signified profit to culture itself, as well as to the public that never paid a penny of the seed gift. At the same time, he viewed copyright—a writer's private property—as an economic and dignitary entitlement that ultimately had to open itself to the public. If treated as rigid monopoly, copyright threatened to halt books at the borders of nations or of individual purchasing power. To be kept from becoming like passports and book tariffs, copyrights had to be leaky—torn pearl-fishing baskets spilling their contents rather than mattresses for hoarding.

Copyright

Like passport regulations, copyright laws had the capacity to inhibit international communication. Backed by law, a rights holder could permit distribution of a work in some countries and deny it in others. And, as with book tariffs, the above-competition pricing that copyrights allowed often discouraged importation of new works. For much of the twentieth century, protectionist US laws empowered customs officials to seize certain books that had not been printed in the United States as mandated by copyright law (Act of March 4, 1909 §§ 31–3). As we saw in Chapter 3, the manufacturing clause of the 1909 Copyright Act required books and magazines to be typeset, printed, and bound on American soil (§ 15). If not complied with, the clause withheld US copyright protection from foreign-origin works, encouraging legalized piracy within the United States. Foreign titles that were seized at the docks under copyright or obscenity laws could thus reappear, sometimes in distorted or mutilated forms, as knockoff copies issued from the shops of legitimate or underground publishers. These items could then compete cheaply with more expensive, copyrighted works by American authors.

The 1909 Copyright Act modified earlier American law by exempting foreign-language works of foreign origin from the manufacturing clause, thus easing their acquisition of copyright protection (§ 15). But foreign-origin works in English still had to be typeset, printed, and bound in America to acquire a US copyright, even though the 1909 Act relaxed this requirement somewhat by providing a thirty-day "ad interim" copyright if a copy of the foreign edition was deposited in the US Copyright Office within thirty days of publication abroad. Once a copy was deposited, the work then had to be manufactured on US soil within the brief ad interim window (§§ 21–2). Failure to do so—and thus give American book artisans their due—would result in the loss of American copyright after the ad interim period had expired. (In 1919, the ad interim window was increased to four months after deposit of the foreign edition.)

These requirements closely paralleled the US book tariff. In 1909, the tariff law allowed foreign-language works to enter duty-free, but levied a 25-percent duty on English-language books less than twenty years old (Payne-Aldrich Tariff Act §§ 416, 517–18). American readers thus suffered from two kinds of price discrimination: tariff-enhanced pricing of imported English-language works and monopolistic pricing of English-language titles manufactured in America and protected by US copyright. Both sets of laws shielded American book industries from foreign competition, at the expense of consumers, and both treated books as if they were articles of commerce—to the detriment of international communication. Together with obscenity statutes, these measures encouraged unauthorized reprinters to supply the public with books that were otherwise banned or overpriced by law. Pound viewed this result as a triumph of capitalism over culture, materialism over mind. "The American copyright regulations, the tariff on books imported into America, are both scandals," he complained in 1917 (*Pound-Anderson* 9–10).

When Pound assailed US copyright law as "originally designed to favour the printing trade at the expense of the mental life of the country" ("Newspapers" 229), he had in mind the codified protection of the domestic book trade that rendered the United States an outcast from the international copyright community. Convinced that something must be done, he took to the pages of the British magazine *New Age* in 1918 to "set down a sketch of what the copyright law ought to be, and what dangers should be guarded against." He began his sketch, entitled "Copyright and Tariff," by declaring that "[t]he copyright of any book printed anywhere should be and remain automatically the author's," and "[c]opyright from present date should be perpetual" (208). Under this proposal, copyright in a work published anywhere in the world would vest automatically and exclusively in the author—tacitly repealing the manufacturing clause and bringing US law closer to the principles of the international Berne Convention for the Protection of Literary and Artistic Works, which protected the rights of authors according to the laws of member countries (art. 2).

Curiously, Pound's scheme would have legislated a "perpetual" copyright, even though this would have been unlawful in the United States where the Constitution empowers Congress to grant copyrights for "limited Times" only (art. I, § 8, cl. 8). His unconstitutional prescription is especially striking in light of his insistence in later years on the plain meaning of the textually proximate clause empowering Congress "[t]o coin Money [and] regulate the Value thereof" (art. I, § 8, cl. 5). He believed that the latter clause gave the power to regulate monetary value exclusively to the federal government, prohibiting banks and other private interests from fixing usurious lending rates or otherwise "arrogat[ing] to themselves unwarranted responsibilities" ("A Visiting" 326–7).

No sooner had Pound announced his perpetual copyright, however, than he hurried to qualify it in the same essay: "BUT the heirs of an author should be powerless to prevent the publication of his works or to extract any excessive royalties." He went on: "If the heirs neglect to keep a man's work in print and at a price not greater than the price of his books during his life, then unauthorised publishers should be at liberty to reprint said works, paying to heirs a royalty not more than 20 per cent. and not less than 10 per cent." ("Copyright" 209). This provision—effectively creating what the law calls a compulsory license (i.e., a license that the copyright owner must grant)—would have stripped heirs of the power to prevent the reprinting of authors' works or to raise book prices above those current during the authors' lifetimes. In effect, heirs would become stewards of their ancestors' works. If they were not diligent in keeping those works in print, their exclusive property right would vanish and their only remedy for unauthorized uses would be a right to damages in the form of royalties withheld by the statute-licensed publisher. Pound's law would have deprived heirs of what legal scholars call a property rule, leaving them with only a liability rule (Calabresi and Melamed 1106–10).

His daring proposal did not end there. Declaring that "the protection of an author should not enable him to play dog in the manger," he added a second, even more aggressive compulsory license ("Copyright" 209). Under this exception, a foreign author would retain exclusive rights to control the reproduction, distribution, and translation of a work in the United States unless the author failed to have it printed in or imported into the country, or did not grant translation rights for an American edition. If the author slumbered on these rights or refused to exercise them, an American publisher or translator could step forward and apply for permission to make use of the work. If the author did not reply within a reasonable time, the publisher or translator could proceed with the proposed use, with the sole duty of paying a royalty of between 10 and 20 percent. Pound had fashioned yet another penalty for a copyright owner's failure to make works available to the public.

In his statute, Pound sought to balance authorial rights with the public interest. Beginning with a grant of perpetual monopoly, he ended by carving out extremely broad exceptions that would permit anyone to issue reprints or translations of works that authors or their heirs had failed to keep in circulation. Pound's law was thus radically free-trade and deeply committed to promoting international understanding and a borderless culture. Around the time he was proposing copyright reform, he praised Henry James for "trying to make two continents understand each other ... to make three nations [Britain, France, and the United States] intelligible one to another" ("In Explanation" 143). James, he observed, was a "hater of tyranny" whose entire career had been a "labour of translation, of making America intelligible, of making it possible for individuals to meet across national borders" (143–4; see also Katz 53–70). Pound viewed his own legal reforms as consistent with James's attempts to remove cultural barriers through the creation of fictional worlds. A reformed copyright law would serve as a legal counterpart to James's efforts to get nations to understand each other, even as it furthered Pound's vision of modern writing as the abolition of geographical and historical borders.

Pound's imaginary statute was a continuation of his theory of patronage; both were systems for distributing benefits to the general public. Just as a patron's largesse should generate spillovers that spread the initial benefaction beyond its particular recipient, so a just copyright law would concern itself with serving readers as much as the proprietary author. Copyrights should be porous, Pound felt, easily converted from strong property rules into public-spirited liability rules whenever authors or their heirs treated their entitlements as an impregnable monopoly rather than a responsibility to keep works in print, translated as needed, and affordable to all. Copyrights were engines for diffusing creativity, not for abetting its stagnation.

Pound's copyright scheme was also consistent with his later theories of money, which were likewise grounded on principles of utility and free circulation. Notably, he championed the German economist Silvio Gesell's system of "stamp scrip" in which paper money would require "affixation of a monthly stamp to maintain its par value." Instead of rewarding individuals for saving or investing, this system "accelerated the circulation of ... money"— that is, encouraged spending—because the monthly stamp imposed a mounting cost for hoarding ("Individual" 276). Pound's copyright proposal was likewise designed to discourage sterile accumulation of property. The threat of compulsory licenses would impose a penalty on misers of copyright: the loss of exclusive control over texts.

The tension in Pound's statute between authorial control and public access, between monopoly and multeity, is enigmatically captured in his Canto IV, first published in 1919, a year or so after his *New Age* article. In the midst of the poem's celebration of the sensuous freedoms of nature, Pound introduces the flattering words of a Chinese poet to his king: "'This wind, sire, is the king's wind, / This wind is the wind of the palace'" (*Cantos* 15). The king's rebuke to this toadying flattery is reported by the poem's disembodied voice-over: "No wind is the king's wind. / Let every cow keep her calf" (16). A public good like the wind, these lines suggest, cannot be annexed to the royal dominions. Yet the reference to cows and calves complicates the anti-monopoly mood here. Pound privately glossed the line "Let every cow keep her calf" as a reference to "copyright" (De Rachewiltz 267–8). Indeed, the line recalls the words of the sixth-century Irish king Diarmid who, the story goes, was asked to determine whether the monk Columba was justified in copying, without permission, the manuscript of a psalter belonging to the abbot Finnian. In a ruling that led to the bloody Battle of the Book, King Diarmid drew upon Brehon law concerning vagrant livestock to declare, "[T]o every cow her calf, so to every book its copy" (Carpenter, *Popular* 27–8). Pound thus juxtaposes contrasting images of the possessive self: a monarch who is humbled by nature's ability to defeat eminent domain; another who draws upon nature and natural law to give judgment in favor of monopoly. Although Pound evinces here some of the solicitude for authorial rights that he manifested in his *New Age* piece, he once again appears to stress the virtues of uncontrolled dissemination, concluding the passage with an ode to the uncolonized wind: "'This wind is held in gauze curtains …' / No wind is the king's …" (*Cantos* 16).

Although he did not pursue his copyright proposal in later years, Pound followed the efforts of others, such as Senator Bronson Cutting, to reform copyright law along similar lines. He admired the attempts of Congressman Albert Henry Vestal in the 1920s and early 1930s to conform American copyright law to international standards. But both Vestal and Cutting died before their reforms could be pushed through. Had Vestal's bills been enacted, they would have extended the copyright term to the author's life plus fifty years, eliminated formalities as conditions of protection, reduced the impact of the manufacturing clause, and permitted the United States to join the Berne Convention. Indeed, Vestal's draft legislation anticipated many features of the 1976 Copyright Act, a law that would not come into force until 1978, more than five years after Pound's death.

Obscenity and censorship

Pound detested laws that regulated literature by turning it into a commodity and subjecting it to the discretion of petty officials. Book tariffs and copyright laws were offenders in this regard, but they could not compare to the abuses made possible by obscenity laws. He felt that unchecked bureaucracy had not quite crippled due process in Britain, where literature could "really only be stopped by the Home Office, though officious magistrates sometimes over[o]de their powers." (He was thinking of the *in rem* prosecution of D.H. Lawrence's *The Rainbow* in 1915.) Printers were the real "curse" in England because, like customs and postal officials in the United States, they could break the communications circuit simply by refusing to set or print any text of which they disapproved (*Pound-Quinn* 142).

Pound's collection of poems, *Lustra*, was subjected to the private censorship of a printer and a publisher in 1916. Like the nervous printer who had alerted Joyce's publisher to the dangers of *Dubliners* ten years before, the London printer William Clowes and Sons raised the alarm over several poems intended for *Lustra*, criticizing them for their impudence and indecorousness, and suggesting that the author "keep his *baser passions* to himself" (qtd. in Moody 285–6; italics in original). Mindful of the prosecution of *The Rainbow* several months before, the publisher Elkin Mathews seconded the printer's complaint and refused to publish *Lustra* without changes, despite Pound's explanation (reminiscent of Joyce's defense of his moral history of Ireland) that his epigrammatic verse was meant to rival the modern novel's edgy diagnosis of "contemporary ethics-in-action" (287).

Arguing for the "freedom of letters," Pound enlisted the literary agent J.B. Pinker and the barrister and politician Augustine Birrell to assure Mathews that none of the poems could be prosecuted for indecency, but Mathews' blue pencil was not to be restrained (qtd. in Moody 287). The publisher objected to "The New Cake of Soap" because it named G.K. Chesterton (libel); to "Epitaph" and other poems because their meaning was "dubious" or "nasty" (indecency); to "The Lake Isle" for its apostrophe "O God" (blasphemy); and to "The Temperaments" with its opening line, "Nine adulteries, 12 liaisons, 64 fornications and something approaching a rape," for obvious reasons (Moody 288; Pound, *Personae* 100–2, 121). In the end, poet, publisher, and printer negotiated a compromise by which two editions would appear: a private edition of 200 copies omitting four poems, to be sold on request, and a regular edition of 800 copies omitting thirteen poems and changing the title of one poem from "Coitus" to "Pervigilium." Both editions banished "The Temperaments," and the title page carried a double-edged definition of "Lustrum" as "an offering for the sins of the whole people, made by the censors at the expiration of their five years of office" (Moody 289–90).

The American appearance of *Lustra* followed the same pattern when John Quinn subsidized two separate impressions of the volume. Alfred A. Knopf of New York issued a public edition at $1.50 per copy, restoring several poems removed from the English editions but following them in omitting "The Temperaments." Quinn had that controversial poem restored, however, in a second impression of sixty copies printed "for private circulation" (Gallup 22–3). He made presents of these copies to select readers, thus avoiding public markets altogether and improvising a gift economy that would bypass prosecutors and purity groups. Some years later, Quinn would vainly urge a private American edition of *Ulysses* to confound the censors (see Chapter 2), but with *Lustra* the plan actually succeeded. Pound at last had a version of his poems that was not "like the Greek statues in the Vatican with tin fig leaves wired onto them" (qtd. in Moody 285).

American bureaucrats were a comparable scourge, Pound thought; empowered by customs and postal laws, their seizures of allegedly immoral books and magazines were virtually unappealable. The 1917 litigation over the *Little Review* number containing Wyndham Lewis's story "Cantelman's Spring-Mate" (see Chapter 2) showed just how hard it was to overturn a postal suppression under section 211 of the US penal laws (the so-called Comstock Act). Pound was disgusted as much by the language of section 211 as by its repressive effects. In prohibiting the mailing of obscene books along with contraceptives and abortifacients, the statute was, he wrote, "amazing, grotesque, and unthinkable"; he wanted to have it printed in every issue of *The Little Review* so that Americans would become aware of it and clamor for its amendment ("Classics" 64). Yet reforming such a promiscuous statutory mélange would be difficult because "a campaign for free literature [should not be] mixed up with a campaign for Mrs Sanger, birth control, etc." (*Pound-Quinn* 142). Pound viewed the Comstock Act as symptomatic, stylistically and substantively, of the degraded state of America. It was a law "obviously made by gorillas for the further stultification of imbeciles" (*Pound-Cutting* 38).

Pound constitutionalized

When Pound decried and Quinn litigated the suppressions of "Cantelman's Spring-Mate" and the "Nausicaa" episode of *Ulysses*, their argument was largely a factual one: these works were not obscene under the law's definition of obscenity; as art, they might stimulate many emotions, but they had no tendency to corrupt any class of readers (see Chapter 2). But Pound also thought they should go free for a strictly legal reason. Writing to Quinn in 1920, he suggested that the Comstock Act was "unconstitutional, from the Jeffersonian angle" (*Pound-Quinn* 199). Quinn rejected Pound's unsolicited brief, pointing out that the New York court that heard the *Little Review* case was not the "place to go into constitutionality and general principles" (202). Quinn was right (though, as Joseph Hassett has noted, he may have blundered in not arguing other legal and aesthetic principles to the judges who convicted the *Little Review* editors [71–115]). As we saw in Chapter 2, even federal courts refused to consider First Amendment challenges to obscenity laws in this period. Pound's idea— that the banning of serious literature unlawfully burdened freedom of speech—was naïve but prescient. Forty years later, constitutional free speech would become the centerpiece for litigating allegedly obscene literature, art, and film in the United States.

Pound could not have known in 1920 that twenty-five years later he would again be driven to invoke free speech as a defense to a criminal charge. In 1943 and again in 1945, the US Department of Justice indicted him on multiple counts of treason; after the fall of Italy to the Allies, he was captured and later flown to Washington, DC. Had he been found mentally competent to stand trial, he would undoubtedly have wanted to base his defense on the US Constitution, although his lawyer would have urged an insanity defense (*Ezra and Dorothy* 109, 204; Cornell 14). After his capture, while he was being held in the US Army Disciplinary Training Center (DTC), he had fantasized about acting as his own counsel, defending himself in court by expounding Confucius, John Adams, and the economic principles that underlay his radio broadcasts. At the DTC, he had obtained an Armed Services edition of Beard's *The Republic* and scoured it for constitutional arguments. Reading Beard's account of legislative powers, he thought that the charges against him might be a bill of attainder, barred by the Constitution as a law "singling out one person or a group of persons by name and condemning them to death or imprisonment without granting them a hearing or public trial of any kind" (Beard 126).

Along the same lines, Pound considered claiming that his treason indictment was tantamount to an ex post facto law, prohibited by the Constitution as violating the principle that "[a]fter we have done and said certain things, no law-maker can, after the fact ... brand our sayings and doings as crimes" (Beard 127). His notion was that he had been assailing FDR and the US government for years before the outbreak of war and had begun broadcasting from Italy before the attack on Pearl Harbor, an event he described as catching him "off sides, but in reach of a microphone" (*Ezra and Dorothy* 73). He even considered telling the DTC's commanding officer that these constitutional guarantees entitled him to return home to Rapallo on "parole" (149). What he failed to notice was that these provisions were limitations on the legislative branch, not the Justice Department, and that in any case he had continued to broadcast after Italy declared war on the United States.

Pound also thought he should be released from the DTC under the constitutional privilege of habeas corpus, which, in Beard's words, prevented the government from "secretly, or openly for that matter, arrest[ing] persons as individuals or groups, throw[ing] them into prisons or concentration camps, hold[ing] them there indefinitely,

FIGURE 5.1 *Ezra Pound, mug shot, US Army Disciplinary Training Center, May 26, 1945. Photograph US Army. Image reproduction courtesy Gina Bradley.*

and do[ing] what it pleases to them" (126). Without access to an attorney, Pound could not invoke the privilege from his DTC tent, but Julien Cornell, the civil liberties lawyer who represented him after his return to the States, actually filed a habeas petition to have him released from St. Elizabeths Hospital, where he had been confined following his competency hearing. Cornell's argument was compelling: if Pound's mental condition was permanent (as seemed likely) though essentially harmless, and he could never be brought to trial, then his hospitalization, not required for treatment, would be the equivalent of indefinite incarceration of a person presumed innocent under the law. This Catch-22 arguably violated Pound's right to due process under the Fifth Amendment to the Constitution (Cornell 46–9, 61–6). The federal trial court denied Cornell's petition, but he was confident of success in the appellate court. A decision was made, however, to withdraw the appeal, and the poet remained confined for ten more years. In 1958, citing logic similar to that in Cornell's petition, the federal court finally dismissed the indictment with the government's consent, and Pound returned to Italy to live out his days in renewed exile (67, 134).

There were weaknesses in the government's case against Pound, including the uncertain value of the Italian-speaking witnesses flown over to testify about his alleged acts of treason, as required by Article III of the Constitution. But Pound's central arguments, repeated again and again, were that his broadcasts were an attempt to educate America, not subvert it; that he had had no treasonous intent; and, most important, as he wrote the US Attorney General in 1943, that "[f]ree speech under modern conditions becomes a mockery if it do not include the right of free speech over the radio" (*Ezra and Dorothy* 369)—or, as he compressed it in his *Pisan Cantos* (1948), "free speech without free radio speech is as zero" (*Cantos* 446). In a thorough legal analysis, Justice Conrad Rushing notes the "carefully reasoned" quality of Pound's contentions (114–15). In particular, Pound pointed to a recorded statement of his own devising, played before each of his broadcasts, that he would "not be asked to say anything whatsoever that [went] against his conscience, or anything incompatible with his duties as a [US] citizen" (*Ezra and Dorothy* 3). He was broadcasting his "OWN stuff," he insisted, mostly economic ideas found in his "pre-war publications," and "always rubbing in certain points in the Constitution" (103, 107, 310). This argument might have appealed even to a postwar

American jury. Other Americans charged with treason—such as Nazi radio broadcasters Robert Best and Douglas Chandler—had been more scripted by their fascist employers (Rushing 127). Pound's transmitted tirades seemed bizarre even to his Italian sponsors. His voice, alternating between smug didacticism and taunting growl, and his rabid, disconnected rhetoric about "Jew-ruin'd" economies, must have puzzled the most patient listeners (*Ezra and Dorothy* 3).

The great lecture on free radio speech that Pound had hoped to deliver to a jury became merely an abstract refrain as the years went by in St. Elizabeths, but he did have one more passage of arms with his old foe, private censorship. In 1946, he learned that Random House had dropped twelve of his poems from a revised anthology of English and American poetry, edited by William Rose Benét and Conrad Aiken, because the firm was "not going to publish any fascist" (qtd. in Carpenter, *A Serious* 791). Aiken had objected to this suppression—"a kind of intellectual and moral suicide which we might more wisely leave to our enemies"—and Random House received protests from the public (qtd. in Norman 416–17). Caving to pressure, Bennett Cerf, head of the firm, announced that Pound's poems would be restored in future editions. A legal issue remained, however: Pound had given no permission for reprinting his copyrighted poems. With calculated lawyerly menace, Cornell warned Cerf that no permission would be granted unless Random House refrained from "derogatory statements" about the untried poet, adding that Pound would agree to accept $300 for the reinstated poems (Cornell 113, 115). Pound, though *hors de combat* in several senses, was once again at the center of three legal problems that had shaped modernism: copyright, libel, and censorship. Treason, never to be tried but always to remain an unlaid ghost, hovered above this brief reunion of lesser laws.

In her account of twentieth-century treason, Rebecca West pointed to the "unsound assumption that the man who possesses a special gift will possess also a universal wisdom which will enable him to impose an order on the state superior to that contrived by the consultative system known as democracy" (141). Although she was not referring specifically to Pound, her formulation acutely diagnoses his self-conception as poet-ambassador-at-large. His Italian broadcasts were a desperate wrong turn in a lifetime devoted to overcoming obstacles to international communication. His "four steps" might have been convenient notation in 1956 for the causes that had led to his reckless transmissions, but in 1940–45 his consuming desire had been to reach war-bound listeners in other countries. Freedom of movement, freedom to import books and ideas—these had dominated his thinking about the law for decades. Now, warped by long-nursed anti-Semitism and ideological hatred, he abandoned Jamesian humanity for a raging rhetoric of demonization. In taking the microphone in Rome, he was still seeking, but now with a savage fixedness, to bypass the "flimsy and damned partition" that had been erected by laws and wars. Quite apart from any legal question of treasonable intent, Pound's radio speeches were often morally indefensible. "A judgment of 'not guilty' occupies no place in the moral sphere" (Rushing 133).

Conclusion

Pound thought he could change bad laws through persistent proselytizing, but the poet who had assailed the law became its captive. Oscar Wilde also saw the flouted law turn on him. Believing that the gross-indecency statute under which he had been convicted was "wrong and unjust," he nevertheless acknowledged an element of rash hypocrisy in his attempt to vanquish Queensberry through litigation. "'Have you been living all this time in defiance of my laws,'" society seemed to ask, "'and do you now appeal to those laws for protection?'" (*De Profundis* 732, 758). In prosecuting the Scarlet Marquess, Wilde had written his first truly unwitty drama, a capitulation to the prosy pragmatism of the legal system. Even in prison, however, he saw himself as an antinomian exception to law's dominion, a connoisseur of juridical chaos, an escapee from concentric normativity. Pound imagined himself, more programmatically, as law's adversary, standing at the edges of the legal system, barking criticisms, exposing the petty tyrannies of law's creature: unchecked bureaucracy. Concluding that liberal democracies had made a wasteland of legal and economic systems, he accepted Italian fascism's claim to have decided on the exception, and he filled law's lacuna with the factive personality of the Duce.

Pound and Wilde wrote perhaps their most powerful works while jailed. *The Pisan Cantos* and *De Profundis* are private narratives constructed from the immediacy of incarceration, weaving reminiscence and regret with the drudgery and indignity of prison life. In the DTC, Pound struggles to understand the "enormous tragedy" that has overtaken fascism and Europe (*Cantos* 445). The poem contrasts the disordered present with the sanity of Paris and London in 1912, "before the world was given over to wars" (526). As Pound hunkers in his cage or rests in his army tent, he feels the consolations of nature: "the wind also is of the process, / sorella la luna" (445). He calls on Kuanon, Chinese goddess of mercy, for solace, as the penal conditions around him confirm the inhumanity of "cages for beasts" (550).

In *De Profundis*, Wilde also deplores the "prison-system" in which he has been condemned to hard labor; for him, too, nature is a respite and a delightful prospect of his eventual release: "'*my brother the wind*' ... '*my sister the rain*'" (754–5; italics in original). Kindness and mercy are found in certain remembered gestures, as when Robert Ross "gravely raise[d] his hat" as Wilde was led, handcuffed, from prison to the bankruptcy court. "Men have gone to heaven for smaller things than that" (722). Although compassion is often displaced to myth in *The Pisan Cantos*, Pound too recalls the particular humanity of a soldier who, against regulations, made him a "table ex packing box" for his tent (538).

Wilde and Pound, exiles in their different ways, stand in the dock of history, flanking modernism as carceral counterparts. They are visible men of law, revealing in their vivid moral anatomy the effects of law's coercions and violence. They brooded on the law, bullied and mocked it, and at last succumbed to it as the destiny to which their heteroclite natures impelled them. Wilde's ill-advised libel prosecution, alleging injurious falsehood, opened the closet to a new concept of male–male desire. Queensberry's justification defense shattered Wilde's attempt to use the law to preserve his own privacy and perpetuate a fiction of self. In later decades, libel law played a strangely similar role in relation to modernism, disciplining texts that bordered too closely on external referentiality, demanding that true likenesses be omitted altogether or disguised so well as to negate any gesture toward the real.

Pound, taking to the airwaves, fulfilled the logic of his thirty years' war with the law and, in doing so, became a perverse summation, a last offering, of modernism's transgressive energies. His arguments for free radio speech recalled his earlier Jeffersonian defense of free literary speech and, further back, Wilde's attacks on the "monstrous theory" that the "Government of a country should exercise a censorship over imaginative literature" (*Complete Letters* 431). Wilde and Pound bookend modernism's agon with the moralistic extension of obscenity laws from scabrous backstreet wares to serious literary and educational works. The ninety years between *Regina v. Hicklin* (1868) and *Roth v. United States* (1957) saw the rise and fall of a crusade to make mid-Victorian morals universal and implicit, to stop any concert that included the singing of the body electric. In a sense, the argument over censorship of serious literature was never really resolved; it was simply cut short with the establishment of a constitutional test of obscenity in the United States and its statutory counterpart in Britain. We live with the salutary wound that obscene modernism never had its full day in court but rather was rescued, decades after its dominance, by a higher law that admits almost all speech to its protection.

Finally, the instinct for property in modernism was rarely a mania for monopoly. Wilde lamented American piracy and was devastated when his copyrights were devoured by his post-conviction debtorship, yet he practiced forms of plagiarism and artfully mocked selfish literary giants who proclaimed, "My own garden is my own garden" ("Selfish" 297). In St. Elizabeths, Pound, the advocate of perpetual copyright, insisted on collecting twenty-five dollars per poem as "the minimum &/or regular anthology fee" (Cornell 90), yet no modernist had so passionately insisted that authors' rights were permeable and readers' rights absolute. Pound and Wilde both decried the transatlantic asymmetry of copyright laws that rendered authors insecure and pirates untouchable. Yet, recognizing that a vast cultural heritage underlay all creativity—that tradition sustained every individual talent—each writer in his way imagined literary production as an echoing green filled with voices of the dead. Modernism practiced what Wilde and Pound preached. Allusion and quotation were often the very brickwork of avant-garde creation. Copyright had no choice but to yield, for a time, to such powerful norms.

ANNOTATED LIST OF STATUTES, TREATIES, AND CASES CITED

Abbreviations are in a modified legal citation format. URLs were visited February 14, 2018.

International treaties and conventions

Copyright

Berne Convention for the Protection of Literary and Artistic Works (September 9, 1886): with ten initial signatories, including Britain, this convention required members to treat works from other member countries at least as well as their own authors' works; to grant a minimum copyright term, for most works, of the author's life plus fifty years; and, as of 1908, not to condition protection of members' authors on legal formalities. Revised 1896, 1908, 1914, 1928, and later. The United States became a member in 1989. Text at https://archive.org/stream/internationalco00offigoog#page/n34/mode/2up.

Buenos Aires Convention on Literary and Artistic Copyright (August 11, 1910): international agreement that governed relations between the United States and Latin American countries; required use of a notice ("All Rights Reserved") on copies of works; eventually superseded in the United States by **Berne Convention** and **UCC**. Text at http://www.wipo.int/wipolex/en/other_treaties/text.jsp?file_id=366495.

Universal Copyright Convention (UCC) (Geneva, September 6, 1952): with forty signatories, including Britain and the United States, this convention was an alternative or supplement to **Berne Convention**, requiring members to protect other members' works without mandating formalities (e.g., deposit, registration, domestic manufacture) other than copyright notices (©). By joining, the United States exempted other UCC members from the manufacturing requirements of **1909 Copyright Act.** Text at http://portal.unesco.org/en/ev.php-URL_ID=15381&URL_DO=DO_TOPIC&URL_SECTION=201.html.

Obscenity

Agreement for the Suppression of Obscene Publications (Paris, May 4, 1910): with signatories including Britain and the United States, this treaty required members to collect and share information about internal laws and other actions taken against obscene materials. Amended 1949. Text at https://treaties.un.org/doc/Treaties/1888/01/18880101%2006-19%20AM/Ch_VIII_06p.pdf.

European Union
Copyright

Council Directive 93/98/EEC, 1990 O.J. (L 290) 9 (EC) (Brussels, October 29, 1993): copyright-harmonizing instrument requiring EU members to grant a minimum term of the author's life plus seventy years, and economic rights to persons who first publish unpublished works whose copyrights have expired. Some members (e.g., Britain and Ireland) implemented this directive with exceptions recognizing the public interest. Text at http://eur-lex.europa.eu/legal-content/EN/ALL/?uri=CELEX:31993L0098.

France
Intellectual property and moral rights

Code de la Propriété Intellectuelle (July 1, 1992): protects, among other things, literary and artistic property (copyrights); authors' moral rights (authorial attribution, artistic integrity, public disclosure and withdrawal); and industrial property (trademarks, patents). Text at https://www.legifrance.gouv.fr/affichCode.do?cid Texte=LEGITEXT000006069414.

United Kingdom

Blackmail

Larceny Act 1861, 24 & 25 Vict. c. 96, §§ 44–47: made it a felony, punishable by penal servitude for life, to demand, or send a letter demanding, with menaces, money or property from another person; or to accuse, threaten to accuse, or send a letter accusing or threatening to accuse, a person of sexual or other crimes for the purpose of extorting money or property. Text at https://books.google.com/books ?id=HMw0AAAAIAAJ&pg=PA54&focus=viewport&output=html.

Larceny Act 1916, 6 & 7 Geo. 5 c. 50, §§ 29–31: similar to preceding but adding a misdemeanor, punishable by up to two years' imprisonment at hard labor, for publishing or threatening to publish, or proposing to abstain from publishing, a libel or other matter concerning a living or dead person, with intent to obtain benefits. Text at http://www.legislation.gov.uk/ukpga/1916/50/pdfs /ukpga_19160050_en.pdf.

Libel Act 1843 (Lord Campbell's Libel Act), 6 & 7 Vict. c. 96, § 3: similar to (and repealed by) the misdemeanor provision in preceding, except that the maximum punishment was three years' imprisonment at hard labor. Text in Folkard 589.

Copyright

Statute of Anne 1710, 8 Ann. c. 19: granted authors, after registering works and depositing copies, exclusive rights to print and reprint works for fourteen years, plus fourteen more if authors were living when the first term expired. Text at http://avalon.law.yale.edu/18th _century/anne_1710.asp.

Copyright Act 1842, 5 & 6 Vict. c. 45: protected works for the longer of forty-two years from first publication or the author's life plus seven years. Text in Seville 258–76.

Copyright Act 1911, 1 & 2 Geo. 5 c. 46: increased the general copyright term to the author's life plus fifty years; provided for compulsory licenses for making sound recordings of musical compositions; codified common-law fair dealing for private study, criticism, and similar activities. Text at http://www.legislation.gov .uk/ukpga/Geo5/1-2/46/enacted.

Donaldson v. Beckett, 1 Eng. Rep. 837 (H.L. 1774): House of Lords' decision rejecting perpetual common-law rights in published works; held that protection was limited to the term provided in **Statute of Anne.** Text at https://www.copyrighthistory.com/donaldson.html.

Southey v. Sherwood, 35 Eng. Rep. 1006 (Ch. 1817): Court of Chancery refused to enjoin the unauthorized publication of Robert Southey's *Wat Tyler* (1817)—a work of political radicalism— unless Southey first established a property right in a law court; acknowledged that equity courts' refusal to enforce copyrights in works considered immoral, defamatory, blasphemous, or seditious enabled unauthorized persons to publish them freely. See Alexander.

Gross indecency

Criminal Law Amendment Act 1885 (Labouchere Amendment), 48 & 49 Vict. c. 69, § 11: inserted into a bill raising the age of consent for young women, this provision made it a misdemeanor, punishable by up to two years' imprisonment at hard labor, for any male, in public or private, to commit, procure, or attempt to procure an indecent act with another male. Text at https://www.parliament.uk/about/living -heritage/transformingsociety/private-lives/relationships/collections1 /sexual-offences-act-1967/1885-labouchere-amendment/.

Regina v. Wilde and Taylor (Central Crim. Ct. [Old Bailey] April 26 to May 1, May 22–25, 1895): Crown prosecution of Oscar Wilde for gross indecency under preceding. The first trial ended in a hung jury, the second in conviction and maximum sentence. For accounts, see Ellmann, *Oscar* 462–78; Hyde.

Libel

Libel Act 1843 (Lord Campbell's Libel Act), 6 & 7 Vict. c. 96: codified aspects of civil and criminal libel; made it a crime, punishable by fine and up to two years' imprisonment, to publish a libel known to be false; allowed defendants to justify libels if true and published for the public benefit; provided for recovery of costs by prevailing parties. Text in Folkard 588–91.

Regina (Wilde) v. Queensberry (Central Crim. Ct. [Old Bailey], April 3–5, 1895): Oscar Wilde's prosecution of the Marquess of Queensberry under preceding. Queensberry, who was acquitted by a conceded jury verdict that found his libel to be justified, forced a sale of Wilde's effects to recover legal costs. Complete trial transcript in Holland.

Obscenity

Customs Consolidation Act 1876, 39 & 40 Vict. c. 36, § 42: prohibited importation of indecent or obscene prints, paintings, and photographs; provided for forfeiture and destruction of same. Text at http://www.legislation.ie/eli/1876/act/36/enacted/en/print.

Obscene Publications Act 1857 (Lord Campbell's Act), 20 & 21 Vict. c. 83: permitted a magistrate or two justices of the peace, upon sworn complaint that obscene materials were being kept for sale, distribution, or exhibition, to authorize search and seizure and then to summon the occupant to show why the materials should not be ordered destroyed. Quasi-criminal, *in rem* forfeiture statute aimed at obscene materials; *in personam* prosecutions of persons proceeded under the common law (non-statutory law) of obscene libel. Text in *Statutes* 1110–12.

Obscene Publications Act 1959, 7 & 8 Eliz. 2 c. 66: replaced the common-law misdemeanor of obscene libel with the statutory offense of publishing an obscene article, punishable by fine and/or up to three years' imprisonment; liberalized *Regina v. Hicklin* test; replaced **Obscene Publications Act 1857** with liberalized search, seizure, and forfeiture procedures; permitted defendants to justify publication as in the interests of science, literature, art or learning (public good); required courts to allow expert opinion. Text at http://www.legislation.gov.uk/ukpga/1959/66/pdfs/ukpga_19590066_en.pdf.

Post Office (Protection) Act 1884, 47 & 48 Vict. c. 76, § 4: made it a misdemeanor, punishable by up to one year's imprisonment at hard labor, to mail or attempt to mail obscene prints, paintings, photographs, and other items. Text in *Public General Statutes* 236–44.

Post Office Act 1908, 8 Edw. 7 c. 48, §§ 16, 63: similar to (and repealing) preceding. Text at http://www.legislation.gov.uk /ukpga/1908/48/pdfs/ukpga_19080048_en.pdf.

Town Police Clauses Act 1847, 10 & 11 Vict c. 89, § 28: made it a crime, punishable by fine or up to two weeks' imprisonment, to offer publicly for sale, distribution, or exhibition profane, indecent, or obscene books, papers, and other items, or to sing profane or obscene songs or ballads, or to use profane or obscene language. Text at http://www.legislation.gov.uk/ukpga/1847/89/pdfs /ukpga_18470089_en.pdf.

Vagrancy Act 1824, 5 Geo. 4. c. 83, § 4: made it a crime, punishable by up to three months' imprisonment at hard labor, and by forfeiture of items, to display publicly obscene prints, pictures, and other matter. Text at http://www.legislation.gov.uk/ukpga/1824/83 /pdfs/ukpga_18240083_en.pdf.

Vagrancy Act 1838, 1 & 2 Vict. c. 38, § 2: amended preceding to clarify that prohibited displays included windows or other parts of shops and buildings in public places. Text in Odgers, *Law* 564.

Regina v. Hicklin, Law Rep. 3 Q.B. 360 (1868): Court of Queen's Bench held, in an appeal from a forfeiture proceeding under **Obscene Publications Act 1857,** that a bookseller's innocent motive was immaterial if matter sold was objectively obscene; established an effects test of obscenity used often by later British and American courts. Text at https://en.wikisource.org/wiki/Regina_v._Hicklin.

Regina v. Penguin Books Ltd., Crim. Law Rep. 176 (1961): prosecution of Penguin Books in 1960 under **Obscene Publications Act 1959** for publishing *Lady Chatterley's Lover*. The jury acquitted after Penguin invoked the "public good" defense and had academics and authors testify as experts. Trial transcript in Rolph, ed.

Regina v. Read, 92 Eng. Rep. 777 (K.B. 1708): Court of King's Bench ruled that obscene libels were ecclesiastical offenses, not punishable in temporal courts, and that libels "must be against some particular person or persons, or against the Government." Not until *Rex v. Curll*, 93 Eng. Rep. 849 (K.B. 1727), were obscene libels punishable at common law as offenses against public morality.

Passports

British Nationality and Status of Aliens Act 1914, 4 & 5 Geo. c.17: amended laws concerning natural-born and naturalized subjects; national status of married women and children; loss of nationality; alien property. Text at http://www.legislation.gov.uk /ukpga/1914/17/pdfs/ukpga_19140017_en.pdf.

Privacy and human rights

Human Rights Act 1998, 46 Eliz. 2 c. 42: incorporates European Convention on Human Rights into UK law; permits lawsuits in British courts for violations of rights; expands remedies for privacy invasion beyond actions for breach of trust and confidence. Text at http://www.legislation.gov.uk/ukpga/1998/42/contents.

Prince Albert v. Strange, 41 Eng. Rep. 1171 (Ch. 1849): Court of Chancery enjoined publication of a catalogue describing Prince Albert's private etchings; established a precedent for personal privacy, based on principles of property, trust, and confidence. Text at http://www.worldlii.org/int/cases/EngR/1849/255.pdf.

Wartime measures

Defence of the Realm Act (DORA), 4 & 5 Geo. 5 c. 29: enacted after Britain entered the First World War; granted the government vast wartime powers to establish criminal offenses and control many aspects of civilian life, including publications and public speaking. Annotated compilation of amendments, regulations, and orders through February 1918 in Pulling, ed.

United States

Constitution

Art. I, § 8, cl. 5: authorizes Congress to "coin money, regulate the value thereof, and of foreign coin." Ezra Pound thought this clause reflected a founding American ideal whereby "the nation controlled the nation's money," as opposed to what he viewed as private and foreign usurious influences ("A Visiting" 314). Text of Constitution and amendments at https://www.law.cornell.edu/constitution/overview.

Art. I, § 8, cl. 8: authorizes Congress to "promote the progress of science and useful arts by securing for limited times to authors and inventors the exclusive right to their respective writings and discoveries." Prohibits perpetual US copyrights and patents.

Art. I, § 9, cls. 2–3: prohibits ex post facto laws, bills of attainder, and suspension of habeas corpus except in extraordinary cases.

Art. III, § 3, cl. 1: defines one form of treason as "adhering to [America's] enemies, giving them aid and comfort"; requires, for conviction, the testimony of at least "two witnesses to the same overt act, or … confession in open court." Had his case gone forward, Ezra Pound would have been tried under these rules and related statutes (see Chapter 5).

Amend. 1: prohibits the government from abridging free speech and press. The centerpiece for constitutionalizing modernism in the United States and, indirectly, Britain (see Chapter 2).

Amends. 5 and 14: provide that federal and state governments shall deprive no person of "life, liberty, or property, without due process of law."

Antitrust

Sherman Antitrust Act, July 2, 1890, ch. 647, 26 Stat. 209: created a private right of action for persons harmed by monopolistic conduct "in restraint of trade or commerce"; made such conduct a misdemeanor punishable by fine and up to one year's imprisonment. Text at https://www.loc.gov/law/help/statutes-at-large/51st-congress /session-1/c51s1ch647.pdf.

Copyright

Act of May 31, 1790, ch. 15, 1 Stat. 124: like Britain's **Statute of Anne,** this first US copyright statute granted authors, upon registering works and depositing copies, protection for fourteen years, plus another fourteen if authors survived the first term. The first of several US statutes expressly denying protection to authors not US citizens or permanent residents. Text at https://www.loc.gov /law/help/statutes-at-large/1st-congress/c1.pdf.

International Copyright Act (Chace Act), March 3, 1891, ch. 565, 26 Stat. 1106: granted protection to non-US authors' works if manufactured from type set in the United States or from plates made from such type ("manufacturing clause") and, in effect, if first or simultaneously printed and published on US soil. Text at https:// www.loc.gov/law/help/statutes-at-large/51st-congress/session-2 /c51s2ch565.pdf.

1909 Copyright Act, March 4, 1909, ch. 320, 35 Stat. 1075: granted protection for twenty-eight years to published works, with possible renewal for another twenty-eight; retained formalities of copyright notice and renewal; provided for compulsory licenses for making sound recordings of musical compositions; abolished the requirement of US manufacture for non-US works in foreign languages; retained it for non-US works in English, with ad interim copyright to ease compliance. Text at https://www.loc.gov/law/help /statutes-at-large/60th-congress/session-2/c60s2ch320.pdf.

Act of August 31, 1954, Pub. L. No. 83–743, 68 Stat. 1030: implemented changes pursuant to **Universal Copyright Convention;** exempted UCC nationals from US manufacturing requirements for works first published abroad in English. Text at https://www.gpo .gov/fdsys/pkg/STATUTE-68/pdf/STATUTE-68-Pg1030.pdf.

1976 Copyright Act, October 19, 1976, Pub. L. No. 94–553, 90 Stat. 2541 (codified at 17 USC §§ 101 et seq.): abolished common-law protection for most works; provided for a term of the author's life plus fifty years for most works; extended terms for already published works to seventy-five years from the year of first publication; codified the judicial doctrine of fair use. Text at https:// www.copyright.gov/history/pl94-553.pdf.

Sonny Bono Copyright Term Extension Act, October 27, 1998, Pub. L. No. 105–298, 112 Stat. 2827 (codified at 17 USC § 304[b]): sought to harmonize US copyright terms with those in European Union; increased terms to the author's life plus seventy years, and, for most works published before 1978, ninety-five years from the

year of first publication. Text at https://www.gpo.gov/fdsys/pkg
/STATUTE-112/pdf/STATUTE-112-Pg2827.pdf.

**Uruguay Round Agreements Act (URAA), Pub. L. No. 103–465,
108 Stat. 4809, 4976–81 (1994) (codified at 17 USC § 104A):**
restored US copyright to foreign works that had not complied
with US copyright formalities (renewal, copyright notice,
American manufacture). Text at https://www.gpo.gov/fdsys/pkg
/STATUTE-108/pdf/STATUTE-108-Pg4809.pdf.

H.R. 6988, 71st Cong., 2nd Sess. (1929): bill (not enacted) proposed
by Congressman Albert Henry Vestal to authorize US adherence
to international copyright conventions and provide US protection
to non-US authors. For Ezra Pound's support, see *Pound-Cutting*
28–9, 45–6.

H.R. 12549, 71st Cong., 2nd Sess. (1930): Congressman Vestal's bill
(not enacted) to extend copyright duration, eliminate formalities,
reduce the impact of manufacturing requirements on non-US
authors, and permit the United States to join **Berne Convention**.

Burrow-Giles Lithographic Co. v. Sarony, 111 US 53 (1884):
copyright infringement action over unauthorized copies of a
photograph of Oscar Wilde; the US Supreme Court held that
photographs were authored writings under art. I, § 8, cl. 8 of
US Constitution. Text at https://supreme.justia.com/cases/federal
/us/111/53/case.html.

**Salinger v. Random House, Inc., 650 F. Supp. 413 (S.D.N.Y. 1986),
reversed, 811 F.2d 90 (2d Cir. 1987):** J.D. Salinger sued for copyright
infringement of private letters quoted in an unauthorized biography;
the trial court deemed the quotations likely a fair use, but the US
Court of Appeals for the Second Circuit reversed, holding that
fair use did not normally apply to unpublished works. Congress
amended the law in 1992 to clarify that there can be fair use of
unpublished works (17 USC § 107). Text of appellate decision at
https://www.law.cornell.edu/copyright/cases/811_F2d_90.htm.

Shloss v. Sweeney, 515 F. Supp. 2d 1068 (N.D. Cal. 2007): English
professor sued the James Joyce estate for a declaratory judgment
that her use of copyrighted and uncopyrighted writings by Joyce and
his daughter Lucia was a fair use, and that the estate had engaged in
copyright misuse by obstructing scholarly use of such materials; the

federal trial court denied the estate's motion to dismiss, and the case promptly settled favorably for the professor. Text at https://www .courtlistener.com/opinion/2579468/shloss- v-sweeney/.

Wheaton v. Peters, 33 US (8 Pet.) 591 (1834): US Supreme Court held that, while unpublished writings enjoyed perpetual common-law protection, published works were limited to terms provided by statute; comparable to British case, **Donaldson v. Beckett.** Text at https://supreme.justia.com/cases/federal/us/33/591/case.html.

Obscenity

Comstock Act (as revised), March 4, 1909, ch. 321, § 211, 35 Stat. 1088, 1129: authorized the Post Office to declare obscene materials, abortifacients, and other items to be nonmailable; made it a crime, punishable by fine and/or up to five years' imprisonment, to use the mails knowingly for circulating prohibited items. Ezra Pound detested "Article 211," as he called it, for suppressing issues of *The Little Review* and other magazines. Anthony Comstock had successfully lobbied for the first version of this law in 1873. Text at http://www.loc.gov/law/help/statutes-at-large/60th-congress /session-2/c60s2ch321.pdf.

Tariff Act of 1922, September 21, 1922, ch. 356, § 305, 42 Stat. 858, 936: prohibited importation of obscene material; provided for judicially warranted search and seizure and for condemnation proceedings and appeals therefrom. Text at https://www.loc.gov/law /help/statutes-at-large/67th-congress/Session%202/c67s2ch356. pdf.

Tariff Act of 1930, June 17, 1930, ch. 497, § 305, 46 Stat. 590, 688: revision of preceding, drafted by attorney Morris Ernst, requiring books seized at customs to be subjected to *in rem* civil forfeiture actions in federal court; permitted parties in interest to demand jury trial and to appeal; an additional provision permitted the Secretary of the Treasury to admit "the so-called classics or books of recognized and established literary or scientific merit" when "imported for noncommercial purposes." *United States v. One Book Entitled Ulysses*, among other cases, was litigated under these provisions. Text at http:// www.loc.gov/law/help/statutes-at-large/71st-congress/c71.pdf.

Massachusetts General Laws, ch. 272, § 28: made it a crime, punishable by fine and up to two years' imprisonment, to import, print, publish, sell, or distribute books or other matter containing "obscene, indecent, or impure language, or manifestly tending to corrupt the morals of youth." Employed in several prosecutions discussed below. Text in *General Laws* 2765–66.

New York Penal Law § 1141: made it a misdemeanor, punishable by fine or up to one year's imprisonment, to sell, lend, give away, or show "any obscene, lewd, lascivious, filthy, indecent, or disgusting" book, magazine, or similar matter. Employed to prosecute the *Little Review* editors in 1920–21 for publishing a portion of Joyce's *Ulysses*. Text in McKinney, ed. 415–16.

Anderson v. Patten, 247 F. 382 (S.D.N.Y. 1917): federal trial court denied Margaret Anderson's motion to enjoin the New York Postmaster from suppressing, under **Comstock Act,** an issue of *The Little Review* containing a Wyndham Lewis story. Text at https://www.ravellaw.com/opinions/64d5d4b9f45a7a4c1c71251686 6f2764.

Attorney General v. Book Named "God's Little Acre," 326 Mass. 281 (Mass. 1950): Massachusetts high court deemed Erskine Caldwell's novel obscene and subject to forfeiture under a Massachusetts *in rem* obscenity statute; refused to entertain **First Amendment** defense. Text at http://masscases.com/cases/sjc/326/326mass281.html.

Commonwealth v. DeLacey, 271 Mass. 327 (Mass. 1930): Massachusetts high court upheld the conviction of a bookstore manager, under **Massachusetts General Laws § 28,** for selling *Lady Chatterley's Lover*. Text at https://casetext.com/case/commonwealth -v-delacey.

Commonwealth v. Friede, 271 Mass. 318 (Mass. 1930): Massachusetts high court upheld a jury conviction of publisher Donald Friede, under **Massachusetts General Laws § 28,** for selling Dreiser's *An American Tragedy*. Text at https://casetext.com/case /commonwealth-v-friede.

Commonwealth v. Holmes, 17 Mass. 336 (Mass. 1821): Massachusetts high court upheld a misdemeanor conviction of a printer, under the common law of obscene libel, for publishing the unedited *Memoirs of a Woman of Pleasure* (*Fanny Hill*).

Grove Press, Inc. v. Christenberry, 175 F. Supp. 488 (S.D.N.Y. 1959), affirmed, 276 F. 2d 433 (2d Cir. 1960): publisher Barney Rosset sued to restrain the New York Postmaster from suppressing the unexpurgated *Lady Chatterley's Lover* under **Comstock Act.** Trial and appellate courts concluded that the Postmaster had acted unconstitutionally under *Roth v. United States.* Text at https:// casetext.com/case/grove-press-inc-v-christenberry-2.

Grove Press, Inc. v. Gerstein, 378 US 577 (1964): US Supreme Court reversed a state-court ruling that Henry Miller's *Tropic of Cancer* was obscene; held, *per curiam*, that it was protected by **First Amendment.** Text at https://supreme.justia.com/cases/federal /us/378/577/.

Heymoolen v. United States, Treas. Decision 42907 (Cust. Ct. 1928): US Customs Court upheld, under **Tariff Act of 1922**, a customs seizure of *Ulysses* and other books as "obscenity of the rottenest and vilest character." Text in Moscato and LeBlanc, eds. 142.

People v. Friede, 133 Misc. 611 (N.Y. Magistr. Ct. 1929): denied publisher Donald Friede's motion to dismiss a charge of possessing and selling, in violation of **N.Y. Penal Law § 1141**, Radclyffe Hall's *The Well of Loneliness*, deeming the book likely obscene under *Regina v. Hicklin* standard. Text at https://casetext.com/case /people-v-friede.

People v. Seltzer, 122 Misc. 329 (N.Y. Sup. Ct. 1924): denied publisher Thomas Seltzer's motion to dismiss a charge of possessing with intent to sell Arthur Schnitzler's *Casanova's Homecoming* (1922) in violation of **N.Y. Penal Law § 1141**; employed *Regina v. Hicklin* standard and rejected expert testimony and views of foreign critics, "for we may assert with pride—though not boastfully— that we are essentially an idealistic and spiritual nation and exact a higher standard than some others." Text of decision at https:// casetext.com/case/people-v-seltzer-2.

Roth v. United States, 354 US 476 (1957): US Supreme Court rejected Samuel Roth's constitutional challenge to **Comstock Act** and affirmed his conviction for mailing obscene advertisements. However, the Court deemed *Regina v. Hicklin* standard "unconstitutionally restrictive of the freedoms of speech and press," and stated that an appropriate test of obscenity (defined as matter "utterly without redeeming social importance" and so unprotected by **First Amendment**) was "whether, to the average person, applying contemporary community standards, the dominant theme of the material, taken as a whole, appeals to prurient interest." This progressive standard, grounded in free-speech principles, transformed US obscenity law. See De Grazia. Text at https:// supreme.justia.com/cases/federal/us/354/476/case.html#F1.

United States v. Dennett, 39 F.2d 564 (2d Cir. 1930): US Court of Appeals for the Second Circuit reversed a federal criminal conviction of Mary Ware Dennett for violating **Comstock Act** by mailing *The Sex Side of Life*; held that this educational pamphlet was non-obscene. Text at http://law.justia.com/cases/federal /appellate-courts/F2/39/564/1543269/.

United States v. One Book Called "Ulysses," 5 F. Supp. 182 (S.D.N.Y. 1933): in a civil forfeiture action under **Tariff Act of 1930**, the federal trial court dismissed the government's libel (i.e., complaint) against a copy of Joyce's *Ulysses* seized at customs, finding the book "sincere and honest" and unlikely, in its entirety, to excite sexual impulses in "a person with average sex instincts." Text at http://law. justia.com/cases/federal/district-courts/FSupp/5/182/2250768/.

United States v. One Book Entitled Ulysses by James Joyce, 72 F.2d 705 (2d Cir. 1934): US Court of Appeals for the Second Circuit affirmed preceding, refusing to apply *Regina v. Hicklin* standard and ruling that the proper test was a book's "dominant effect" in light of the "relevancy of the objectionable parts to the theme, the established reputation of the work in the estimation of approved critics, if the book is modern, and the verdict of the past, if it is ancient." Dissent by Judge Martin T. Manton. Text at http://law. justia.com/cases/federal/appellate-courts/F2/72/705/1549734/.

United States v. One Obscene Book Entitled "Married Love," 48 F.2d 821 (S.D.N.Y. 1931): in a civil forfeiture action under **Tariff Act of 1930**, the federal trial court dismissed the government's libel (i.e., complaint) against a seized copy of Marie Stopes's book about marital sex, finding nothing "exceptionable anywhere," since the book would not be "obscene or immoral" to "a normal mind." Text at http://law.justia.com/cases/federal/district-courts /F2/48/821/1569043/.

Passports

Act of May 22, 1918, ch. 81, 40 Stat. 559: authorized presidential proclamations regulating aliens' departure from or entry into the United States and requiring US citizens to bear valid passports for international travel; violations punishable by fine and/or up to twenty years' imprisonment. Text at https://www.loc.gov/law/help/statutes-at-large/65th-congress/session-2/c65s2ch81.pdf.

Passport Act of 1926, July 3, 1926, ch. 772, 44 Stat. 887: authorized the US Secretary of State to issue passports and empower other officials to do so; limited the validity of passports and visas to two years, unless shortened by the Secretary of State. Text at https://www.loc.gov/law/help/statutes-at-large/69th-congress/c69.pdf.

Executive Order No. 2285 (December 15, 1915): required all persons, American or foreign, leaving the United States for foreign countries to bear "passports of the Governments of which they are citizens," and prescribed rules for applying for US passports. Text at http://www.presidency.ucsb.edu/ws/?pid=75392.

Privacy

New York Civil Rights Law § 51: permitted anyone, whose name, portrait, or picture had been used for advertising or trade purposes without written permission, to sue for injunctive relief and damages; provided exceptions, including for use of a person's name, portrait, or picture "in connection with his literary, musical or artistic productions which he has sold or disposed of with such name, portrait or picture used in connection therewith." Text quoted in full in *Jackson v. Consumer Publications*, 169 Misc. 1022 (N.Y. Sup. Ct. 1939), at https://casetext.com/case/jackson-v-consumer-publications-inc-1.

Fairbanks v. Winik, 119 Misc. 809 (N.Y. Sup. Ct. 1922), reversed, 206 A.D. 449 (N.Y. App. Div. 1923): film actor sued under N.Y. Civil Rights Law § 51 to prevent a movie company from violating his privacy rights by reediting his films in an objectionable manner. Text of appellate decision at https://casetext.com/case/fairbanks-v-winik-2.

Joyce v. Roth and Two Worlds Publishing Co. (N.Y. Sup. Ct. filed March 14, 1927; consent decree entered in clerk's office January 2,

1929): James Joyce's lawsuit against publisher Samuel Roth, alleging that Roth had violated his privacy rights under **N.Y. Civil Rights Law § 51** by appropriating his name for commercial purposes. Partly an attempt to get around the lack of clear US copyright for *Ulysses*. See Spoo, *Without* 193–232, 277–8.

Publicity rights

Oklahoma Stat. tit. 12, §§ 1448–1449: private right of action for unauthorized use of a deceased personality's name, voice, signature, photograph, or likeness for advertising or commercial purposes; similar right of action for the knowing use of a living person's name, voice, signature, photograph, or likeness for similar purposes. Publicity rights for deceased personalities last for 100 years. Texts at http://www.oscn.net/applications/oscn/Index.asp?ftdb=STOKST12&level=1.

Tennessee Code Annotated § 47–25–1105: private right of action, similar to preceding, for unauthorized commercial use of a person's name, photograph, or likeness in any medium; makes such use a Class A misdemeanor and declares products or goods involved to be contraband, subject to forfeiture. Text at http://law.justia.com/codes/tennessee/2014/title-47/chapter-25/part-11/section-47-25-1105.

Haelan Laboratories, Inc. v. Topps Chewing Gum, Inc., 202 F.2d 866 (2d Cir. 1953): US Court of Appeals for the Second Circuit, in a case involving a ballplayer's photograph, held that, "in addition to and independent of [a] right of privacy ... a man has a right in the publicity value of his photograph, i.e., the right to grant the exclusive privilege of publishing his picture." Text at http://law.justia.com/cases/federal/appellate-courts/F2/202/866/216744/.

Tariffs

Act of June 30, 1864, ch. 171, § 13, 13 Stat. 202, 213: imposed a 25-percent duty on imported books, periodicals, pamphlets, and similar items. Text at https://www.loc.gov/law/help/statutes-at-large/38th-congress/session-1/c38s1ch171.pdf.

Act of October 1, 1890, ch. 1244, § 513, 26 Stat. 567, 604: declared duty-free status of books and pamphlets printed exclusively in languages other than English. Text at https://www.loc.gov/law/help /statutes-at-large/51st-congress/session-1/c51s1ch1244.pdf.

Payne-Aldrich Tariff Act, August 5, 1909, ch. 6, §§ 416, 470, 517–18, 36 Stat. 11, 64, 70, 73–4: imposed a 25-percent duty on imported English-language books and other printed matter less than twenty years old; a 15-percent duty on paintings and other artworks; declared duty-free status of books and pamphlets printed chiefly in languages other than English. Text at https://www.loc.gov /law/help/statutes-at-large/61st-congress/session-1/c61s1ch6.pdf.

Underwood Tariff Act, October 3, 1913, ch. 16, §§ 325, 329, 331, 425–7, 652, 38 Stat. 114, 145–6, 155: imposed a 15-percent duty on imported English-language books and printed matter less than twenty years old; set duty rates for wood pulp, labels, playing cards, cigar bands, and similar items; declared duty-free status of imported books and pamphlets printed wholly or chiefly in languages other than English, as well as books imported by public libraries and educational institutions, and original paintings, drawings, and other artworks. Text at https://www.loc.gov/law/help/statutes-at -large/63rd-congress/session-1/c63s1ch16.pdf.

Wartime measures

Espionage Act of 1917, June 15, 1917, ch. 30, 40 Stat. 217: enacted shortly after the United States entered the First World War; prohibited acts of interference with American military operations or recruitment as well as activities supporting enemies during wartime. Title I, § 3 made it a crime, punishable by fine and/or up to twenty years' imprisonment, willfully to cause or attempt to cause insubordination, disloyalty, mutiny, or refusal of duty in US armed forces, or to obstruct the recruiting or enlistment service. Title XII, §§ 1–3 declared nonmailable any letter, book, newspaper, or other writing in violation of the statute, and made it a crime, punishable by fine and/or up to five years' imprisonment, to use or attempt to use the mails for such purposes. Text at https://www.loc.gov/law /help/statutes-at-large/65th-congress/session-1/c65s1ch30.pdf.

Sedition Act of 1918, May 16, 1918, ch. 75, 40 Stat. 553: amended preceding to make it a crime, punishable by fine and/or up to twenty years' imprisonment, during wartime willfully to "utter, print, write, or publish any disloyal, profane, scurrilous, or abusive language" about the form of US government, its Constitution, or armed forces, as well as many other kinds of written and spoken dissent concerning US war efforts. Text at https://www.loc.gov/law /help/statutes-at-large/65th-congress/session-2/c65s2ch75.pdf.

Soldier Voting Act, April 1, 1944, ch. 150, § 22, 58 Stat. 136, 148: prohibited the US executive branch and military from distributing to troops any book, periodical, film, or other material "containing political argument or political propaganda of any kind designed or calculated to affect [presidential or congressional elections]." Text at   https://www.loc.gov/law/help/statutes-at-large/78th-congress /c78s2.pdf.

Masses Publishing Co. v. Patten, 246 F. 24 (2d Cir. 1917): US Court of Appeals for the Second Circuit upheld the New York Postmaster's suppression of an issue of the magazine, *The Masses*, under **Espionage Act.** Reversing trial judge Learned Hand's ruling that the issue did not violate the Act and was protected as free speech, the Second Circuit concluded that the Postmaster had not abused his discretion in deeming the issue "an attempt to cause insubordination, disloyalty, mutiny, or refusal of [military] duty." Text at https://www.thefire.org/u-s-court-of-appeals-for-the -second-circuit-opinion-for-masses-publishing-co-v-patten/.

WORKS CITED

Agamben, Giorgio. *State of Exception*. Trans. Kevin Attell. Chicago: U of Chicago P, 2005.

Alexander, James R. "Evil Angel Eulogy: Reflections on the Passing of the Obscenity Defense in Copyright." *Journal of Intellectual Property Law* 20.2 (April 2013): 209–314.

Alldridge, Peter. "'Attempted Murder of the Soul': Blackmail, Privacy and Secrets." *Oxford Journal of Legal Studies* 13.3 (Autumn 1993): 368–87.

Anderson, E.H. "Tax on Ideas." *Bulletin of the American Library Association* 8.4 (July 1914): 73–7.

Anderson, Margaret C. Affidavit. Anderson v. Patton, No. E14–379, 247 F. 382 (S.D.N.Y. 1917).

Baldwin, Peter. *The Copyright Wars: Three Centuries of Trans-Atlantic Battle*. Princeton, NJ: Princeton UP, 2014.

Barendt, Eric. "Defamation and Fiction." *Law and Literature: Current Legal Issues*. Vol. 2. Ed. Michael Freeman and Andrew Lewis. Oxford: Oxford UP, 1999. 481–98.

Barlow, John Perry. "The Economy of Ideas." *Wired* 2.03 (March 1994), https://www.wired.com/1994/03/economy-ideas/?topic=online_commerce&topic_set=neweconomy. Visited February 14, 2018.

Bartholomew, Mark. "A Right Is Born: Celebrity, Property, and Postmodern Lawmaking." *Connecticut Law Review* 44.2 (December 2011): 301–68.

Beard, Charles A. *The Republic: Conversations on Fundamentals*. New York: Viking, 1943.

Beckerman-Rodau, Andrew. "The Problem with Intellectual Property Rights: Subject Matter Expansion." *Yale Journal of Law and Technology* 13.1 (2011): 35–89.

Beebe, Barton. "*Bleistein*, the Problem of Aesthetic Progress, and the Making of American Copyright Law." *Columbia Law Review* 117.2 (March 2017): 319–97.

Birmingham, Kevin. *The Most Dangerous Book: The Battle for James Joyce's Ulysses*. New York: Penguin, 2014.

Black's Law Dictionary. 6th ed. St. Paul, MN: West, 1990.

Boyer, Paul S. *Purity in Print: Book Censorship in America from the Gilded Age to the Computer Age.* 2nd ed. Madison: U of Wisconsin P, 2002.

Boyle, James. *The Public Domain: Enclosing the Commons of the Mind.* New Haven, CT: Yale UP, 2008.

Brainard, Morgan. Letter to Judge John M. Woolsey (March 29, 1934). John Munro Woolsey Papers, Yale Law School.

Briggs, Julia. *Virginia Woolf: An Inner Life.* Boston, MA: Harcourt, 2005.

Broun, Heywood, and Margaret Leech. *Anthony Comstock: Roundsman of the Lord.* New York: Literary Guild of America, 1927.

Calabresi, Guido, and A. Douglas Melamed. "Property Rules, Liability Rules, and Inalienability: One View of the Cathedral." *Harvard Law Review* 85.6 (April 1972): 1089–1128.

Calkins, Raymond. Letter to Samuel Roth (February14, 1927). Samuel Roth Papers, Columbia University.

Carpenter, Humphrey. *A Serious Character: The Life of Ezra Pound.* Boston, MA: Houghton Mifflin, 1988.

Carpenter, William Boyd. *Popular History of the Church of England from the Earliest Times to the Present Day.* London: John Murray, 1900.

Cerf, Bennett. *At Random: The Reminiscences of Bennett Cerf.* New York: Random House, 2002.

Chew, Samuel C. *Swinburne.* Boston: Little, Brown, 1929.

Chisholm, Hugh. "How to Counteract the 'Penny Dreadful.'" *Fortnightly Review* 58 (n.s.) (November 1, 1895): 765–75.

Christopher, Russell. "Meta-Blackmail." *Georgetown Law Journal* 94 (March 2006): 739–85.

Coase, Ronald. "Blackmail." *Virginia Law Review* 74.4 (May 1988): 655–76.

Cohen, Ed. *Talk on the Wilde Side: Towards a Genealogy of a Discourse on Male Sexualities.* New York: Routledge, 1993.

Cole, John Y. "The Armed Services Editions: An Introduction." *Books in Action: The Armed Services Editions.* Ed. John Y. Cole. Washington, DC: Library of Congress, 1984. 3–11.

Collier, Patrick. "Virginia Woolf in the Pay of Booksellers: Commerce, Privacy, Professionalism, *Orlando.*" *Twentieth Century Literature* 48.4 (Winter 2002): 363–92.

Comstock, Anthony. *Frauds Exposed; Or, How the People Are Deceived and Robbed, and Youth Corrupted.* New York: J. Howard Brown, 1880.

Comstock, Anthony. *Traps for the Young.* 3rd ed. New York: Funk and Wagnalls, 1883.

Conan Doyle, Arthur. "Adventure of Charles Augustus Milverton." *Strand Magazine* 27 (April 1904): 373–83.

Cooley, Thomas M. *Treatise on the Law of Torts*. Chicago: Callaghan, 1879.

Cornell, Julien. *Trial of Ezra Pound: A Documented Account of the Treason Case by the Defendant's Lawyer*. London: Faber and Faber, 1966.

Cox, David J. *Public Indecency in England 1857–1960: "A Serious and Growing Evil."* London: Routledge, 2015.

Danson, Lawrence. *Wilde's Intentions: The Artist in His Criticism*. Oxford: Clarendon, 1997.

Darling, Kate, and Aaron Perzanowski, eds. *Creativity without Law: Challenging the Assumptions of Intellectual Property*. New York: New York UP, 2017.

Darnton, Robert. "What Is the History of Books?" *Daedalus* 111.3 (Summer 1982): 65–83.

Davis, Lennard J. *Factual Fictions: The Origins of the English Novel*. Philadelphia: U of Pennsylvania P, 1983.

Decherney, Peter. *Hollywood's Copyright Wars: From Edison to the Internet*. New York: Columbia UP, 2012.

De Grazia, Edward. *Girls Lean Back Everywhere: The Law of Obscenity and the Assault on Genius*. New York: Vintage, 1993.

Delany, Paul. "Who Paid for Modernism?" *New Economic Criticism: Studies at the Interface of Literature and Economics*. Ed. Martha Woodmansee and Mark Osteen. London: Routledge, 1999. 335–51.

De Rachewiltz, Mary. "Mens Sine Affectu." *Modernism and Copyright*. Ed. Paul K. Saint-Amour. New York: Oxford UP, 2011. 265–71.

DeSalvo, Louise A. *Virginia Woolf's First Voyage: A Novel in the Making*. Totowa: NJ: Rowman and Littlefield, 1980.

Dickens, Charles. *Speeches of Charles Dickens*. Ed. Richard Herne Shepherd. London: Chatto and Windus, 1884.

Diepeveen, Leonard. *Changing Voices: The Modern Quoting Poem*. Ann Arbor: U of Michigan P, 1993.

Dore, Florence. *The Novel and the Obscene: Sexual Subjects in American Modernism*. Stanford, CA: Stanford UP, 2005.

Edel, Leon. *Henry James: A Life*. New York: Harper & Row, 1985.

Eliot, T.S. "*From* Philip Massinger." *Selected Prose of T.S. Eliot*. Ed. Frank Kermode. New York: Harcourt, 1975. 153–60.

Eliot, T.S. "*Ulysses*, Order, and Myth." *Selected Prose of T.S. Eliot*. Ed. Frank Kermode. New York: Harcourt, 1975. 175–8.

Eliot, T.S. *The Waste Land. Collected Poems 1909–1962*. New York: Harcourt, 1970. 51–76.

Ellmann, Richard. *James Joyce*. Rev. ed. New York: Oxford UP, 1982.

Ellmann, Richard. *Oscar Wilde*. New York: Alfred A. Knopf, 1988.

Ernst, Morris L. *The Best Is Yet ....* New York: Harper and Brothers, 1945.

Ernst, Morris L., and Alexander Lindey. *The Censor Marches On: Recent Milestones in the Administration of the Obscenity Law in the United States*. New York: Da Capo, 1971.

Ernst, Morris L., and Alan U. Schwartz. *Censorship: The Search for the Obscene*. New York: Macmillan, 1964.

Ernst, Morris L., and William Seagle. *To the Pure ... : A Study of Obscenity and the Censor*. New York: Viking, 1928.

Fargnoli, Nicholas A., ed. "Oral History: B. W. Huebsch." *Dictionary of Literary Biography Yearbook 1999*. Ed. Matthew J. Bruccoli. Detroit, MI: Gale, 2000. 193–219.

Farley, David G. *Modernist Travel Writing: Intellectuals Abroad*. Columbia: U of Missouri P, 2010.

Foley, Kathryn M. "Protecting Fictional Characters: Defining the Elusive Trademark-Copyright Divide." *Connecticut Law Review* 41.3 (February 2009): 921–61.

Folkard, Henry Coleman. *Law of Slander and Libel*. 7th ed. London: Butterworth, 1908.

Ford, Hugh. *Published in Paris: American and British Writers, Printers, and Publishers in Paris, 1920–1939*. New York: Macmillan, 1975.

Friedman, Susan Stanford. *Psyche Reborn: The Emergence of H.D.* Bloomington: Indiana UP, 1981.

Frischmann, Brett M. "Evaluating the Demsetzian Trend in Copyright Law." *Review of Law and Economics* 3.3 (2007): 649–77.

Frischmann, Brett M., and Mark A. Lemley. "Spillovers." *Columbia Law Review* 107.1 (January 2007): 257–302.

Fysh, Stephanie. *Work(s) of Samuel Richardson*. Newark: U of Delaware P, 1997.

Gagnier, Regenia. *Idylls of the Marketplace: Oscar Wilde and the Victorian Public*. Stanford, CA: Stanford UP, 1986.

Gaines, Jane M. *Contested Culture: The Image, the Voice, and the Law*. Chapel Hill: U of North Carolina P, 1991.

Gallup, Donald. *Ezra Pound: A Bibliography*. Charlottesville: UP of Virginia, 1983.

Galoob, Stephen. "Coercion, Fraud, and What Is Wrong with Blackmail." *Legal Theory* 22.1 (March 2016): 22–58.

Galsworthy, John. "Blackmail." *Captures*. London: Heinemann, 1923. 127–46.

General Laws of the Commonwealth of Massachusetts. Vol. 2. Boston: Wright and Potter, 1921.

Genette, Gérard. *Paratexts: Thresholds of Interpretation*. Trans. Jane E. Lewin. Cambridge, UK: Cambridge UP, 1997.

Gertzman, Jay A. *Bookleggers and Smuthounds: The Trade in Erotica, 1920–1940*. Philadelphia: U of Pennsylvania P, 1999.

Gertzman, Jay A. *Samuel Roth: Infamous Modernist*. Gainesville: UP of Florida, 2013.

Gillers, Stephen. "A Tendency to Deprave and Corrupt: The Transformation of American Obscenity Law from *Hicklin* to *Ulysses II*." *Washington University Law Review* 85.2 (2007): 215–96.

Gillespie, Michael Patrick. *Oscar Wilde and the Poetics of Ambiguity*. Gainesville: UP of Florida, 1996.

Glass, Loren. *Counterculture Colophon: Grove Press, the Evergreen Review, and the Incorporation of the Avant-Garde*. Stanford, CA: Stanford UP, 2013.

Glass, Loren. "Redeeming Value: Obscenity and Anglo-American Modernism." *Critical Inquiry* 32.2 (Winter 2006): 341–61.

Goldman, Jonathan. *Modernism Is the Literature of Celebrity*. Austin: U of Texas P, 2009.

Greene, Graham. *The Power and the Glory*. New York: Compass Books, 1966.

Groves, Jeffrey D. "Courtesy of the Trade." *History of the Book in America, Vol. 3, The Industrial Book 1840–1880*. Ed. Scott E. Casper et al. Chapel Hill: U of North Carolina P, 2007. 139–48.

Hall, Radclyffe. *The Well of Loneliness*. New York: Covici Friede, 1928.

Harris, Frank. *George Bernard Shaw: An Unauthorised Biography*. Ware, UK: Wordsworth, 2008.

Hassett, Joseph M. *The* Ulysses *Trials: Beauty and Truth Meet the Law*. Dublin: Lilliput, 2016.

Haynes, Christine. "The Politics of Publishing during the Second Empire: The Trial of *Madame Bovary* Revisited." *French Politics, Culture and Society* 23.2 (Summer 2005): 1–27.

Heap, Jane. "Art and the Law." *Little Review* 7.3 (September–December 1920): 5–6.

Heller, Michael A. "Tragedy of the Anticommons: Property in the Transition from Marx to Markets." *Harvard Law Review* 111.3 (April 1998): 621–88.

Hemingway, Ernest. *In Our Time*. 1925. New York: Charles Scribner's Sons, 1930.

Hofer, Matthew, and Gary Scharnhorst, eds. *Oscar Wilde in America: The Interviews*. Urbana: U of Illinois P, 2010.

Holland, Merlin. *The Real Trial of Oscar Wilde*. New York: Fourth Estate, 2003.

Holt, Henry. "Competition." *Atlantic Monthly* 102 (October 1908): 516–26.

Houston, Lloyd. "(Il)legal Deposits: *Ulysses* and the Copyright Libraries." *Library* 18.2 (June 2017): 131–51.

Hyde, H. Montgomery. *The Trials of Oscar Wilde*. New York: Dover, 1973.

Hynes, Samuel. *A War Imagined: The First World War and English Culture*. New York: Collier, 1990.

Hynes, Samuel. *Edwardian Turn of Mind*. Princeton, NJ: Princeton UP, 1968.

Ibsen, Henrik. *Four Major Plays*. Vol. 1. Trans. Rolf Fjelde. New York: Signet, 1965.

Irr, Caren. *Pink Pirates: Contemporary American Women Writers and Copyright*. Iowa City: U of Iowa P, 2010.

James, Henry. "The Aspern Papers." *Novels and Tales of Henry James*. Vol. 12. New York: Charles Scribner's Sons, 1908. 3–143.

James, Henry. "The Birthplace." *Novels and Tales of Henry James*. Vol. 17. New York: Charles Scribner's Sons, 1909. 131–213.

James, Henry. *Bostonians*. London: Macmillan, 1886.

James, Henry. "In the Cage." *Novels and Tales of Henry James*. Vol. 11. New York: Charles Scribner's Sons, 1908. 367–507.

James, Henry. *Notebooks of Henry James*. Ed. F.O. Matthiessen and Kenneth B. Murdock. Chicago: U of Chicago P, 1947.

James, Henry. "The Private Life." *Novels and Tales of Henry James*. Vol. 17. New York: Charles Scribner's Sons, 1909. 217–66.

James, Henry. "The Real Right Thing." *Novels and Tales of Henry James*. Vol. 17. New York: Charles Scribner's Sons, 1909. 411–31.

James, Henry. "She and He: Recent Documents." *Yellow Book* 12 (January 1897): 15–38.

Joyce, James. "Communication de M. James Joyce sur le Droit Moral des Écrivains." *Critical Writings*. Ed. Ellsworth Mason and Richard Ellmann. New York: Viking, 1959. 274–5.

Joyce, James. *Letters of James Joyce*. Vol. 1. Ed. Stuart Gilbert. New York: Viking, 1957.

Joyce, James. "Oscar Wilde: The Poet of 'Salomé.'" *Critical Writings*. Ed. Ellsworth Mason and Richard Ellmann. New York: Viking, 1959. 201–5.

Katz, Daniel. *American Modernism's Expatriate Scene: The Labour of Translation*. Edinburgh: Edinburgh UP, 2007.

Keymer, Thomas. "Obscenity and the Erotics of Fiction." *The Cambridge History of the English Novel*. Ed. Robert L. Caserio and Clement C. Hawes. Cambridge, UK: Cambridge UP, 2012. 131–46.

Kinkead-Weekes, Mark. "Introduction." D.H. Lawrence, *The Rainbow*. Part I. Ed. Mark Kinkead-Weekes. Cambridge, UK: Cambridge UP, 2002. xix–lxxvi.

Koestenbaum, Wayne. *Double Talk: The Erotics of Male Literary Collaboration*. London: Routledge, 1989.

Latham, Sean. *Art of Scandal: Modernism, Libel Law, and the Roman à Clef*. New York: Oxford UP, 2009.

Lawrence, D.H. "A Propos of *Lady Chatterley's Lover.*" *A Selection from Phoenix.* Ed. A.A.H. Inglis. Harmondsworth, UK: Penguin, 1979. 327–61.

Lawrence, D.H. *Letters of D.H. Lawrence.* Vol. 3. Ed. James T. Boulton and Andrew Robertson. Cambridge, UK: Cambridge UP, 1984.

Lawrence, D.H. *Letters of D.H. Lawrence.* Vol. 4. Ed. Warren Roberts et al. Cambridge, UK: Cambridge UP, 1987.

Leaffer, Marshall. "The Right of Publicity: A Comparative Perspective." *Albany Law Review* 70.4 (Fall 2007): 1357–74.

Leavell, Linda. *Hanging on Upside Down: The Life and Work of Marianne Moore.* New York: Farrar, Straus and Giroux, 2013.

Lefebvre, Louis. "René Char et le Droit de Divulgation Post Mortem." *Revue Générale du Droit* (December 2014), http://www.revuegeneraledudroit.eu/blog/2014/12/11/rene-char-et-le-droit-de-divulgation-post-mortem/. Visited February 14, 2018.

Lemley, Mark A. "IP in a World without Scarcity." *New York University Law Review* 90.2 (May 2015): 460–515.

Lemley, Mark A. "Romantic Authorship and the Rhetoric of Property." *Texas Law Review* 75 (March 1997): 873–906.

Lewis, Lloyd, and Henry Justin Smith. *Oscar Wilde Discovers America.* New York: Benjamin Blom, 1936.

Lewis, Wyndham. *Tarr.* New York: Alfred A. Knopf, 1918.

Macaulay, Thomas Babington. *Works of Lord Macaulay Complete.* Vol. 8. Ed. Lady Trevelyan. London: Longmans, Green, 1871.

Madison, Charles A. *Book Publishing in America.* New York: McGraw-Hill, 1966.

Manchester, Colin. "Lord Campbell's Act: England's First Obscenity Statute." *Journal of Legal History* 9.2 (September 1988): 223–41.

Marshik, Celia. *British Modernism and Censorship.* Cambridge, UK: Cambridge UP, 2006.

Marshik, Celia. "History's 'Abrupt Revenges': Censoring War's Perversions in *The Well of Loneliness* and *Sleeveless Errand.*" *Journal of Modern Literature* 26.2 (Winter 2003): 145–59.

Marshik, Celia. "Thinking Back through Copyright: Individual Rights and Collective Life in Virginia Woolf's Nonfiction." *Modernism and Copyright.* Ed. Paul K. Saint-Amour. New York: Oxford UP, 2011. 65–86.

Mason, Stuart. *Bibliography of Oscar Wilde.* Intro. Robert Ross. London: T. Werner Laurie, 1914.

Mason, Stuart. *Oscar Wilde: Art and Morality.* London: J. Jacobs, 1908.

Max, D.T. "Injustice Collector: Is James Joyce's Grandson Suppressing Scholarship?" *New Yorker* (June 19, 2006): 34–43.

McCleery, Alistair. "Trials and Travels of *Lady Chatterley's Lover.*" *Reading Penguin: A Critical Anthology.* Ed. William Wootten and

George Donaldson. Newcastle upon Tyne, UK: Cambridge Scholars, 2013. 27–48.

McKinney, William M., ed. *Consolidated Laws of New York, Annotated.* Bk. 39. New York: Edward Thompson, 1917.

McLaren, Angus. *Sexual Blackmail: A Modern History.* Cambridge, MA: Harvard UP, 2002.

Mead, Frederick, and A.H. Bodkin. *Criminal Law Amendment Act, 1885, with Introduction, Notes, and Index.* London: Shaw and Sons, 1885.

Medina Casado, Carmelo. "Sifting through Censorship: The British Home Office *Ulysses* Files (1922–1936)." *James Joyce Quarterly* 37.3–4 (Spring–Summer 2000): 479–508.

Moody, A. David. *Ezra Pound: Poet, A Portrait of the Man and His Work. Volume I: The Young Genius 1885–1920.* New York: Oxford UP, 2007.

Moore, George. *Literature at Nurse, or Circulating Morals.* London: Vizetelly, 1885.

Morrisson, Mark S. *Public Face of Modernism: Little Magazines, Audiences, and Reception, 1905–1920.* Madison: U of Wisconsin P, 2001.

Moscato, Michael, and Leslie LeBlanc, eds. *United States of America v. One Book Entitled* Ulysses *by James Joyce: Documents and Commentary.* Frederick, MD: U Publications of America, 1984.

"Mr. Oscar Wilde's 'Dorian Gray.'" *Pall Mall Gazette* (June 26, 1890): 3.

Mullin, Katherine. *James Joyce, Sexuality and Social Purity.* Cambridge, UK: Cambridge UP, 2003.

Mullin, Katherine. *Working Girls: Fiction, Sexuality, and Modernity.* Oxford: Oxford UP, 2016.

Murray, Douglas. *Bosie: A Biography of Lord Alfred Douglas.* New York: Hyperion, 2000.

Netanel, Neil Weinstock. *Copyright's Paradox.* New York: Oxford UP, 2008.

Norman, Charles. *Ezra Pound.* Rev. ed. New York: Minerva, 1969.

North, Michael. "The Picture of Oscar Wilde." *PMLA* 125.1 (January 2010): 185–91.

Novak, Daniel A. "Sexuality in the Age of Technological Reproducibility: Oscar Wilde, Photography, and Identity." *Oscar Wilde and Modern Culture: The Making of a Legend.* Ed. Joseph Bristow. Athens: Ohio UP, 2008. 63–95.

Nowlin, Christopher. *Judging Obscenity: A Critical History of Expert Evidence.* Montreal: McGill-Queen's UP, 2003.

Odgers, W. Blake. *Law of Libel and Slander.* Vol. 1. Philadelphia: Blackstone, 1887.

Odgers, W. Blake. *Outline of the Law of Libel.* London: Macmillan, 1897.

Painter, George D. *Marcel Proust: A Biography.* Vol. 1. New York: Vintage, 1978.

Parkes, Adam. "Censorship and the Novel." *Encyclopedia of Twentieth-Century Fiction*. Vol. 1. Ed. Brian W. Shaffer. Oxford: Ailey-Blackwell, 2011. 63–8.

Parkes, Adam. *Modernism and the Theater of Censorship*. New York: Oxford UP, 1996.

Pater, Walter. *The Renaissance: Studies in Art and Poetry*. 3rd ed. London: Macmillan, 1888.

Patterson, L. Ray, and Stanley W. Lindberg. *Nature of Copyright: A Law of Users' Rights*. Athens: U of Georgia P, 1991.

Paul, James C.N., and Murray L. Schwartz. *Federal Censorship: Obscenity in the Mail*. New York: Free P of Glencoe, 1961.

Pease, Allison. *Modernism, Mass Culture, and the Aesthetics of Obscenity*. Cambridge, UK: Cambridge UP, 2000.

Pennell, E.R., and J. Pennell. *Life of James McNeill Whistler*. Vol. 1. Philadelphia: J. B. Lippincott, 1908.

Plath, Sylvia. *The Bell Jar*. New York: Harper Perennial, 2006.

Plath, Sylvia. *Unabridged Journals of Sylvia Plath: 1950–1962*. Ed. Karen V. Kukil. New York: Anchor, 2000.

"The Poet and the Peanut Boy." *Fort Collins Courier* (May 4, 1882): 1.

Posner, Richard A. *Law and Literature: A Misunderstood Relation*. Cambridge, MA: Harvard UP, 1988.

Posner, Richard A. "The Right of Privacy." *Georgia Law Review* 12.3 (Spring 1978): 393–422.

Potter, Rachel. *Obscene Modernism: Literary Censorship and Experiment, 1900–1940*. Oxford: Oxford UP, 2013.

Pound, Ezra. "ABC of Economics." *Selected Prose 1909–1965*. Ed. and Intro. William Cookson. New York: New Directions, 1973. 233–64.

Pound, Ezra. "American Book Pirates." *Poetry and Prose Contributions to Periodicals*. Ed. Lea Baechler et al. 11 vols. New York: Garland, 1991. 4:383.

Pound, Ezra. "A Visiting Card." *Selected Prose 1909–1965*. Ed. and Intro. William Cookson. New York: New Directions, 1973. 306–35.

Pound, Ezra. *Cantos*. New York: New Directions, 1995.

Pound, Ezra. "The Classics 'Escape.'" *Poetry and Prose Contributions to Periodicals*. Ed. Lea Baechler et al. 11 vols. New York: Garland, 1991. 3:63–4.

Pound, Ezra. "Copyright and Tariff." *Poetry and Prose Contributions to Periodicals*. Ed. Lea Baechler et al. 11 vols. New York: Garland, 1991. 3:208–9.

Pound, Ezra. *Ezra and Dorothy Pound: Letters in Captivity, 1945–1946*. Ed. Omar Pound and Robert Spoo. New York: Oxford UP, 1999. Cited as "*Ezra and Dorothy*."

Pound, Ezra. *Ezra Pound and Margaret Cravens: A Tragic Friendship, 1910–1912*. Ed. Omar Pound and Robert Spoo. Durham, NC: Duke UP, 1988. Cited as "*Pound-Cravens*."

Pound, Ezra. *Ezra Pound and Senator Bronson Cutting: A Political Correspondence, 1930–1935*. Ed. E. P. Walkiewicz and Hugh Witemeyer. Albuquerque: U of New Mexico P, 1995. Cited as "*Pound-Cutting*."

Pound, Ezra. "Four Steps." *Poetry and Prose Contributions to Periodicals*. Ed. Lea Baechler et al. 11 vols. New York: Garland, 1991. 10:186–93.

Pound, Ezra. "The Individual in His Milieu." *Selected Prose 1909–1965*. Ed. and Intro. William Cookson. New York: New Directions, 1973. 272–82.

Pound, Ezra. "In Explanation." *Poetry and Prose Contributions to Periodicals*. Ed. Lea Baechler et al. 11 vols. New York: Garland, 1991. 3:142–3.

Pound, Ezra. *Letters of Ezra Pound to James Joyce*. Ed. Forrest Read. New York: New Directions, 1970. Cited as "*Pound-Joyce*."

Pound, Ezra. *Letters of Ezra Pound to Margaret Anderson:* The Little Review *Correspondence*. Ed. Thomas L. Scott and Melvin J. Friedman. New York: New Directions, 1988. Cited as "*Pound-Anderson*."

Pound, Ezra. "Newspapers, History, Etc." *Poetry and Prose Contributions to Periodicals*. Ed. Lea Baechler et al. 11 vols. New York: Garland, 1991. 5:227–30.

Pound, Ezra. "Patria Mia." *Selected Prose 1909–1965*. Ed. and Intro. William Cookson. New York: New Directions, 1973. 99–141.

Pound, Ezra. *Personae: The Shorter Poems*. Rev. ed. Ed. Lea Baechler and A. Walton Litz. New York: New Directions, 1990.

Pound, Ezra. "Pound for President." *Poetry and Prose Contributions to Periodicals*. Ed. Lea Baechler et al. 11 vols. New York: Garland, 1991. 4:393.

Pound, Ezra. *Pound, Thayer, Watson, and* The Dial: *A Story in Letters*. Ed. Walter Sutton. Gainesville: UP of Florida, 1994. Cited as "*Pound*-Dial."

Pound, Ezra. *Selected Letters of Ezra Pound to John Quinn, 1915–1924*. Ed. Timothy Materer. Durham, NC: Duke UP, 1991. Cited as "*Pound-Quinn*."

Pound, Ezra. "Tariff and Copyright." *Poetry and Prose Contributions to Periodicals*. Ed. Lea Baechler et al. 11 vols. New York: Garland, 1991. 3:226–9.

Pound, Ezra. "Things to Be Done." *Poetry and Prose Contributions to Periodicals*. Ed. Lea Baechler et al. 11 vols. New York: Garland, 1991. 2:190.

Pound, Ezra. "This Approaches Literature!" *Poetry and Prose Contributions to Periodicals*. Ed. Lea Baechler et al. 11 vols. New York: Garland, 1991. 2:283.

"Praises Underwood for Free Art Fight: Removal of Tariff on Modern Works Largely Due to His Efforts, Says John Quinn." *New York Times* (September 26, 1913): 10.

Prosser, William L. "Privacy." *California Law Review* 48.3 (August 1960): 383–423.

Public General Statutes Passed in the Forty-Seventh and Forty-Eighth Years of the Reign of Her Majesty Queen Victoria. London: Queen's Printing Office, 1884.

Pulling, Alexander, ed. *Defence of the Realm Manual.* 5th ed. London: His Majesty's Stationery Office, 1918.

Quinn, John. Brief on Behalf of Complainant in Support of Motion for Injunction Pendente Lite. Anderson v. Patton, No. E14–379, 247 F. 382 (S.D.N.Y. 1917).

Quinn, John. Letter to James Joyce (August 15, 1920). John Quinn Memorial Collection, New York Public Library, Manuscripts and Archives Division.

Quinn, John. Letter to James Joyce (April 13, 1921). John Quinn Memorial Collection, New York Public Library, Manuscripts and Archives Division.

Rainey, Lawrence. *Institutions of Modernism: Literary Elites and Public Culture.* New Haven, CT: Yale UP, 1998.

Raustiala, Kal, and Christopher Sprigman. *Knockoff Economy: How Imitation Sparks Innovation.* New York: Oxford UP, 2012.

Reid, B. L. *Man from New York: John Quinn and His Friends.* New York: Oxford UP, 1968.

Rembar, Charles. *End of Obscenity: The Trials of* Lady Chatterley, Tropic of Cancer *and* Fanny Hill. New York: Random House, 1968.

Report from the Select Committee of the House of Lords Appointed to Consider the Law of Defamation and Libel. N.p., 1843.

Richards, Neil M., and Daniel J. Solove. "Privacy's Other Path: Recovering the Law of Confidentiality." *Georgetown Law Journal* 96.1 (November 2007): 123–82.

Rimmer, Matthew. "Bloomsday: Copyright Estates and Cultural Festivals." *SCRIPTed* 2.3 (September 2005): 383–428.

Roberts, Warren, and Paul Poplawski. *Bibliography of D.H. Lawrence.* 3rd ed. Cambridge, UK: Cambridge UP, 2001.

Robertson, Geoffrey. *Obscenity: An Account of Censorship Laws and Their Enforcement in England and Wales.* London: Weidenfeld and Nicolson, 1979.

Rolph, C.H., ed. *Trial of Lady Chatterley: Regina v. Penguin Books Limited: The Transcript of the Trial.* London: Penguin, 1961.

Rose, Mark. *Authors and Owners: The Invention of Copyright.* Cambridge, MA: Harvard UP, 1993.

Rose, Mark. *Authors in Court: Scenes from the Theater of Copyright.* Cambridge, MA: Harvard UP, 2016.

Rosenblatt, Elizabeth L. "Adventure of the Shrinking Public Domain." *University of Colorado Law Review* 86 (Spring 2015): 561–630.

Roth, Samuel. *Stone Walls Do Not: The Chronicle of a Captivity.* New York: William Faro, 1930.

Rushing, Conrad L. "'Mere Words': The Trial of Ezra Pound." *Critical Inquiry* 14.1 (Autumn 1987): 111–33.

Saint-Amour, Paul K. *The Copywrights: Intellectual Property and the Literary Imagination*. Ithaca, NY: Cornell UP, 2003.

Saint-Amour, Paul K. "Introduction: Modernism and the Lives of Copyright." *Modernism and Copyright*. Ed. Paul K. Saint-Amour. New York: Oxford UP, 2011. 1–36.

Saint-Amour, Paul K. Review of William M. Landes and Richard Posner, *Economic Structure of Intellectual Property Law*. *Modernism/ modernity* 12.3 (September 2005): 511–13.

Saint-Amour, Paul K. *Tense Future: Modernism, Total War, Encyclopedic Form*. New York: Oxford UP, 2015.

Salmon, Richard. *Henry James and the Culture of Publicity*. Cambridge, UK: Cambridge UP, 1997.

Salter, Mark B. *Rights of Passage: The Passport in International Relations*. Boulder, CO: Lynne Riener, 2003.

Sax, Joseph L. *Playing Darts with a Rembrandt: Public and Private Rights in Cultural Treasures*. Ann Arbor: U of Michigan P, 1999.

Schmitt, Carl. *Political Theology: Four Chapters on the Concept of Sovereignty*. Trans. George Schwab. Cambridge, MA: MIT P, 1985.

Schwartz, Paul M., and Karl-Nikolaus Peifer. "Prosser's Privacy and the German Right of Personality: Are Four Privacy Torts Better than One Unitary Concept?" *California Law Review* 98.6 (December 2010): 1925–87.

Scott, Bonnie Kime, ed. *Gender in Modernism: New Geographies, Complex Intersections*. Urbana: U of Illinois P, 2007.

Seshagiri, Urmila. *Race and the Modernist Imagination*. Ithaca, NY: Cornell UP, 2010.

Seville, Catherine. *Literary Copyright Reform in Early Victorian England: The Framing of the 1842 Copyright Act*. Cambridge, UK: Cambridge UP, 1999.

Shelden, Michael. *Graham Greene: The Man Within*. London: Heinemann, 1994.

Sherry, Norman. *The Life of Graham Greene. Volume One: 1904–1939*. London: Jonathan Cape, 1989.

Shloss, Carol Loeb. "Privacy and Piracy in the Joyce Trade: James Joyce and Le Droit Moral." *James Joyce Quarterly* 37.3–4 (Spring-Summer 2000): 447–57.

Showalter, Elaine. *Sexual Anarchy: Gender and Culture at the Fin de Siècle*. New York: Viking, 1990.

Sinfield, Alan. *Wilde Century: Effeminacy, Oscar Wilde, and the Queer Moment*. London: Cassell, 1994.

Slocum, John J., and Herbert Cahoon. *Bibliography of James Joyce*. Westport, CT: Greenwood, 1971.

Smethurst, James. *African American Roots of Modernism: From Reconstruction to the Harlem Renaissance*. Chapel Hill: U of North Carolina P, 2011.

Solove, Daniel J. "A Taxonomy of Privacy." *University of Pennsylvania Law Review* 154.3 (January 2006): 477–560.

Spoo, Robert. "Copyright Protectionism and Its Discontents: The Case of James Joyce's *Ulysses* in America." *Yale Law Journal* 108.3 (December 1998): 633–67.

Spoo, Robert. "Courtesy Paratexts, Informal Publishing Norms and the Copyright Vacuum in Nineteenth-Century America." *Stanford Law Review* 69.3 (March 2017): 637–710.

Spoo, Robert. "Three Myths for Aging Copyrights: Tithonus, Dorian Gray, Ulysses." *Cardozo Arts and Entertainment Law Journal* 31.1 (2012): 77–112.

Spoo, Robert. "The Uncoordinated Public Domain." *Cardozo Arts and Entertainment Law Journal* 35.1 (2016): 107–51.

Spoo, Robert. *Without Copyrights: Piracy, Publishing, and the Public Domain*. New York: Oxford UP, 2013.

Statutes, Vol. IX, from the Session of the Sixteenth and Seventeenth to the Session of the Twentieth and Twenty-First Years of Queen Victoria. 2nd rev. ed. London: Her Majesty's Stationery Office, 1895.

Stern, Simon. "Wilde's Obscenity Effect: Influence and Immorality in *The Picture of Dorian Gray*." *Review of English Studies* 68.286 (September 2017): 756–72.

Stevenson, Robert Louis. *Strange Case of Dr. Jekyll and Mr. Hyde*. London: Longmans, Green, 1886.

Taylor, Richard C. *Goldsmith as Journalist*. Cranbury, NJ: Associated UP, 1993.

"Testimony of Mr. John Quinn, on Behalf of the Association of American Painters and Sculptors, Inc." *Tariff Schedule: Hearings before the Committee on Ways and Means, House of Representatives*. 62nd Congress, 3rd Session, Doc. No. 1447. Vol. V, Ed. Sched. M and N. Washington, DC: Government Printing Office, 1913. 5692–708.

Tushnet, Rebecca. "Economies of Desire: Fair Use and Marketplace Assumptions." *William and Mary Law Review* 51.2 (November 2009): 513–46.

"Unfair Enterprise." Editorial. *Nation* 108 (January 4, 1919): 7.

Vanderham, Paul. *James Joyce and Censorship: The Trials of "Ulysses."* New York: New York UP, 1998.

Veblen, Thorstein. *Theory of the Leisure Class*. 1899. New York: Penguin, 1979.

Veeder, Van Vechten. "History and Theory of the Law of Defamation. II." *Columbia Law Review* 4.1 (January 1904): 33–56.

Vermeule, Adrian. "Our Schmittian Administrative Law." *Harvard Law Review* 122.4 (February 2009): 1095–1149.

Vivian, Herbert. "Reminiscences of a Short Life." *Oscar Wilde: Interviews and Recollections.* Vol. 1. Ed. E.H. Mikhail. London: Macmillan, 1979. 154–8.

Vizetelly, Ernest Alfred. *Émile Zola: Novelist and Reformer.* London: John Lane, 1904.

Warren, Samuel D., and Louis. D. Brandeis. "The Right to Privacy." *Harvard Law Review* 4.5 (December 15, 1890): 193–220.

Weinrib, Laura M. "Sex Side of Civil Liberties: *United States v. Dennett* and the Changing Face of Free Speech." *Law and Historical Review* 30.2 (May 2012): 325–86.

West, Rebecca. *New Meaning of Treason.* New York: Viking, 1964.

Wexler, Joyce Piell. *Who Paid for Modernism? Art, Money, and the Fiction of Conrad, Joyce, and Lawrence.* Fayetteville: U of Arkansas P, 1997.

Whistler, James McNeill. *Gentle Art of Making Enemies.* London: William Heinemann, 1904.

Wilde, Oscar. "A Few Maxims for the Instruction of the Over-Educated." *Complete Works of Oscar Wilde.* New York: Perennial, 1989. 1203–4.

Wilde, Oscar. *An Ideal Husband. Complete Works of Oscar Wilde.* New York: Perennial, 1989. 482–551.

Wilde, Oscar. "The Canterville Ghost." *Complete Works of Oscar Wilde.* New York: Perennial, 1989. 193–214.

Wilde, Oscar. "The Case of Warder Martin: Some Cruelties of Prison Life." *Complete Works of Oscar Wilde.* New York: Perennial, 1989. 958–64.

Wilde, Oscar. *Complete Letters of Oscar Wilde.* Ed. Merlin Holland and Rupert Hart-Davis. New York: Henry Holt, 2000.

Wilde, Oscar. "The Critic as Artist." *Complete Works of Oscar Wilde.* New York: Perennial, 1989. 1009–59.

Wilde, Oscar. "The Decay of Lying." *Complete Works of Oscar Wilde.* New York: Perennial, 1989. 970–92.

Wilde, Oscar. *De Profundis. Complete Letters of Oscar Wilde.* Ed. Merlin Holland and Rupert Hart-Davis. New York: Henry Holt, 2000. 683–780.

Wilde, Oscar. *Importance of Being Earnest. Complete Works of Oscar Wilde.* New York: Perennial, 1989. 321–84.

Wilde, Oscar. "Impressions of America." *Oscar Wilde in America: The Interviews.* Ed. Matthew Hofer and Gary Scharnhorst. Urbana: U of Illinois P, 2010. 177–82.

Wilde, Oscar. *Lady Windermere's Fan. Complete Works of Oscar Wilde.* New York: Perennial, 1989. 385–430.

Wilde, Oscar. "On the Sale by Auction of Keats' Love Letters." *Complete Works of Oscar Wilde.* New York: Perennial, 1989. 815.

Wilde, Oscar. *The Picture of Dorian Gray. Lippincott's Monthly Magazine* 46 (July 1890): 1–100. Cited as "1890."

Wilde, Oscar. *The Picture of Dorian Gray.* 1891. *Complete Works of Oscar Wilde.* New York: Perennial, 1989. Cited as "1891."

Wilde, Oscar. "The Selfish Giant." *Complete Works of Oscar Wilde.* New York: Perennial, 1989. 297–300.

Wilde, Oscar. "Soul of Man under Socialism." *Complete Works of Oscar Wilde.* New York: Perennial, 1989. 1079–1104.

Wilson, Nicola. "Circulating Morals (1900–1915)." *Prudes on the Prowl: Fiction and Obscenity in England, 1850 to the Present Day.* Ed. David Bradshaw and Rachel Potter. Oxford: Oxford UP, 2013. 52–70.

Wise, Thomas J. *Bibliographical List of the Scarcer Works and Uncollected Writings of Algernon Charles Swinburne.* London: privately printed, 1897.

Woolf, Virginia. *A Room of One's Own.* New York: Harcourt, 1957.

Woolf, Virginia. *Diary of Virginia Woolf.* Vol. 1. Ed. Anne Olivier Bell. New York: Harcourt, 1977.

Woolf, Virginia. *Letters of Virginia Woolf.* Vol. 1. Ed. Nigel Nicolson and Joanne Trautmann. New York: Harcourt, 1975.

Woolf, Virginia. *Letters of Virginia Woolf.* Vol. 2. Ed. Nigel Nicolson and Joanne Trautmann. New York: Harcourt, 1976.

Woolf, Virginia. *Letters of Virginia Woolf.* Vol. 3. Ed. Nigel Nicolson and Joanne Trautmann. New York: Harcourt, 1977.

Woolf, Virginia. *Night and Day.* New York: Harcourt, 1948.

Woolf, Virginia. "The Patron and the Crocus." *Common Reader.* New York: Harcourt, 1953. 211–5.

Worthen, John. "D.H. Lawrence and the 'Expensive Edition Business.'" *Modernist Writers and the Marketplace.* Ed. Ian Willison, Warwick Gould, and Warren Chernaik. London: Macmillan, 1996. 105–23.

INDEX

Abercrombie, Lascelles 105
Acker, Kathy 81
Adams, John 145
affirmative defense. *See under*
   Wilde, Oscar
Agamben, Giorgio 6
Agreement for the Suppression of
   Obscene Publications 64
Aiken, Conrad 148
Aldington, Richard 106
Alfred A. Knopf (publisher) 96,
   97, 143. *See also* Knopf,
   Alfred
Allatini, Rose
   Despised and Rejected 69
Anderson, Margaret 7, 50, 59,
   67, 71
anticommons 39–40, 44, 100
Armed Services Editions.
   See under Pound, Ezra

Barnes, Djuna 83, 93
   Nightwood 50
Baudelaire, Charles 42, 64
Beach, Sylvia 2, 87, 88, 89. *See
   also* Shakespeare and
   Company
Beard, Charles A.
   *The Republic: Conversations
   on Fundamentals* 134, 145,
   147
Beasley, Gertrude 89
   My First Thirty Years 65
Beckett, Samuel 101, 119

Benét, William Rose 148
Bennett, Arnold
   The Old Wives' Tale 91
Berne Convention for the
   Protection of Literary and
   Artistic Works 85, 138, 142
Best, Robert 148
Bible 67, 132
Birrell, Augustine 143
blackmail 4–5, 10, 11, 12, 25–8,
   104, 108–17, 126
   badger game 25–6
   laws 109, 113, 117
   as murder 113
   paradox of 109
   prior restraint 10, 108
   renting 109, 110, 114, 126
   and reputation 4, 9–10, 25, 29,
   115
   and sexuality 109, 110, 111
   as vampirism 113–15
   and working classes 10, 27,
   111–12, 114–15
   See also Conan Doyle, Arthur;
   Wilde, Oscar
blasphemy 1–2, 16, 42–43,
   62, 143. *See also* Lord
   Chamberlain; Wilde, Oscar
Boccaccio, Giovanni 7, 67
   The Decameron 66
Boni and Liveright (publisher) 57,
   64, 96
book tariffs 131–4, 137–8, 142.
   See also under Pound, Ezra

Boston Booksellers' Association 48

Brandeis, Louis D. *See* Warren, Samuel D., and Louis D. Brandeis

Bridson, D.G. 127

British Broadcasting Corporation (BBC) 106, 127

Bryher (Annie Winifred Ellerman) 88

Buenos Aires Convention 88–9

Bushel, Judge Hyman 58, 61

Byron, Lord 90

Cabell, James Branch
Jurgen: A Comedy of Justice 64

Caldwell, Erskine
God's Little Acre 76

Candy (novel by Terry Southern and Mason Hoffenberg) 91

Carnevali, Emanuel 93

Carson, Edward 22–4, 40–41, 42, 43, 74

Cather, Willa 134

censorship. *See* obscenity

Cerf, Bennett 95, 96–7, 148.
See also Random House

Chandler, Douglas 148

Chaplin, Charlie 48, 125

Char, René 99

Chatterton, Thomas 39

Chesterton, G.K. 143

Churchill, Winston 129

circulating libraries 13, 46, 47, 49–50, 58. *See also* Mudie's; W.H. Smith

Circulating Libraries Association 50. *See also* circulating libraries

Clarke, Edward 25, 53

Cleland, John
Memoirs of a Woman of Pleasure (*Fanny Hill*) 56–7, 72

Clibborn, Robert 109

Coke, Sir Edward 128

Comstock, Anthony 48, 49, 58, 65–6. *See also* New York Society for the Suppression of Vice

Comstock Act (US Criminal Code § 211) 58–9, 73, 75–6, 77, 129, 143–4. *See also* obscenity, customs laws

Conan Doyle, Arthur
"The Adventure of Charles Augustus Milverton" 5, 10, 11, 104, 113–17, 126

Confessional Unmasked 55

confidentiality (tort) 31, 117–18, 119

Confucius 11, 145

Contact Editions (publisher) 65

contract law 35, 37, 97, 106, 110, 113, 117, 119, 125

Cooley, Judge Thomas 126

copyright (general) 9, 12, 13, 28–9, 33–40, 79–102, 137–42
  Australia 100
  Canada 100
  common law (or natural rights) 7, 89
  compulsory license 139–41
  and creativity 52, 86
  duration 9, 79, 97–102, 138–9
  European Union 99–100
  fair use and fair dealing 29, 80
  heirs 2, 80, 99, 101–2, 123, 139
  incentive theory 3, 34, 49, 79, 84
  in personam proceedings 16
  in rem proceedings 16
  as monopoly 4, 78, 87, 136, 137, 138, 140, 141, 151
  and obscenity 4, 9, 43–4, 46, 65–7, 78, 81, 87–8, 89–93, 137

orphan works 101, 102
and piracy 4, 16, 17, 33–8,
    86–97, 137
and privacy 2, 31, 118, 122–4
proprietary turn 79–80, 81
public domain (*see* public
    domain)
restored rights 99–100
spillover effects 136, 140
as stunting modernism 9, 78,
    101–2
as tax 3, 82
transatlantic asymmetries 4,
    81, 85–9, 98, 100–1, 151
United Kingdom (*see* copyright
    (UK))
United States (*see* copyright
    (US))
copyright (UK)
    1842 Act 97–8
    1911 Act 85
    Statute of Anne (1710) 79,
        81–2
copyright (US)
    1790 Act 79
    1891 Act 3–4, 33, 90, 92, 95
    1909 Act 90, 95, 98, 137
    1976 Act 98, 142
    formalities 44, 86, 89, 97, 98
    and international agreements
        16, 81, 85, 88–9, 98–9
    isolationism and protectionism
        81, 85, 98–9, 138
    manufacturing clause 85,
        89–93, 94–5, 98, 137–8
    Sonny Bono Act 98, 100
    See also trade courtesy
Cornell, Julien 147, 148
Cornhill Company (publisher) 95–6
courtesy of the trade. *See* trade
    courtesy
Covici, Pascal 57
Crane, Hart 83
Cravens, Margaret 83, 97, 134–5

Criminal Law Amendment
    Act 1885 (Labouchere
    Amendment) 25, 109
Cutting, Senator Bronson 60,
    141–2

Darantiere, Maurice 88
Debs, Eugene 69
defamation. *See* libel; slander
Defence of the Realm Act (UK)
    68–9
Defoe, Daniel 79
Dennett, Mary Ware
    The Sex Side of Life 59
Dial (magazine) 85
Diarmid (Irish king) 141
Dickens, Charles 34, 82, 92
    A Tale of Two Cities 94
    Our Mutual Friend 94
Douglas. Lord Alfred 16, 19,
    21, 24, 32
    blackmail 25, 26, 27
    libel actions 18, 20, 104
D'Oyly Carte, Richard 35, 37
Dreiser, Theodore 48, 50
    An American Tragedy 57, 58,
    61
Du Maurier, George 37

Edward VII (Britain) 106
Egoist Press (publisher) 72
Eldon, Lord 90
Eliot, George 92
Eliot, T.S. 3
    Bel Esprit 136
    copyright 80, 86–7, 123
    as editor 50
    libel 106–7
    patronage 83–4, 87, 97
    piracy 7, 86–7, 93
    writings and magazines
        Criterion 83, 97
        Sweeney Agonistes 86
        The Waste Land 100, 136

elitism 8, 24, 74
Elkin Mathews (publisher) 142–3
Ernst, Morris 7, 45, 51, 57, 59,
    61, 64, 76
  customs laws 60, 72, 76
  obscenity and classics 67–8
  use of experts 8, 57–8
Espionage Act of 1917 (US)
    69–70
Evans, Caradoc 93

Faber and Faber (publisher) 50
Fairbanks, Douglas 125
Falconer, John (printer) 106
Farrar and Rinehart (publisher)
    97
Farrell, James 47
Faulkner, William 47
Field, Eugene 38
Fielding, Henry 67
First World War 45, 68–70, 108,
    130
Fitzgerald, F. Scott 134
Flaubert, Gustave 42, 45–6, 64
  Madame Bovary 45
Forster, E.M. 56, 78
  Maurice 111
Frankfurter Zeitung (newspaper)
    125
Franklin, Benjamin
  "Advice on Choosing a
    Mistress" 48
Friede, Donald 57

Galsworthy, John
  "Blackmail" 113
George H. Doran (publisher) 86
Gesell, Silvio 140–1
Gilbert and Sullivan 37
  Patience, or Bunthorne's Bride
    35, 37, 38, 126
Gill, Charles 43
Goldsmith, Oliver 82
Greene, Graham 1–2

  The Power and the Glory 1–2
  Stamboul Train 1
gross indecency. *See* Criminal
    Law Amendment Act 1885;
    Wilde, Oscar
Grove Press v. Christenberry
    77–8

Hall, Radclyffe
  The Well of Loneliness 5, 45,
    50, 51, 55–6, 57–8, 61,
    107–8
Hand, Judge Augustus 76
  on classics 7, 67–8
  on expert witnesses 7
  obscenity rulings 59, 67–8,
    69–70, 74, 75, 77
Hand, Judge Learned 74
Harris, Frank 19, 39, 48, 93, 105,
    125
  Mr. and Mrs. Daventry 39
Hays, Arthur Garfield 59
H.D. (Hilda Doolittle) 83, 88–9,
    119
  Kora and Ka 88–9
Heap, Jane 9, 62, 71, 74, 76
Hemingway, Ernest 47, 134
  In Our Time 107
  To Have and Have Not 107
Henry IV (France) 133
Henry Holt (publisher) 34.
    See also Holt, Henry
Heseltine, Philip ("Peter
    Warlock") 105
Higginson, Thomas Wentworth 42
Hogarth Press (publisher) 50–1,
    86
Holmes, Peter 56
Holt, Henry 94. *See also* Henry
    Holt
Home Office (British) 65, 70–1,
    75, 142
Home Secretary (British) 55, 69
honor, culture of 18–21, 104–5

Horace Liveright, Inc. (publisher) 97. *See also* Liveright, Horace

Houghton Mifflin (publisher) 97

Howell, Charles Augustus 10

Hudson, W.H.
  Green Mansions 91, 95

Huebsch, B.W. 63, 64, 95–6

Hughes, Langston 83

Hughes, Ted 123

Human Rights Act 1998 (UK) 118

Hurston, Zora Neale 83

Huysmans, Joris-Karl
  À Rebours 24

Ibsen, Henrik 109–10
  A Doll's House 110
  Hedda Gabler 110, 114

Incorporated Society of Authors, Playwrights and Composers (UK) 75

informal norms 13, 79–80, 151.
  See also trade courtesy

James, Henry 140, 149
  privacy 2, 6, 10–11, 103, 123, 126
  publicity 10
  writings
    "The Aspern Papers" 5, 119, 121
    "The Birthplace" 121–2
    The Bostonians 119–20
    "In the Cage" 111–12, 115
    "The Private Life" 111
    "The Real Right Thing" 5, 120–1, 122
    The Reverberator 119

James, Norah
  Sleeveless Errand 45

Jim Crow 12

Jonathan Cape (publisher) 55–6

Joyce, James 48, 50, 93, 105

copyright 65, 80, 86, 89, 99, 100, 123

estate 99, 101–2, 123

international protest 88, 125

libel 51, 106–7

obscenity 51, 52, 106

patronage 83–4, 86, 87, 88

piracy 7, 75, 87–8, 124

privacy lawsuit against Roth 2, 88, 89, 124–5, 126

trade courtesy 95–6, 96–7

writings
  A Portrait of the Artist as a Young Man 95
  Chamber Music 95–6
  Dubliners 6, 51, 95, 106, 142
  Exiles 95
  Finnegans Wake 51
  "Gas from a Burner" 106
  "Oscar Wilde: The Poet of 'Salomé'" 30
  Ulysses (*see Ulysses* (Joyce))

Joyce, Michael 125

Kafka, Franz 119

Kant, Immanuel 118

Keats, John 30

Kipling, Rudyard 56

Knopf, Alfred 95. *See also* Alfred A. Knopf (publisher)

Labouchere Amendment. *See* Criminal Law Amendment Act 1885

law and economics 4, 12

Lawrence, D.H. 47, 48, 50, 65, 83, 93
  copyright and piracy 92, 93, 96
  libel 105
  obscenity 92, 102
  writings
    "A Propos of *Lady Chatterley's Lover*" 92

Lady Chatterley's Lover 57,
    63, 72, 77–8, 91, 92, 96
The Rainbow 5, 55, 63, 69,
    142
Sons and Lovers 96
Women in Love 105
Lawrence, Frieda 96
League of Nations 130
Le Gallienne, Richard 93
Le Guin, Ursula K. 81
Lewis, Wyndham
    libel 105–6, 107
    writings
        The Apes of God 106
        "Cantelman's Spring-Mate"
            58–9, 70, 75, 77, 143–4
        The Roaring Queen 105
        Tarr 105
libel (civil) 1, 12, 18, 104–8, 117,
    119, 125, 148
    deceased persons 19, 20
    in personam proceedings 5
    in rem proceedings 5, 107
    publication 20, 46
    regulation of literature 3, 150
    and reputation 4–5, 9, 20
    truth defense 21
libel (criminal) 5, 18, 19, 104
    deceased persons 20–21
    feuding and violence 19–21, 104
    justification defense 21, 22, 40,
        117, 150
    publication 20
    and reputation 20
    See also Queensberry,
        Marquess of; Wilde, Oscar
Lindey, Alexander 57, 59, 72
Little Review 50, 58–9, 62, 64, 67,
    70, 71, 74, 83–4, 85–6, 135,
    143–4
Liveright, Horace 95. *See also*
    Boni and Liveright; Horace
    Liveright, Inc.
Lord Chamberlain 12, 42, 49

Lorrain, Jean 104–5
Louÿs, Pierre 27
    Aphrodite 72

Macaulay, Thomas 10, 82
Malleson, Miles
    *Two Short Plays: Patriotic and
        Unpatriotic* 69
Manton, Judge Martin T. 8, 74
Martin Secker (publisher) 105
Mason, Stuart 16
    Bibliography of Oscar Wilde
        15
Masses (magazine) 69–70
Mathers, E. Powys 93
Maunsel and Company
    (publisher) 106
Mendès, Catulle 93, 105
Methuen (publisher) 55, 56
Middleton, Richard 93
Miller, Henry 102
    Tropic of Cancer 77
Mirbeau, Octave
    A Chambermaid's Diary 93
Modern Library (publisher) 95
Monroe, Harriet 50
Moore, George 49, 54
    A Story-Teller's Holiday 64
Moore, Marianne 80, 101, 123
moral rights 12, 99, 100
Mudie's (circulating library) 49,
    50. *See also* circulating
    libraries
Mussolini, Benito 127, 149

name appropriation 2, 12, 19, 29–
    33, 103, 105, 118, 124–6.
    See also privacy; publicity
Nation (magazine) 96
National Social Purity Crusade
    47. *See also* purity groups
National Vigilance Association 47,
    53. *See also* purity groups
New Age (magazine) 138, 141

New Deal 8, 127, 134
New Statesman (magazine) 89
New York Society for the
    Suppression of Vice 48,
    49, 53, 57, 63, 71. *See
    also* Comstock, Anthony;
    purity groups; Sumner, John
    Saxton

obscene libel (common law) 5,
    53–4, 56–7, 62
Obscene Publications Act 1857
    (Lord Campbell's Act) (UK)
    5, 54–6, 67, 69
  as *in rem* mechanism 46, 54–5
Obscene Publications Act 1959
    (UK) 78
obscenity 16, 17, 40–4, 45–78,
    142–4
  average person standard 72,
    75, 76
  children and vulnerable readers
    7, 41, 56, 61–2, 63, 66, 72
  classics 7–8, 67–8
  and copyright 4, 9, 43–4, 46,
    65–7, 78, 87–8, 89–93, 101,
    137
  customs laws 3, 8, 47, 59–61,
    65, 70–1, 72, 76, 142, 143
  expert witnesses 7–8, 56, 57–8,
    75, 78
  free speech and First
    Amendment 9, 12, 74–8, 151
  indiscriminate circulation 7,
    62–5
  in personam proceedings
    52–61, 71, 78
  in rem proceedings 52–61, 71,
    78, 142
  Massachusetts law 57, 76
  net effect test 72, 75
  New York law 8, 57, 64, 71

patchwork regulation 8, 70–3,
    77
postal laws 3, 8, 47, 54, 58–9,
    67–8, 69–70, 71, 72, 75,
    77–8, 142, 143–4
printers and publishers 51,
    142–3
prior restraint 10, 48, 49, 50,
    58
private and limited editions 7,
    41, 63–5, 88–9, 106, 143–4
self-censorship 6–7, 50–1
as stunting modernism 9, 78,
    102
  See also Comstock Act;
    obscene libel; Obscene
    Publications Act 1857;
    Obscene Publications Act
    1959; *Regina v. Hicklin*
O'Hara, John 47
Orioli, Pino 63

Pankhurst, Sylvia 68–9
passport laws 130–1.
    See also under Pound, Ezra
Pater, Walter
  *Studies in the History of the
    Renaissance* 41
patronage 64, 81–4, 97, 102,
    134–6
  and copyright 9, 81–4, 87–9
  private 82, 83–4, 88
  public 82–3, 84
  spillover effects 11, 135–6, 140
P.E.N. (author collective) 75
Penguin Books (publisher) 78
Plath, Sylvia 2, 123
  The Bell Jar 91, 123
Poetry (magazine) 50, 85
posing. *See under* Wilde, Oscar
Pound, Dorothy 134
Pound, Ezra 4, 81, 93, 105,
    127–51

anti-Semitism 11, 129, 148, 149
Armed Services Editions 134, 145
book tariffs 11, 91, 129, 130, 131–4, 136, 137–8, 142
copyright 7, 9, 11, 80, 85–6, 89, 90–1, 129, 137–42, 148, 151
    as editor 50, 85–6, 135
    free speech 9, 144, 150–1
    magazines 50, 85–6
    money and usury 11, 128, 138–9, 140–1
    obscenity 7, 11, 50, 58, 67–8, 129, 142–4
    passports 11, 129, 130–1, 136, 137
    patronage 11, 83–4, 134–6, 140
    radio broadcasts 127, 145, 148–9, 150–1
    treason 11, 12, 127, 128, 145–9
    US Army Disciplinary Training Center (DTC) 134, 145–7, 150
    and US Constitution 11, 127, 128, 129, 134, 138–9, 144–9
    writings
        A Lume Spento 85
        A Quinzaine for this Yule 85
        "Cantico del Sole" 68
        Canto IV 141
        Canto VII 130
        The Cantos 128
        "Coitus" 143
        "Copyright and Tariff" 138–41
        "Epitaph" 143
        Exultations 85
        "Four Steps" 127–8
        Instigations 85
        Introductory Text Book 127

"The Lake Isle" 143
Lustra 85, 142–3
"The New Cake of Soap" 143
Pavannes and Divisions 85
Personae 85
"Pervigilium" 143
The Pisan Cantos 149–50
"The Temperaments" 143
"This Approaches Literature!" 70
"The Priest and the Acolyte" (Bloxam) 23, 42
Priestley, J.B. 1
Prince Albert v. Strange 117–18
privacy 12, 17, 31, 35, 102, 103–4, 117–23, 126
    and honor 31–2, 35, 117
    and intellectual property 11, 118, 122–3, 124
    laws 4, 30, 44, 103, 117–19, 122, 124, 125
    as property 2, 26, 29
    and reputation 5, 9, 10, 102, 115
    See also name appropriation; Warren, Samuel D.
private editions. See under obscenity
Prohibition 52, 60, 129
Proust, Marcel 104–5
    Les Plaisirs et les jours 104–5
public domain 3, 13, 39, 78, 79, 89, 94–5
    death and mourning 80, 101, 102
    transatlantic asymmetries 4, 81, 85–9, 98, 100–1
publicity 11, 12, 102, 124–6
    laws 4, 12, 30, 31, 44, 103, 124, 125–6
    and reputation 5, 9, 102, 115
    as self-display 5, 30, 104, 115, 126
    See also name appropriation

Punch (magazine) 37
Pure Literature Society 47. *See
    also* purity groups
purity groups 7, 13, 43, 46–9, 53,
    63, 65–7, 74, 106, 143

Queensberry, Marquess of
    calling card for Wilde 20–21,
        22, 29
    prosecuted for libel by Wilde
        5, 6, 20–21, 29, 40–41, 104,
        117, 129, 149, 150
    threats of violence 19, 20
Quinn, John
    art tariffs 133
    obscenity litigation 64, 67, 71,
        75, 84
    as patron 83–4, 86, 97, 135,
        143

Rabelais, François 7, 67
Random House (publisher) 8, 57,
    72, 95, 96–7, 123, 148. *See
    also* Cerf, Bennett
Regina v. Hicklin 7, 41, 55, 56, 65,
    74, 75, 76, 78, 151
    children and vulnerable readers
        61–2, 72
    classics 67
    effects test 61–2
    indiscriminate circulation 62–3
    portions of texts 61
Rhys, Jean 50
Richardson, Samuel 92
Rilke, Rainer Maria
    Duino Elegies 86
Roberts Brothers (publisher) 35
Roosevelt, Franklin Delano (FDR)
    127, 129, 145
Ross, Robert 15–16, 150
Rosset, Barney 77
Roth, Samuel 48–9, 72
    Joyce's privacy lawsuit against
        2, 88, 89, 124–5, 126

as lawful pirate 4, 86–8, 92–3,
    96, 99
magazines
    American Aphrodite 75
    Beau 48
    Casanova Jr's Tales 65
    Good Times 75
    Two Worlds Monthly 48,
        86–8, 93, 124
Rothermere, Lady 83, 97
Roth v. United States 75–7, 151
Ruskin, John 18
Russell, Bertrand 69
    "The German Peace Offer" 69

Sackville-West, Vita 86
Salinger, J.D. 2, 123
Sandburg, Carl 93, 134
Sanger, Margaret 48, 144
Santayana, George
    *Persons and Places: The
        Background of My Life* 134
Sarony, Napoleon 35–8
Schmitt, Carl 6, 17
Schwob, Marcel 105
Scott, Henry 55
Scott, Sir Walter 92
Scribner's (publisher) 34, 107
Seaside Library (publisher) 33,
    35
Second World War 127, 134
Sedition Act of 1918 (US) 69
Shakespeare, William 39, 67, 84,
    121–2
Shakespeare and Company
    (publisher) 64, 87. *See also*
    Beach, Sylvia
Shaw, George Bernard 125
    copyright 19, 105
    libel 19, 105
    writings
        *The Shewing-Up of Blanco
            Posnet* 43
Shelley, Percy Bysshe 90

Sherman Antitrust Act 95
Silko, Leslie Marmon 80
Sinclair, Upton 50
slander 104
Smollett, Tobias 67
Society for the Suppression of Vice
    (UK) 47. *See also* purity
    groups
Soldier Voting Act (US) 134
Southey, Robert 90
Spirit Lamp (magazine) 27
Stationers' Company 82
Steinbeck, John 134
St. Elizabeths Hospital 127, 147,
    148, 151
Sterne, Laurence 67
Stevenson, Robert Louis
    *The Strange Case of Dr. Jekyll
        and Mr. Hyde* 110, 111
Stopes, Marie
    Contraception 60
    Married Love 60
Strachey, Lytton 86
suffragism 12
Sumner, John Saxton 48, 49,
    53, 57, 64, 71. *See also*
    New York Society for the
    Suppression of Vice
Swinburne, Algernon
    "A Word for the Navy" 10
Synge, John M. 84, 93

Tariff Acts (US) 59–61, 68, 72, 74,
    76, 96
    classics exception 68
    See also book tariffs; obscenity,
        customs laws
Temple, Shirley 1
trade courtesy 13, 16, 34–5, 37,
    81, 93–7
trademark and unfair competition
    37, 125, 126
Treason. *See under* Pound, Ezra
Tree, Herbert Beerbohm 27

Ulysses (Joyce) 143
    British ban 70–1, 72
    and copyright 80, 84, 87–8, 91,
        92, 93, 96–7
    and libel 106–7
    in *Little Review* 50, 71, 74, 84,
        144
    Paris edition 51, 64–5, 72, 87,
        93, 136
    Roth's unauthorized version 2,
        48, 87–8
    US customs forfeiture case
        8–9, 57, 60–1, 68, 71, 72–3,
        74–5, 76, 96–7
*United States v. One Book
    Entitled Ulysses. See
    Ulysses*, US customs
    forfeiture case
Universal Copyright Convention
    98
US Constitution 11, 82, 127, 129,
    138–9, 144–7. *See also*
    obscenity, free speech and
    First Amendment
US Supreme Court 8–9, 37, 73,
    75–8, 127

Veblen, Thorstein 20
Vestal, Congressman Albert Henry
    141–2
vice crusaders or societies. *See*
    purity groups
Viereck, George Sylvester
    The House of the Vampire 80
Vivian, Herbert 31, 32
Vizetelly, Henry 5, 47, 53–4

Warren, Samuel D., and Louis D.
    Brandeis
    "The Right to Privacy" 11,
        31–2, 118–19, 122, 124, 126
wartime regulations 12, 68–70,
    134. *See also* Defense of
    the Realm Act; Espionage

Act of 1917; Sedition Act of
    1918; Soldier Voting Act
Watch and Ward Society 47, 48–9,
    57. *See also* purity groups
Weaver, Harriet Shaw 72, 83, 87
West, Rebecca 78, 148
Whistler, James McNeill
    libel action 18
    writings
        *The Gentle Art of Making
            Enemies* 18
Whitman, Walt
    Leaves of Grass 47
W.H. Smith (distributor) 1, 49
Wilde, Constance 31
Wilde, Oscar 9, 15–44, 53, 63,
    125, 129
    affirmative defense 28–9
    American lecture tour 6, 33–4,
        126
    anticommons 39–40, 44
    bankruptcy and forced sale 30,
        32, 33, 38–9, 151
    blackmail 6, 25–8, 30, 31, 39,
        109, 110
    blasphemy 42–3
    copyright 6, 15, 33–40, 66,
        151
    elitism 24, 74
    as exception 6, 17–18, 149
    free speech 4, 9, 40, 74, 151
    homosexuality 6, 44, 109, 110
    honor 6, 18–21, 31–2, 35
    obscenity 6, 40–44
    piracy 6, 7, 16, 33–8, 43
    plagiarism 18, 39
    posing 6, 20, 22–24, 74
    privacy 6, 29–33, 35, 126
    prosecuted for gross indecency
        5–6, 11, 18, 29, 105, 149
    prosecutes Queensberry for
        libel 5–6, 11, 16, 20–24, 25,
        29, 38, 40–41, 42, 43, 104,
        117, 129, 150

publicity 6, 29–33, 37, 126
    and renters 24, 27–8, 109, 110,
        111
    writings
        An Ideal Husband 26
        The Ballad of Reading Gaol
            6, 33
        "The Canterville Ghost" 38
        "Charmides" 42
        "The Decay of Lying" 37–8
        De Profundis 17, 32, 39, 43,
            149–50
        *The Importance of Being
            Earnest* 26, 27, 32, 111
        Lady Windermere's Fan 26
        "On the Sale by Auction of
            Keats' Love Letters" 30,
            32, 42
        The Picture of Dorian Gray
            6–7, 10, 16, 22–3, 24,
            25, 26, 27, 28, 32–3, 38,
            40, 41–2, 43, 51, 66,
            111
        Poems 33–4, 35, 42
        "The Portrait of Mr. W.H."
            33, 39, 80
        "The Soul of Man under
            Socialism" 30, 33, 41
        Vera; or, the Nihilists 34
William Clowes and Sons (printer)
    142
Wilson, Woodrow 131
women's property rights 12
Woolf, Leonard 50–1, 56
Woolf, Virginia 69
    circulating libraries 50
    copyright 52, 86, 91, 92
    obscenity 56
    patronage 82–3, 135
    privacy 117
    as publisher 50–1, 86
    writings
        A Room of One's Own 56,
            80, 117

Night and Day 86, 91, 117
Orlando 51
The Voyage Out 86, 91, 92
Woolsey, Judge John M. 8, 71, 72–3, 74, 75, 76, 96–7. *See also Ulysses*, US customs forfeiture case
Wordsworth, William 34

Yeats, W.B. 83, 86, 95
Young Men's Christian Association (YMCA) 48. *See also* purity groups

Zola, Émile 5, 47, 53–4
Nana 53
Pot-bouille 53
La Terre 53